D0816463

114723356

NO LONGER
PROPERTY OF PPLD

THE BACKCOUNTRY
HANDBOOK

AN ILLUSTRATED GUIDE TO THE TECHNIQUES
AND JOYS OF THE WILDERNESS EXPERIENCE
BY THE EDITORS OF MOTHER EARTH NEWS
INTRODUCTION BY EDWARD ABBEY

A FIRESIDE BOOK
PUBLISHED BY SIMON & SCHUSTER INC.

NEW YORK   LONDON   TORONTO   SYDNEY   TOKYO

790.0973
B126

Fireside / Simon & Schuster
Simon & Schuster Building
Rockefeller Center
Avenue of the Americas
New York, NY 10020

Copyright © 1989 by Mother Earth News
Partners

All rights reserved including the right of
reproduction in whole or in any form.

Grateful acknowledgment is made for
permission to reprint "Peter Cottontail"
by Steve Nelson and Jack Rollins on
pages 98–101. Copyright © 1950
(Renewed) Hill and Range Songs. Used
by permission of Warner Chappell Music, Inc. All rights reserved.

FIRESIDE and SIMON & SCHUSTER
and colophon are registered trademarks of
Simon & Schuster Inc.

Designed by John Baxter Design
Manufactured in the United States of
America

10 9 8 7 6 5 4 3 2 1
10 9 8 7 6 5 4 3 2 1 PBK

Library of Congress Cataloging in Publication Data

ISBN 0-671-68369-1
ISBN 0-671-65791-7   (PBK)

PROPERTY OF
PIKES PEAK LIBRARY DISTRICT
P.O. BOX 1579
COLORADO SPRINGS, CO 80901

Acknowledgments

Putting together a book like this is, not unlike the running of a good group camp, an exercise in cooperation. Because of this, we're deeply grateful for the team we had with us on this adventure and the teamwork displayed by one and all.

For sharing wisdom accumulated along countless miles of trail, we'd like to thank Edward Abbey ("Forward!"), Tom Gresham ("Safe Shooting"), Tom Brown, Jr. ("Survival: Shelter," "Survival: Water," "Survival: Fire"), Hugh M. Johnson ("Looking Into Binoculars"), Ron Spomer ("The Incredible Beanbag Tripod"), David del Junco ("Giardiasis in Paradise"), Mark D. Coburn, ("Low-Cost Backpacking Foods"), Lance Olsen ("The Bear Facts"), Christopher Nyerges and Dolores Miller Nyerges ("Using Nature's Bounty"), Tom Turner ("Farewell, Fellow Travelers"), Sierra Adare ("More Backcountry Cooking"), Lyman Products ("Some Words of Caution"), Pat Stone ("The Right Boat"), Terry Krautwurst ("Camp Coffee Traditions"), Richard Freudenberger, Don Osby, David Swift ("Tents"), Bill McLarney ("Freshwater Game Fish"), Dennis Burkholder ("A Basic [and Beautiful] Boat"), Clarence Goosen ("Consolidated Camper," "A Basic [and Beautiful] Boat"), Maurie Hoekstra ("Take a Wok!") and Alfred Meyer. Design and art direction came from John Baxter, with the able assistance of Linda Patterson Eger, Kathleen Seabe, Bill Lessner, Sandra McKee, Robert Graf, Kay Holmes Stafford, Kathy Tomlin, Helen P. McAuliffe, Richard Muehleman and Laura A. Greenburg. Editorial assistance, without which valuable information might have been lost in the telling, was supplied by Assistant Managing Editor Liz Brennan and Chief Copy Editor Lorna K. Loveless, assisted by Klara Blair, Julie Brown, Wilma Dingley, Joanne Dufilho, Judy Gold, Deborah Henry, Judy Janes, Alexis Lipsitz, Christie Lyon, Betty N. Mack, Karen Murray, Rita Norton and Ingrid Sterner. Finally, we'd like to thank Tim Watkins, Managing Editor, *Mother Earth News*, for picking up the pack when no one else would carry it, and hauling *The Backcountry Handbook* into print.

David Petersen
Senior Editor, West, Mother Earth News
David Schoonmaker
Senior Editor, Mother Earth News
Bruce Woods
Editor-in-Chief, Mother Earth News

THE BACKCOUNTRY HANDBOOK

Contents

Forward!
By Edward Abbey

Edward Abbey—active outdoorsman and author of Desert Solitaire, The Monkey Wrench Gang *and 17 other popular novels and essay collections—is one of America's most powerful and relentless spokesmen for the environment and certainly its most uninhibited. Here, at Abbey's curmudgeonly best, is his introduction to* The Backcountry Handbook.

If there's one thing that gripes me in my lurching about in America's blessed but overcrowded backcountry, it's those androids from the moronic inferno of contemporary technoculture who apparently learned outdoors etiquette from *The Boy Scout Handbook* of 1928. I mean the cretins who build their campfires with green logs laboriously chewed from living trees with dull hatchets. And then erect a corral of rocks to enclose a fire about 10 times bigger than even a White Man needs. And then, upon departure from the scene of their felonies, pile all their garbage upon the smoldering remains—including such noncombustibles as tinfoil and wet tin cans, wet condoms and Pampers—let it smoke and blacken and stink for a while, and conclude the infamy by heaping this mess with a pile of mud and stones.

Everywhere we go in what's left of natural America, we find these miniature trash dumps. The intention, no doubt, was to prevent forest fires, as Smokey the Bore has been instructing us for 50 years. But fires are natural, inevitable and good for the forest;

any Native American can tell you that. If you can find one. (The true terror of the modern forest is not the wildfire but the logger with his chain saw, the road builder with his bulldozer, the cowboy with his cow. These types wreak far more destruction upon our forests than any wildfire ever did or could. And wreak it at our expense, financed by our tax dollars.)

Why *do* these Ralph Lauren he-man Campfire Girls build giant fire rings filled with half-baked rubbish? I don't know. No one knows. They are the product not of thought but of ritual, spastic reflex, ancient ideologies conceived in sin and whelped by bureaucrats. One discovers such mementos even in the sand and rock of the desert, where the nearest tree may be a scrubby juniper four feet tall, 10 feet away. Mysteries of the Wild.

But irksome. There are many things that irk, actually, not only me but you, but this is not the place for a complete listing. I mention this one item merely as an example of a practice that *The Backcountry Handbook* may help bring to an end, I hope, if it is read by the right people. If they can read.

Having freed myself of this grievance, I shall now praise the book still further. It is packed with good and useful information, written and compiled by outdoorsmen and -women who seem to know what they are talking about. One of the writers and editors, a friend of mine, is an expert bowhunter, a man who gets his deer, his elk, his caribou in the difficult and Paleolithic manner, rely-

ing more on skill, knowledge, intuition and sympathy for the prey than on firepower, alcohol and the latest O.R.V. And he does it every year, legally and honorably. In other words, there are good hunters as well as the better-known and—sad but true—more numerous slob hunters. Study this book, and, if you don't already know, you'll learn the difference. The difference is important, a matter not of degree but of principle, of purpose, of tradition.

And so on. Hunting, fishing, fire building, camping, getting lost and finding yourself; these and many another craft of fundamental interest are spelled out for us here. Even the oldest and the wisest can learn something useful from this book.

Can learn everything but the simplest and most basic, which is, of course, love. Love for the land and its wild inhabitants and the spirit of the landscape itself. That kind of love, while expressed in the pages of this book, can be experienced fully and enjoyed only through adventure—by getting out there, *out there,* far beyond the walls of the urban, suburban, small-town, merely cultural cage in which most of us waste away our tedious, imprisoned lives. Cities and towns are the Gulag of modern life. Our true home lies outside, deep in the wilderness of forest and mountain, river and desert and sea, the source of our being and the destiny of our great meandering blundering dreaming journey through time. Like Odysseus in his wanderings, we are homeward bound whether we know it or not.

At the Head of the Trail

Not so long ago, learning the skills and pleasures of camping, fishing and hunting was, for most young Americans, one of the few types of education to be entered into eagerly. The great outdoors, to generations of children, was as seductive a playground as are today's video parlors. And teachers, whether they were simply more experienced peers or true old masters, were widely available and eagerly attended.

Most of today's adults, though, never had such opportunities. For us, the cities and suburbs provided their own special educations, their own teachers, which were often no less valuable, but *different*. So we mastered the necromancy of the food processor rather than the simple magic of the Dutch oven, learned road maps rather than game trails, angled for raises while the trout rose freely to mayfly hatches, and forced ourselves to find poor rest in strange motel beds rather than rejuvenation under the wild jewelry of the night sky.

And such skills have had their values. Indeed, for many of us, mastery of the urban lore of job and home have brought together an opportunity and a *need*, and have led us—either as vacationers or new dwellers in rural areas—to the wilderness we've missed. Happily, too, there are still teachers, still peers who've turned experience into wisdom, still oldsters whose skills have become polished with use, like the handles of old knives. In this book, we've collected some of their teachings into an introduction to the ways of the wild.

We begin with a chapter on gearing up, since outdoor neophytes will need to buy the tools of their chosen activity, and since most experienced woods-wanderers have just a touch of the equipment junkie about them. We can't cover every possible piece of backcountry paraphernalia here, but we do present a variety of equipment choices, covering a wide range of outdoor activities, and do so in a manner that demonstrates *how*

one goes about shopping for the great outdoors. And therein are some lessons well worth learning. Fashion and fad influence this market as they do every one, but impeccable styling won't mean much when your tent fails in the first rainstorm.

From basic gear we move on to entry-level skills. By going a bit more deeply into exactly how your equipment will be used, this chapter serves to both support and expand upon the first. Would-be nimrods will encounter information on firearms safety, on zeroing-in a scope, even on expanding their horizons to include primitive muzzle-loading weapons, virtually identical to those that explored the American West. Hopeful anglers (is there any other kind?) will get a tackle-boxful of fishing how-to, including in-depth studies of the various species they'll be seeking. (After all, an understanding of piscine behavior will fill more stringers than any "wonder" lure.) And, for those who simply like to wander the wilderness, we provide some hard-learned tips on *what* to pack for your next outing and—almost as important—*how* to organize the gear within your backpack for easy walking and quick access to the things you'll need to get at "right now."

Of course, there'd be little charm and wonder to the backcountry without the creatures that make those forests, deserts or tundras their homes. So we've included a chapter describing the natural history of some of the most fascinating of North America's residents . . . most of which very likely share your preferred stomping grounds.

And you'll see more wild creatures, whether you're a hunter, a photographer or just an entranced observer, if you build the tree stand we detail in our "Wilderness Workshop" chapter. Many of the larger items available to enhance outdoor experiences are pretty costly, so why not use some of your spare time (when the weather keeps you out of the woods, maybe) to build your own simple boat, ice-fishing shack, or camper?

Many people view the great outdoors with fear, and if this volume does nothing else, we hope that it will help a few overcome that intimidation. After all, those who are most frightened of the wild are most likely to try to dominate or destroy it. We don't have enough wilderness left to tolerate that sort of nonsense anymore.

Fear, of course, is often simply a lack of knowledge. Our fifth chapter draws upon the know-how of a number of America's foremost wilderness experts. With the help of these teachers, you'll learn survival skills, first-aid techniques, methods of weather forecasting, the basics of land navigation with map and compass, and even how to create one of a series of custom-designed carry-along survival kits—emergency packets created by people who make their livings teaching others how to thrive in the wild. When you *know* you can make a fire, purify water and find your way home in comfort wherever your travels take you, you can truly relax and enjoy the wonders of the American backcountry.

As relaxation around the fire or cookstove is the traditional end to any outdoor day, we've wrapped up our book with a chapter on cooking. *Anything* tastes better in the wild, but we're confident that the recipes included here will help you start many a day with enthusiasm, and end as many with contented sighs.

So there you have it: the best package of useful backcountry information that we can put together. Use it with our blessings and with our hopes that it helps you become a lover, steward and even champion of the American wilderness. You should know, however, that no book could contain everything you'll ever want to know about outdoor recreation. In the end, even the best of teachers must leave you at the trail head after pointing a direction. The education continues—and the adventure unfolds—as you walk that trail yourself.

—*The Editors*

PART ONE

Gearing Up

A guide to the
selection of appropriate
outdoor equipment
for the hunter, angler
and hiker

Tents

A backcountry bargain abode is one that keeps you dry in the wet, warm in the cold and sheltered in a blow.

Today there's no reason to buy a tent that won't set up in a jiffy, won't be moved off that danged root in half a jiffy and won't thwart claustrophobia after you've been penned in for a few days in bad weather. While the chances of getting a real bargain in a tent have never been better, the issues have never been more complex.

The term *bargain* is used not in the discount sense but in the spirit of perpetuating this scenario: You're *way out there*. A sideways rain shower pelts your tent in the middle of the night. The poles are shivering and the rain fly is moaning, and you hear mud flowing. No matter, your tent mate is purring, and you don't feel so bad yourself. That tent, friend, is a bargain, no matter what you paid.

Not all tents can offer as much. Here are some tent issues to consider:

Brand name: Competition born of the outdoor-equipment boom of the '70s has brought to market a bounty of excellent designs and executions. Tent manufacturers have done such a thorough job of stealing refinements from one another that the best reasons for brand loyalty probably concern service. Most popular (and unpopular) brands still offer service in the baby-boom outdoor-gear tradition: They're embarrassed when something goes wrong and fix it quickly—and for free if they're really embarrassed.

Design: The Gospel of Dome is writ large across the landscape. Like the song "Proud Mary," a dome tent is great when done right. Variations on the dome are manifold. There are countless ways to emulate the arched

One advantage of the dome tent is that the frame is outside, leaving more space inside for people and gear.

form of a frightened cat, but each includes poles that are fastened to grommets at the tent's lower periphery and that arch and push up and out.

Bill Moss, the nation's foremost designer of what he likes to call "tensioned fabric," is pretty much responsible for the way tents look today. His first dome tent was a "pop tent," an item that made a page in a 1955 *Life* magazine because of its novelty.

The one significant exception to the dome trend is called the hoop, or tunnel, style and is the latest design that hard-core mountaineers covet. It consists of two or three hoops holding open a tube, vestibules on either end and a tug-of-war means of holding it up.

Seasoning: No arm of the Department of Agriculture regulates the wording in the brochures of tent manufacturers. Most tents are deemed "three-season"; when they are labeled "four-season," they are usable in winter. A four-season tent, usually tagged "expedition" as well, is supposed to take snow loads, shed high winds and have a vestibule or two (optional or standard) for extra closet space and to offer a spot to perform cooking chores on bare ground.

Sleeping capacity: When all you're going to do in a tent is sleep, and those involved don't move much at night, the tentmaker's number will stand. If you're new at this, subtract one from that number; if just you and another will be using it, a three-person tent is wonderfully roomy with minimal weight increase. (Unless, of course, much backpacking is involved; then every ounce is significant.)

Weight: You'll drive yourself nuts if you squint too hard when comparing advertised weights. Even though the competition to have the lightest, largest tent is dogged, reputable manufacturers tend to keep their advertised figures in the ballpark—although the caveat that "weight does not include pegs, seam sealer, . . ." is standard fare.

Weight is as weight does. Heavier is stronger, materials and design being equal. Extra reinforcement, in the form of double-needle stitching, bar tacking, lined stress points and so on, adds ounces. Careful shopping means knowing which are the ounces of prevention.

Fabric: Nylon. It comes in more varieties than snow. Heavier (taffeta, Oxford) nylon better withstands shearing, puncture and abrasion. Thinner nylon is lighter. Urethane-coated nylon is waterproof and less drafty to boot. Ripstop nylon is designed to do just that with its grid of heavier threads. (The benefits of Gore-Tex are moot thanks to one quirk: Gore-Tex does not currently pass the tent industry's fire-retardancy regulations.)

Nylon's weight, or thickness, is measured in ounces per square yard, with 1.2 and 2.5 the most common at the extremes. One-point-two-ounce nylon is wispy stuff, perfect for inner walls. Coated 2-point-something sheeting is commonly used for floors, while rain flies are likely to be 1.7- or 1.9-ounce coated ripstop. "No-see-um" nettings segregate the bugs from the bags. The finer

the mesh, the fewer insects get in your ear.

Poles: Many tentmakers boast high-grade aluminum (7075, for example), usually made by Easton. This is tried and true stuff, guaranteed for life. On some tents, you get the cheaper option of glass-composite poles, which are lighter and more compact.

Never, never believe any salesperson or brochure that claims a pole is unbreakable. There's no such thing. Somewhere there blows a wind that will snap any pole, shred any tent.

Shock-corded poles assemble themselves in a magician's trick. This is no small convenience when wind-driven graupel is rolling down your neck. Beware of flimsy cord—threading a broken one is the real trick.

Zippers: YKK has done its part to eliminate the world's concern for reliable zippers. Its plastic-coil models are preferred for tent use and do an admirable job—although the clever salesperson who coined the term "self-healing" deserves an award only for enthusiasm. If you expect perfection, you'll learn a lesson in the nature of things.

Cost: All companies want your business. Now that the market has flattened, some are desperate for it. It's a double-edged sword. You might be getting more for your money; you might be getting newer short-cut manufacturing methods.

Manufacturers right and left are knocking a hundred bucks off their tents just by having them sewn overseas. Furthermore, a tent sewn overseas may or may not be made of American fabric.

Finishing the product: That's your job. Needles poke holes in nylon—it's called sewing. Those holes will leak a bit unless you take the trouble to seal them; tents usually come with a tube of seam sealer, and you're foolish not to spend an evening applying the stuff.

The Real World

It takes practice to learn to pitch any tent with a modicum of grace and efficiency. A

Most quality tents have somewhat thicker material on their floors than on their walls.

helpful hint is to spread the tent on its proposed site and roll around on it, miming your repertoire of sleeping positions—a practical drill that assures smooth ground, or at least tells you on which side you should sleep. This sort of Prone Position Efficacy Testing can be postponed, of course, with freestanding tents, which can readily be moved.

Tent brochures like to point out how thus-

and-so can be set up in 90 seconds while you stir your Spaghetti-Os with the other hand. Generally speaking, any *tent* can be set up by one person in a jiffy—it's the rain fly that gets you. The tents made by small, dedicated companies offer not only shelter but a little bit of smug enjoyment every time out. They cost more; you get it all.

Luckily, there are any number of fine three-person-plus tents in the under-$400 range and some plausible ones for under $300. Unless a tent is to be used as a storage shed for the kids over summer, being finicky about visual and practical aesthetics will pay off in due time. If you want to compound misery, try weathering a storm in a loose, gloomy tent. To use a tent is to place yourself in a situation where the senses become acute and more than a little fussy.

Every time we take a friend, a lover or a tent on a trip, we can't help but scrutinize strengths and weaknesses. (Just don't dwell on the fact that a friend or lover is probably doing the same thing.) We can change people if they need changing, or at least try. With a tent we can only get mad. Wet, too.

Your First Boat

In 1949, while outfitting themselves to look for oil in the jungles of Guatemala, Russ Schoonmaker and his partner, E.B. Shade, were shopping for an outboard motor in Guatemala City. In Guatemala at that time, shopping for American items was by brand name—accompanied by a whole lot of gesturing. They went into a sporting goods store and asked the proprietor in their limited Spanish if he had Johnson. The owner shook his head (thinking that they were asking for Johnson & Johnson athletic supplies), but said he had Bauer & Black. Schoonmaker answered, "Vamanos a ver" (Let's see!). The shopkeeper returned with a box of first-class athletic supporters.

Chances are good that your initiation into the language of boating won't be quite so difficult. Ask for an outboard and you'll get one. Still, you'll be a lot more likely to obtain a package that suits your needs and finances if you learn to talk nautical. The lingo of the sailor—boatspeak, if you will—is a bunch of fun, and it's also key to being accepted in the ritualistic clan of seafarers.

There's a wealth of information contained in the minds of enthusiastic skippers; all you've got to do is ask. You'll find that boat owners enjoy expounding on the merits of their vessels almost as much as they do running them. Visit marinas, boatyards and shops, and ask questions. There you'll learn as much as a person can hope to secondhand.

The aim of the following advice is to offer enough background to allow you to converse with those who know more. Only small powerboats are covered, but you'll find that much of the terminology will apply equally well to the larger vessel you may someday have the luxury of owning.

A primer on the language and lore of boating

FLAT BOTTOM

TUNNEL HULL

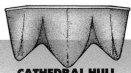

CATHEDRAL HULL

V- HULL

Hull Types

On the best of all possible waters, the ideal boat would be fast, stable, dry and able to knife through chop with comfort. On a real lake, river or stream, however, boat design is a compromise. The type of hull that's right for you will depend on what you'll do with the boat and where you plan to do it.

If there's anything approaching an absolute in hull design, it's the distinction between displacement and planing hulls. Viewed from the front (bow), displacement hulls are rounded or shaped in a deep V to push water out of the way, rather than rising onto it, as a planing hull does. Most recreational small powerboats have planing hulls, because skipping along on top of the water allows you to wring more speed from a given amount of power. Displacement-hulled powerboats are the province of commercial saltwater fishermen, who value the ability to move smoothly in big water.

The concept of a displacement hull is still important to the recreational powerboat owner, though, because every boat runs slowly (at hull or displacement speed) at times—when maneuvering in crowded harbors, approaching a dock or preparing to beach, for example. A boat's handling at hull speed—the quickness and predictability of its response to the helm and its resistance to side winds—is a very important aspect of its performance. Don't succumb completely to the thrill of velocity and fail to check out slow-speed manners.

The majority of small powerboats sold today have modified-V hulls. This shape tapers from a fairly steep V at the stem (bow at water line) to practically flat at the stern. The pointed front allows the boat to move water aside at slower speeds, while the squared-off aft (rear) becomes the platform for planing at speed. The flatter bottom aft also adds lateral stability. A boat with a broad, flat bottom is less inclined to rock (sailors say it is less *tender* or more *stiff*) than a round or V hull. Among other things, however, a flat bottom is slow and rides poorly in waves. Flat bottoms are thus used mainly for small utility craft, called johnboats or punts, which do a fine job of moving the angler or hunter over calm, shallow waters at slow speeds.

As with just about every other niggling de-tail of boating, naval architects have a unique way of talking about the degree of the V in a hull. *Dead rise* is the angle that one leg of the V forms with horizontal, measured from the *keel* (the ridge at the bottom) to the *chine* (the line above which the hull is rising more or less vertically to the gunnel). On a flat-bottomed boat, where the chine is *hard*, dead rise is zero. On modern powerboat hulls, where the chine is *soft* (rounded) forward and becomes more distinct aft, an average dead rise would be in the 15° to 20° range. In general, a steeper V works best in big waves, while a shallower one planes more quickly and may be faster. A boat for towing water-skiers, for example, would probably have a shallow V, emphasizing acceleration rather than handling in rough seas.

The angle of the *stem* from vertical also tells you something about a boat's purpose. A *plumb* (vertical) stem is found on a dis-placement hull, while one that's *raked* well back is probably built for speed.

Multihulls

In the mid-'70s, the *cathedral* hull, which has a central V hull and two smaller outrig-ger V hulls, was all the rage because it offered the lateral stability of a flat bottom without its liabilities. Since then, the design has been extensively refined, producing offshoots such as the *twin* (or *tunnel*) hull, while the basic cathedral has been largely abandoned.

Specific design details—the naval ar-chitect's expertise—are more important than characteristics common to all multihulled boats, but there are a few generalizations that can be made about them. The total breadth of the bottoms of cathedral and tunnel hulls makes them very stable, provides them with large load capacities and offers roomy interi-ors (because of the boats' rectangular shapes). What's more, the multiple-V hulls slice smoothly through calm water and light chop.

Likewise, there are liabilities to multihulls: First, when they rock at a certain angle, they lose lateral stability quickly and are inclined to roll upside down (turn turtle). (A V hull will rock more easily initially but will increas-ingly resist the motion.) Second, the shape offers more surface (wetted) area to the water and so tends to be slower than a modified V. Third, because they lean very little into a corner, flat hulls have wider turning radii at

speed. And fourth, they pitch (rock fore and aft) and ride harshly in heavy seas. The mix of advantages and disadvantages of cathedral and tunnel hulls makes them particularly popular with people who enjoy inland and coastal fishing.

Hull Materials

Boats are made from wood, steel, alumi-num, fiber-reinforced plastic (fiberglass) and even cement, but the majority of small powerboats being built today are either alu-minum or fiberglass. Both materials are suitable for fresh water, but in salt water alu-minum requires more attention to protect it from electrolytic reactions and corrosion. Some sailors find that fiberglass requires slightly less maintenance in fresh water, as well, and it is somewhat more resistant to damage from gentle collisions. It's also un-questionably easier to repair fiberglass once the damage is done.

In general, you'll find that simpler and smaller hull forms are likely to be made from aluminum, which has good stiffness, while the more exotic shapes of sporty runabouts are easier to mold in fiberglass.

Power

Power systems for small boats nowadays are almost exclusively outboard or inboard-outboard—where the engine is against the in-side of the transom (the back of the hull), and the propeller is mounted on a steerable column resembling the lower section of an outboard. Strictly inboard power systems are rare on boats shorter than 20 feet. Inboards don't trailer well, because the propeller shaft and propeller are fixed to the bottom of the hull; they are less responsive to the helm, be-cause the propeller doesn't change its di-rection of thrust; and the motor has to be mounted somewhere near midships, taking up valuable passenger space.

With a few exceptions, small-boat motors operate in two cycles, in which there is com-bustion each time the piston rises. (By con-trast, gasoline automobile engines are four-cycle, firing every other time the piston rises.) Two-cycle engines are lighter and mechanically less complex than the four-cycle variety, but they require that oil be mixed in the gasoline for lubrication.

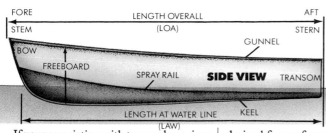

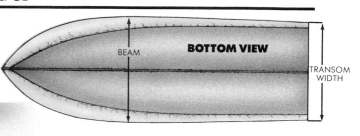

If your association with two-cycle engines is limited to balky chain saws and smoky motorcycles, modern outboard motors are likely to surprise you. In the past two decades, they've advanced tremendously in everyday manners and reliability. Except for units with less than 10 horsepower, outboards typically have multiple cylinders for smoothness, water cooling for reliability, oil injection to preclude hand mixing of oil and gas and, on larger models, amenities such as electric starting, electronic ignition, power steering and power trim to adjust the boat's attitude for best performance. At the upper, hot-rod end of the scale, there are 600-pound, V-8 outboards that displace 4,000 cubic centimeters (244 cubic inches) and produce 300 horsepower.

In years past, outboards got the nod to inboard-outboards on price, but recently that difference has largely disappeared. In part, this is because of changes in the way boat and motor companies are doing business. The trend today is toward boat-and-motor packages designed for each other and sold under the same name. Boats that start on the design tables as inboard-outboards, and that are manufactured under the same corporate umbrella as their power plants, are quite cost-competitive with mix-and-match boat-motor combinations.

Very briefly, the main advantages offered by an inboard-outboard configuration are better weight distribution (since the motor is inside the hull and down low), protection of the motor from the elements, and cleaner visual lines. The outboard takes up no room inside the boat, however, and is much easier to upgrade to higher power at a later date.

Power Requirements

Most recommendations concerning the size of motor for a boat are directed at how much weight and power the craft can stand, not how much is ideal. The former concern has to do with safety and speed, while the latter is a matter of economy and personal need. Make no mistake, though, an underpowered boat can be nearly as dangerous as an overpowered one if you get caught in heavy currents, powerful seas or strong winds.

Every boat built since October 31, 1972, should have a metal plaque listing maximum load and power capacities. These figures are derived from a formula that calculates hull displacement by multiplying the length at water line by the width of the transom. The formula doesn't take into consideration the design of the hull, and there may be boats that can safely handle more power than recommended, but it does provide a good rule of thumb.

The horsepower capacity chart that follows shows what powers can be used according to the displacement factor, but there are a number of modifications that may have to be made to the numbers.

First, if yours is a flat-bottomed boat, such as a johnboat, with a displacement factor of

HORSEPOWER CAPACITY

Displacement Factor

(water-line length × transom width)

0–35	36–39	40–42	43–45	46–52
HP: 3	5	7½	10	15

To determine a "rule of thumb" maximum horsepower rating for your boat, multiply the water-line length by the width of the transom, then refer to the table above. Additional factors may also influence the proper mating of boat to motor.

less than 52, move back one horsepower category. Thus if you have a 10-foot-long johnboat with a 4-foot-wide transom, the displacement factor is 40, but you must move down into the 36–39 category and use a 5 hp motor.

Second, if your boat has a displacement factor greater than 52, has remote steering (which balances the boat better), and has a transom height of at least 20 inches, double your displacement factor and subtract 90 to arrive at the horsepower. For example, an 18-foot runabout with a 6-foot transom has a displacement factor of 108, which, when doubled, equals 216. Subtract 90, and you arrive at a maximum horsepower rating of 126, which can be rounded up to 130 hp.

To complicate matters further, for a boat with a displacement factor greater than 52 but *without* remote steering or a 20-inch-high transom, multiply the displacement factor by 0.8 and subtract 25—unless the boat has a flat bottom, in which case you multiply by 0.5

and subtract 15 to find the maximum horsepower rating.

Obviously, a boat with the largest possible motor may not be the most economical. For a general-purpose planing runabout, an ideal motor will maintain a reasonable speed—say 20 to 30 mph—at around two-thirds of the engine's maximum rpm. The 3,500 to 4,000 rpm range is usually the most fuel-efficient, avoids undue stress and maintains a reserve of power.

To illustrate how important this can be, a motor run at full throttle, rather than two-thirds, may use twice as much fuel and gain only 10 mph in top speed. Twice as much fuel in even a medium-large 100-hp motor may mean a drop from 6 mpg to 3 mpg. (Fuel consumption of really big outboards is measured in gallons per mile.)

Another question to be answered by the person looking for a boat with 100 or more horsepower is whether to use one engine or two. There are many factors to consider, but here are a few of the most important. Two engines not only cost more to buy than one, but they use roughly half again as much fuel as a single engine of equivalent total horsepower. With two engines, one can be shut off when fishing at trolling speeds. (Many inland fishermen outfit their boats with a single large motor for getting to the spot and a tiny, quiet electric trolling motor for moving around while there.) Twin motors are available with counter-rotating props, to counteract the twisting force of a single prop and provide better handling. Twin motors also provide an extra margin of reliability, though today's outboards are generally very trustworthy.

Boating has become a bit more involved, but a lot more satisfying, since those petroleum geologists ventured onto the rivers of Central America. As soon as they managed to acquire a 10-hp Johnson and bolt it to a canoe, they spent a day shearing the entire region's supply of the pins that secure the propeller to the engine, and returned to poling and paddling their way down the jungle freeways. It wasn't what you'd call an unqualified nautical success.

Nonetheless, it was a learning experience. If you happen to be looking for an outboard motor in a Spanish-speaking country, you might ask for a *motor de bote*—and be sure to gesture a lot.

Looking Into Binoculars

How to make
visionary choices when power
isn't everything

Good binoculars are an investment that can magnify your enjoyment of almost all outdoor, and a good many *indoor*, experiences. But there are more than a few points to consider before plunging into what can be a sizable purchase (top-line binocs go for several hundred dollars). Factors such as weight, size, magnification power, image brightness, field of view, focusing, lens construction and coating, and—most important—your own particular needs, all deserve careful thought.

The Basics

Before we jump into the nitty-gritty of long-range optics, we need to get a few terms and definitions under our belts. The first of these is the most basic, and frequently the least understood: the differences between *binoculars* and *field glasses*. Though the two terms are often used interchangeably, there *is* a distinction. Field glasses are the ancestors of binocs, and they're simply two Galilean-type telescopes—each with two in-line lenses hooked together with a common focusing apparatus—fraught with several optical defects. Not least among the shortcomings of field glasses is a field of view (the area visible through the lenses at a given distance) that decreases dramatically as magnification increases. Consequently, field glasses are useful only for low-magnification applications, usually not to exceed a power of four (4X). But if you can get by with such moderate magnification, field glasses do have the singular advantage of being far less expensive than binoculars—more correctly called *prism* binoculars—to which we'll turn our attention in a moment.

But first we need to learn two lens-defining terms: *Ocular lenses* are the small ones on the eye end of binoculars (in fact, they're often called eye lenses, or eyepieces), while *objective lenses* are the big ones at the front, where light enters.

Binoculars are capable of optically precise magnification far beyond that of field glasses because they employ prisms as well as magnifying lenses. The most common prism arrangement used in binoculars is called the *porro* system, which utilizes two prisms in each barrel; the first magnifies and inverts the image, while the second turns what you see right side up again. In addition to increased power, the prism setup allows for wider separation of the objective lenses, thus increasing binocular vision.

And there's another term to learn—*binocular vision*. In simpler words, this means two-eyed vision: seeing the same object through two eyes set a distance apart, thus allowing the brain to compute estimates of depth and distance from the two slightly different images. The greater the separation of those two images, the greater the depth of field (the amount of image that can be sharply focused). With field glasses, that separation is minimal, limited to the width of the two parallel telescopes, or about the normal distance between human eyes. But with porro prism binoculars, the reflecting prisms allow the front, or objective, lenses to be mounted farther apart, while the ocular (eyepiece) lenses remain a comfortable distance from each other.

Magnification

All binoculars have a pair of numbers stamped into one of the barrels and separated by an X, like so: 7X35, 8X35, 10X40 and so on. The first of those numbers tells you the magnification power, while the second gives the diameter of the objective lenses in millimeters. For example, a pair of glasses marked 7X35 provides a magnification of seven and has objective lenses each measuring 35 mm.

Lower-powered glasses are more forgiving of movement and thus are the best bet for viewing from a moving vehicle—a car, boat or aircraft—or if you intend to "sweep" the glasses to follow a big buck bounding across a field or a hawk in flight. The dividing line between hand-held glasses and those requiring a tripod is about 8X. Above that, you'll need some method of anchoring things down.

Image Brightness

If you hold a pair of binoculars at arm's length with the objective lenses pointing at a light, then look *at* the ocular lenses (not through them), you'll see a bright circle of light on each of the lenses. Those circles are the *exit pupils*, which represent the area, or amount, of light that exits from the glasses.

For purposes of comparison, the exit pupil is expressed in millimeters, signifying the diameter of the circle of light leaving the binoculars. But you don't have to *measure* those little orbs. Instead, there's a formula: Just divide the magnification power into the diameter of the objective lens. For example, the exit pupil of a pair of 7X35s is 5 mm (35 mm divided by 7). But occasionally the light-emitting capabilities of optics are expressed as a second measurement, or guide number, known as *relative brightness*, and it's important to know what both ratings mean. Relative brightness is nothing more than the exit pupil (in the above example, 5) squared. Continuing the same example, it would be 5 times 5, or 25. Since some binoculars gather and pass much more light than others, the exit pupil's relative brightness can be an important gauge for selecting night-viewing glasses.

But regardless of how much light exits from a given pair of binocs, the amount that can enter the human eye is limited by Mother Nature. Everyone knows that the pupils in our eyes adjust to available light by expanding and contracting, opening under conditions of dim illumination and closing down when exposed to bright light. But there *are* limits: No matter how bright your surroundings may be, your pupils won't contract below about 2 mm, and in total darkness they'll open to a maximum of only some 7 mm. At dawn and dusk, our pupils are "set" at about 5 mm.

What all that means is that any pair of 7X glasses having an exit pupil of 5 mm (that's a relative brightness of 25, remember) can be used effectively from dawn to dusk. And for *night* viewing, if the exit pupil of your binocs is 7 mm (relative brightness of 49), you've again reached the usable limit.

Remember those numbers when you go shopping, because most good manufacturers list their products' exit pupils (and/or relative brightness) in their literature. And even

Whether you hunt or simply watch wildlife, good binoculars will add to your enjoyment.

if they don't, you can figure it out for yourself, now that you know the formula.

Field of View

As mentioned before, field of view is simply the area that's visible through a pair of binoculars at a given distance. It's sometimes expressed as an angle, but field of view is generally noted as a linear measurement, in feet, at 1,000 yards. And, except in special wide-angle glasses, field of view diminishes as power of magnification goes up. In other words, 7X glasses have a larger field of view than do 9X optics. Field of view is another measurement that's usually included in the manufacturer's literature.

Unfortunately, not all manufacturers label their glasses accurately. The best insurance is a reputable brand name. Or you can check relative field of view yourself by taking two pairs of binoculars of the same power and focusing them on a distant object (such as a sizable parking lot) that is bigger than the visual area either set of glasses can cover. Note how much you can see through each pair; the binocs that span the larger area have the wider field of view.

For buyers wanting maximum viewing area, many major binocular manufacturers offer *wide-angle* glasses in addition to their standard models. For example, one maker offers three 7X35s, with fields of view of 420′, 520′ and 578′ (all measured at 1,000 yards).

Lens Construction

Sometimes the makers of binoculars with a wide field of view rob Peter to pay Paul.

That is, the field of view may be increased at a sacrifice of clear resolution around the edges of the lenses. So another thing to look for when examining glasses is *edge sharpness*. If the image fuzzes out around the edges, look for another pair. (Again, buying name brands offers some degree of protection, since quality binocs employ lenses that have been honed for clarity right to the extreme edges.)

To perform an in-store test of the overall image quality of a pair of binoculars, pick out a viewing target with lots of straight lines and angles (a group of buildings, for example). If the edges of the target's lines bulge outward or bend in, the glasses have lens distortion and are best returned to the display case.

Be sure to check that the edges and the center of the image are clear *at the same time*. If you focus so that the center of the target image is clear and the edges become fuzzy, or if you focus on the edges and the center loses sharpness, hand the binoculars back to the clerk and try another pair.

Do you wear corrective eyeglasses? If so, then by all means wear them when you look through a pair of binoculars you're thinking of buying. Some binocs restrict the field of vision of eyeglass-wearers, while others don't. The spectacle-wearer can enjoy a full field of view with binocs equipped with fold-down rubber eyecups.

A final lens consideration is *coating*. Whenever an image passes through a lens, it loses some of its brightness. If you wear eyeglasses, for instance, about 8% of the incoming light is lost through reflection before it reaches your eyes. And the same concept applies to binoculars: When light passes through a lens or prism, the glass "eats" between 4% and 6% of the brightness. Since modern binoculars may have as many as 12 lenses, half of the incoming illumination may be lost before it reaches you.

To improve light transmission and reduce reflection, modern optical lenses are coated with a molecular layer of special metallic salt that increases light transmission by as much as 50%. And lens coating, if done properly, has the added ability to eliminate flat and hazy images and produce crisp detail in which dark areas appear *dark* and light areas appear *light*.

While coating of the exterior lenses is important, it's even more essential to vision quality that the inside optics get the treatment. To be sure a manufacturer hasn't cut corners by coating only the outside lenses, hold the suspect glasses backward in front of you, with a bright light in the background. Now look through the objective lenses (they're the large ends, remember), and pivot the glasses until you can see a reflection. Properly coated lenses glint purple or blue, while uncoated interior optics show up as a bright glare.

Focus

Though you can buy binoculars that require separate focusing for each barrel, they're largely impractical. Stick to the standard, center-focusing type. To focus center-adjusting glasses, the first step is to set the hinged barrels to fit the distance between your eyes (the $10 term here is "interpupillary distance"). Fold or unfold the two barrels at the hinge until the split images come together to form one crisp picture.

It's always best to focus on a clearly defined target, such as a sign or building. Close your right eye (or cover the right objective lens), and, using only your left eye, turn the focusing wheel until you see the target clearly. Now close your left eye, and turn the adjustable eyecup on the right barrel until the target comes into sharp focus. (The right-eye adjusting wheel will have marks to either side of its center. By memorizing or making note of your personal setting, you can adjust it quickly, should it get changed somehow, without having to go through the entire procedure again.) Now your binocs are set, and all further focusing for distance changes can be done with only the hinge wheel.

Parting Thoughts

Outdoorspersons, such as backpackers, climbers and hunters, often must be weight- and bulk-conscious when selecting equipment. Thus the recent popularity of ultralight and compact "minibinocs." Are they as good as their larger kin? They *can* be, if you're willing to pay for the technology of reduced-size quality. Use the procedures outlined earlier, whether testing the big guys or their smaller counterparts.

Darrell Pace, two-time gold medalist for the U.S. Olympic archery team and enthusiastic bowhunter, draws on a practice target.

Equipment for Bowhunting

Archery equipment is inexpensive and easy to care for.

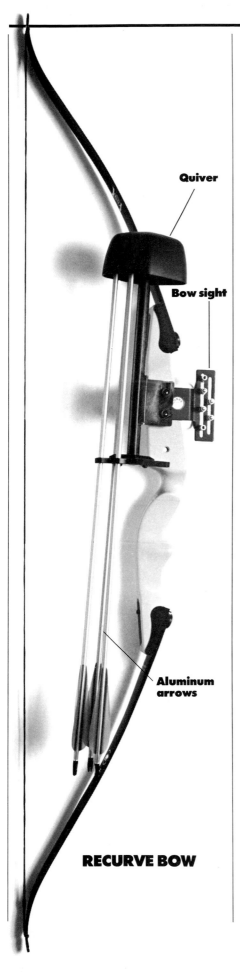

Quiver

Bow sight

Aluminum arrows

RECURVE BOW

The lure of archery, whether it involves the pursuit of game or simply the Zen of doing a relatively simple thing very well, is an old one. And the gear needed to participate in this sport is comparatively inexpensive and easy to use. Here's what you'll need to get started.

Bows

Of basic designs in bows there are but three: longbow, recurve and compound. The longbow is a venerable weapon and deadly in the hands of an expert. But the longbow is a poor choice for the beginner. With an average length of nearly six feet, such a weapon is clumsy under the best of conditions and all but impossible to maneuver in tight quarters, such as a ground blind or tree stand. Longbows also launch arrows at low velocity, which means a high-arcing flight trajectory that works against accuracy. Choosing to hunt with a bow rather than a gun is sufficient handicap in itself; better to perfect your skills before experimenting with this, the hard-core purists' tool.

The recurved bow, also an ancient weapon, is decidedly superior to the longbow in design technology. With its laminated limbs and forward-turned tips, the recurve is capable of delivering substantially more velocity to arrows, and doing so with a foot less length. It's a streamlined, lightweight, reliable weapon and the favorite of many old-line bowhunters. Archery equipment manufacturer Fred Bear, for a prime example, has taken virtually every big-game animal in the accessible world with a recurve.

The compound bow has been around only since the late 1960s. It employs a wheel or cam attached to the end of each limb, between and around which a steel cable is laced. A bowstring is stretched between the cable ends, and tension is applied and balanced via screw adjustments on the limbs. This space

age setup allows a very short bow, four feet on the average, to launch arrows 5% to 10% faster than a recurve having an equivalent draw weight. (Draw weight is the force, measured in pounds, required to pull the bowstring back a distance of 28 inches from the arrow rest.) A further advantage of compounds is that, on most models, draw weight is adjustable through a range of 10 to 15 pounds. This allows you to start out light and gradually increase the draw weight as your shooting muscles tone up with practice. But the single greatest advantage of the compound is a phenomenon known as draw weight let-off.

Both longbows and recurves "stack" as they are drawn. That is, they come back easily the first few inches but become increasingly more difficult to pull as they approach full draw. The last couple of inches can be tough to pull and tougher to hold, inducing shooter fatigue and potential inaccuracy. The magic of the compound is that it offers its maximum resistance at about half draw, beyond which point it releases as much as half its tension, allowing the shooter to complete and hold a draw with ease.

Because of these advantages—flatter trajectory, adjustable draw weight and let-off—many experienced archers encourage novice bowhunters to learn the basics on a compound before experimenting with other designs. However, unless a compound bow is set up and tuned properly, it will never shoot well. And setting up and tuning a compound can be a bear. For that reason, start out with a compound only if you have a knowledgeable friend or archery salesperson to help you get your equipment tuned. If you'll be learning on your own, consider starting with a recurve.

A compound bow will cost more than an equivalent-quality recurve. Other considerations: A recurve is light in weight; simple and hassle-free; traditional and graceful;

23

quieter; and it must be strung for each use. A compound is heavy; in need of complex tuning; technologically superior; shorter; and it always remains strung.

Don't worry about "what everybody else is shooting," but test-shoot both designs, and decide for yourself which is best for you. A couple of hints: If you hunt primarily from a ground blind or tree stand, the shortness of a compound will prove convenient and you won't be bothered by its extra weight. Conversely, inveterate stalkers and still-hunters can grow lopsided after miles of toting a heavy compound around the boonies.

Arrows

Contemporary bowhunter consensus favors aluminum arrow shafts over wood or fiberglass. The leading shaft manufacturer is Easton Aluminum. The top-of-the-line Easton shaft is the XX-75 (anodized in your choice of camo or orange). One step down in quality and price is the Game Getter (in camo or green), with the economy model being the Eagle (green only). The more expensive shafts are harder and thus less likely to bend. But harder shafts are no less likely to become lost. Any competent archery equipment dealer can help you determine what length and weight of arrows suit you.

Arrowheads

There are two basic types of arrowheads: field points for practice, broadheads for hunting. Field points look like bullets and have no cutting blades. They're designed to cause

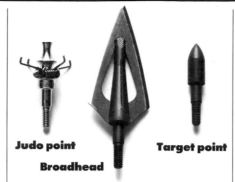

Judo point   **Target point**

Broadhead

minimal damage to target backstops and to pull easily from same. While field points can be used to hunt small game and birds, several specialty points—such as hard rubber blunts and the space age Judo point—are superior.

For big-game hunting (including wild turkey) you'll need broadheads equipped with two or more cutting blades. Back in the days when cedar arrows were the archer's only choice, broadheads were designed to glue directly to the shafts. Modern aluminum shafts, which are hollow tubes, employ threaded inserts that allow the use of screw-in points.

Many bowhunters shun broadheads having permanent blades because they must be resharpened after each hunting shot (hunting with dull broadheads is both nonproductive and cruel). The only alternative to resharpening is to purchase generally more expensive and less streamlined broadheads that use replaceable blades—just pull the old blades out after a hunting shot (whether you hit or missed, they'll be too dull to use again), and insert a replacement set.

Accessories

Three accessories are basic to bowhunting: quiver, arm guard and shooting glove or finger tab.

Most bowhunters own at least two types of quivers. The first is a simple tube that attaches to your belt to hold arrows when practicing. For hunting, you'll want a bow-mount quiver that fastens directly to your bow's handle riser. Five to eight arrows snap firmly into rubber grips at each end of such a quiver, with a hood over the front to protect the points from contacting dulling objects—such as your body during a fall or

Arm guard

other graceless moment.

Two disadvantages of bow quivers are that they add weight to your bow and hold but a few arrows. In their favor, properly mounted bow quivers are silent (as opposed to the rattle of loose arrows in a traditional back quiver), your arrows are always close at hand, and you have one less item dangling from your bod to get snagged in the brush.

An arm guard is a brace made of stiff leather or vinyl and generally measuring three to four inches wide by six or seven inches long. Elastic straps hold the guard

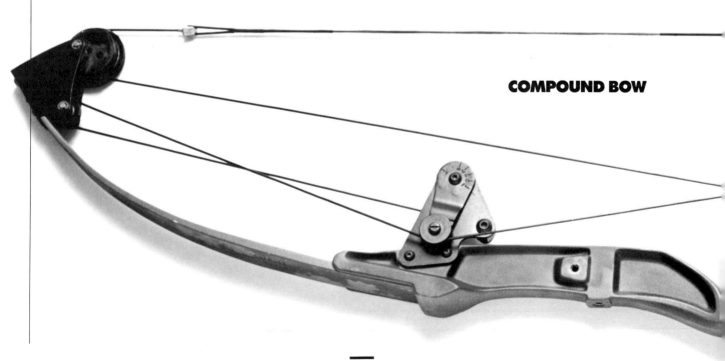

COMPOUND BOW

firmly to the inside forearm of your bow hand. This device not only protects against painful string slap when shooting bare-armed, but keeps long sleeves from interfering with the action of the bowstring.

Shooting glove

Shooting gloves versus finger tabs: Neither is expensive, so try both and decide for yourself. A tab, which slips over the middle finger of your string hand, offers a slight advantage in smooth release and, thus, accuracy. A shooting glove straps around your wrist and covers the index, middle and ring fingers of your string hand up to the second joint. For hunting, most archers prefer a glove.

Accouterments

In this category we have incredible numbers of items proffered to improve the bowhunter's shooting or hunting or both. Many are useful. Others are junk.

Most bowhunters these days shoot with bow sights. Although popular, they're not essential to successful hunting and may in some cases even prove detrimental. To use a bow sight, you simply hold the sight pin on the target and release. If your equipment is tuned and your form is good, your arrow will strike where the sight indicates. But because each of several pins on a bow sight is set for a specific range, when shooting at a target at an unknown distance, you have to estimate the range in order to know which pin to sight with.

Recognizing in this ranging problem a new market, optics manufacturers recently have come out with a little item called a bowhunting range finder. Most work well.

Another recent bowhunting innovation is the trigger release. The front of this device snaps to the bowstring, while the back is a handle with which to draw the bow (rather than fingers on string). It's said to improve accuracy by eliminating the need to develop a smooth release—you simply squeeze a trigger. A significant potential problem with the

Finger tab

trigger release for hunting is that it's just one more thing to think about, one more thing to go wrong.

Other bowhunting accouterments include stabilizers that protrude wandlike from the front of your bow, bowstring nock-point locaters (essential), string silencers (recommended), lighted bow sights (yuck!), arrow-tracking devices (they dispense a trail of colored string—double yuck!) and bow cases (handy). A visit to a well-stocked archery shop will entertain you for hours.

In addition to basic shooting gear, you'll need a compact pair of binoculars. Good binoculars are essential, and compacts are, well, compact.

Bowhunting clothing should be of a camouflage design—such as the innovative Trebark pattern (which looks just like what it sounds like) or a leaf pattern suitable to your hunting environs—and of a soft material that won't whistle when you walk and hiss when you drag it through the brush. Wool and soft cotton are both excellent choices. You'll also need quiet, comfortable footwear; many bowhunters are turning to camouflaged running shoes for fair-weather, easy-terrain hunts.

Finally, you'll need some sort of pack system with which to haul a hunter's essentials—extra clothing, snacks, water and survival basics such as rain gear, first-aid kit, maps, compass and waterproofed matches.

Parting Shot

Beyond gearing up, becoming a successful bowhunter is simply a matter of practice, perseverance and perspective. Of the three, perspective is by far the most important: If a quick, easy kill means more to you than the varied and subtle pleasures of a long, challenging hunt, you'll never be content, or worth a damn, as a bowhunter. With the right perspective—the easygoing attitude that the hunt is more important than the kill—you're bound to enjoy many a good bowhunt.

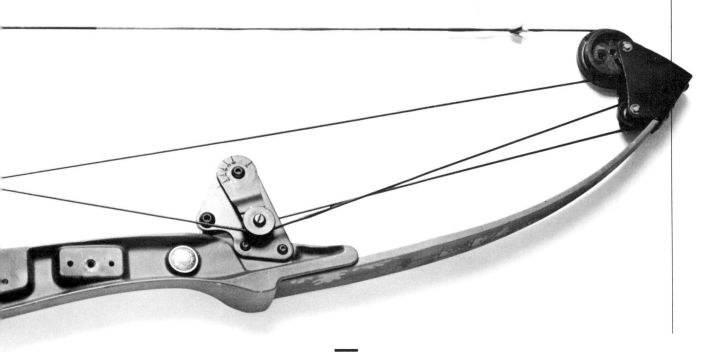

Loren got it almost right. There *is* magic on this planet, and it's contained in *fast-moving* water. Whitewater. The feisty foam of a river dropping over rocks. The whitecaps created when rushing water gets squeezed so tight that waves pop out on top. The frothy turbulence of cresting current curling back in a breaker that never stops dancing in place. *That's* magic.

To touch this magic firsthand, you must paddle it. Riding a wild river is entering a spell of joy, beauty, excitement and satisfaction. It's one of the finest outdoor experiences.

About a Boat

The crucial link between you and this enchantment is your boat. The craft that you choose to paddle will determine the nature of your relationship with the river. It will both create and limit your whitewater experience. So even before you start learning river skills, you need to consider which boat will be most suitable for you.

But first be warned about one thing: Every paddler is extremely biased toward his or her favorite craft. For example, here's what whitewater humorist (and guidebook writer) William Nealy has to say about kayaks and canoes: "Easily recognizable by their grace, finesse and seemingly divine inspiration, expert kayakers are far more tolerant and levelheaded than their expert canoeist brothers and sisters . . . and realize the whole [canoe vs. kayak] controversy boils down to the canoeists' feelings of sexual inadequacy and insecurity." (The canoeists counter Nealy's ribbing with the cry: "Half the paddle, twice the paddler!")

Kayak

The smallest, and in many ways most remarkable, whitewater craft is the kayak, that little, double-pointed, single-passenger boat that darts down, around and through the fiercest of rapids. The kayaker is a hybrid, centaurlike creature: upper half human, lower half water bug. (Legs and hips are hidden away in the boat, essential for leaning and balancing the craft but superfluous for transportation.) The two halves are united by a spray skirt, a neoprene girdle that fastens around the kayaker's waist and over the rim of the boat's cockpit.

The kayaker is the most agile river runner. With those two blades of the double-bladed paddle, he or she can duck into the smallest eddy (a patch of still water behind a boulder). Darting carefully among these nooks of calm, the paddler can work across or even up the river. (Some kayakers paddle *up* seven-mile whitewater runs!)

A decent kayaker can even get flipped upside down by a wave and then right the boat with an Eskimo roll. Indeed, you will never feel truly at home in a kayak until you can roll it in a river. While not a hard maneuver to execute, the roll is a bit tricky to learn—it's hard to listen to instructions when you're sitting upside down and underwater. (By the way, if you can't roll, you're not trapped. It's easy, after a minimum of practice, to somersault out of a flipped kayak.)

Then there are kayaking's playful pleasures. Low in the water, the K-1 paddler gets joyfully drenched as he or she plows through the waves. In the right hydraulic (a standing curling wave), a kayaker can happily surf in place for minutes on end. What's more, if the boater paddles up into certain holes (drops), the bow will get pushed down, and then the whole boat will pop into the air (a "pop-up"). Some holes will actually flip the boat end over end in the air (an "ender").

Kayaks are tippy boats—any beginner is bound to do a good bit of swimming before mastering the aggressive leans required to balance the craft in fast water. They're quite "turny," too: Most novices can maneuver around a boulder more easily than they can paddle in a straight line. Still, it's surprisingly easy to kayak entry-level whitewater. And since successful kayaking doesn't require a great deal of strength, older children and small adults can paddle the boats without difficulty.

Solo Canoe

Paddling a solo canoe down a whitewater river is so different from kayaking that it's actually like going down two different rivers. It's not just that a canoeist kneels instead of sits and uses a single-bladed paddle instead

Whitewater means exhilaration, no matter which boat you choose.

The Right Boat

"If there is magic on this
planet, it is contained in water."
Loren Eiseley

A kayak is probably best suited to the needs of the aggressive, adventurous "cowboy" paddler.

of a double-bladed one. No, the main difference is that solo canoeing is more riding up *on* the water than *in* it. A kayaker maintains control by going faster than the river flow—that vessel is so much in the water that the paddler needs to overcome its force with speed. An open canoeist will sometimes use speed as well (especially when trying to avoid a bad rock or drop), but that person needs to hit waves slowly so the boat will ship less water. After all, the open boater has one limitation always staring over the old shoulder—swamping. A water-filled canoe is a serious one-ton problem.

Does it sound like the thrill-seeking K-1 water bug has all the fun, while the stodgy canoe cruiser spends his or her paddling hours avoiding trouble? Take a second look. Canoes can also dart into eddies. They can surf hydraulics. And now that the best open boats have advanced designs and are stuffed with extra flotation, they can handle the same really big water the kayaks can. Good whitewater canoeists can actually roll a

flipped boat upright and continue on with just a few inches of water inside. Solo canoeists have even paddled the Grand Canyon!

But even that's missing the point. Here's a secret: There's a special pleasure derivable from open boating that no closed-boat paddler can match. The best canoeists learn the art of riding *with* the river. They learn how to read the lines of movement in all that turbulent water. Then they deftly catch a piece of that flow and artfully—almost effortlessly—ride atop the river's back. (Every paddler talks about "reading the water." Most really mean "read the rocks and drops"—i.e., learn to spot the obstacles. Good open canoeists, however, take the phrase literally.)

The best open canoeing is not so much the machismo experience of challenging nature, but one of, to a degree, merging with it. (Not mindless merging, though. You have to stay constantly alert for those moments when strong paddling may be required.)

All of which means that both kayaking and open canoeing have mighty powerful virtues. The aggressive, bronco-busting kayak style isn't better or worse than the strong, with-the-river finesse of the open canoeist. But it's surely different.

Enough about those two. Let's talk about the other paddling possibilities.

C-1

What do you get if you cross a kayak with an open canoe? A C-1: It's fully decked and pointy-ended like a kayak, but you paddle it kneeling and with a single blade like a canoe. Now you can look at that as the perfect combination ("At last, an unswampable canoe!") or as a bizarre paddling mutation ("Why should I go and stick myself in one of those tippy little boats with only one blade to lean on?").

It's hard to know how to feel about the C-1. It does have some advantages over its kayak kin: A C-1 paddler sits higher up, resulting in a much better view downstream. And some people prefer paddling from a kneeling position rather than a sitting one. (It's better for your back, but harder on your knees and feet.) The C-1 does have some advantages compared to an open canoe, too. It's easier to maneuver and play in big waves and

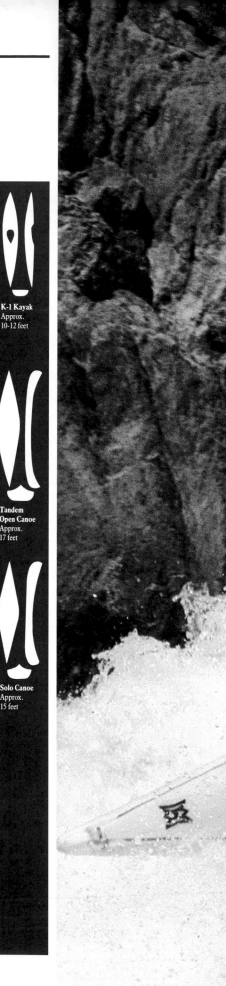

K-1 Kayak
Approx.
10-12 feet

Tandem Open Canoe
Approx.
17 feet

Solo Canoe
Approx.
15 feet

More people start paddling in a tandem open canoe than in any other craft, for good reasons!

holes. And you can roll it back up when it flips. But the nagging feeling that the C-1 paddler is unnecessarily handicapped by "cutting off his right blade to spite his left" still remains.

The main pull of the C-1 is for people who love the distinctive single-blade paddling style yet prefer the aggressive riverbusting pace of closed boating. It does (devout kayakers, please pardon this) take more paddling expertise to C-1 a hard river than to kayak it. It also takes a good bit of strength to paddle a closed, in-the-water boat with only one blade. Hence, C-1 paddlers tend to be young men with big upper bodies.

Tandem Open Canoe

Now, here's the all-time favorite beginner's craft: the tandem open canoe. (You know, "Let's go rent a canoe and see if we can have an adventure like those guys in that *Deliverance* movie did!") More people start out paddling open tandem than any other way. And there is a special thrill that comes from sharing the excitement, and nervousness, of whitewater with a cohort—and a special poetry if both paddlers learn to work as a single unit.

A tandem canoe is a more versatile boat than a solo or decked one. Two people can paddle calm stretches more easily than one, and the open craft has more storage room for gear than a closed boat does. So the tried and true Indian canoe is great for long lake or river paddles and camping trips, as well as whitewater runs.

One of the distinct features of tandem paddling is the difference between being in the bow (front) or the stern (back). Typically, the bow paddler makes those instant "dodge that rock to the right or left" decisions, while the stern person has to power and pivot the length of the boat into the opening the bow finds. The bow gets the best crash-into-the-waves splashes, while the stern (generally the more experienced paddler) is responsible for the placement of the boat as a whole in the rapid.

Drawbacks? If the two of you don't paddle well together (pretty much a given until you're experienced), you're going to make a lot of mistakes due to miscommunication. So beware of the "tandem temper tantrums." In addition, since a tandem canoe is a heavy canoe, it's more likely to swamp than a solo canoe. So it can't tackle some of the big water that decked and solo boats can. One last disadvantage: If you own a tandem canoe, all your friends are going to ask you to take them down some exciting river, and escorting complete novices through treacherous rapids gets old fast. (A hint for when you do get stuck in that situation: If your rookie partner is fairly strong, try teaching him or her the stern strokes and taking the bow yourself. Then, at least, you won't have to yell directions all the time.)

C-2

A tandem *closed* boat, the C-2, is an even rarer sight than a C-1. The banana-shaped two-holer is an amazing paddling craft. It maneuvers sharply and can smash through all the really big stuff that an open tandem boat has to avoid—after all, it won't swamp. But, boy oh boy, the two paddlers really have to be experienced and compatible, because C-2s are just as tippy as their solo closed kin. (Enough husband-and-wife teams have suffered together in C-2s that the craft is sometimes dubbed "the divorce boat.") Good C-2 paddlers don't need to talk much to get down a river; they respond instinctively to each other's actions. And since they *can't* talk un-

Getting Started

There's really only one sensible way to begin learning how to paddle whitewater. Find a paddling club or river outfitter that gives lessons, and take them. Why? Because, for safety reasons, whitewater paddling's a group sport. Because that way you can find out how much you like river running before you spend several hundred dollars on equipment. Because you can receive first-class instruction. And because through a club you can hook up with fellow paddlers, people who will—in all likelihood—soon become good comrades.

The governing body of American whitewater canoeing and kayaking is the American Canoe Association (P.O. Box 1190, Newington, VA 22122; 703/550-7523). The people there will kindly send out, on request, a list of whitewater paddling clubs in your state and a "canoe sport information packet."

derwater, they really need to have a well-practiced Eskimo roll.

C-2 paddling is neat, but it's definitely not for beginners. You should have both solid closed and open boat experience before you and your (even-tempered) partner enter one.

Raft

There's no way to avoid stepping on some paddling fingers here. A raft is a despicable "rubber bus" or "pig boat" to William Nealy. On the other hand, another whitewater writer, Ron Watters, is so devoted to the big floaters that his definitively titled *The White-Water River Book* is entirely about rafts and kayaks. (Open canoes get two paragraphs.)

Why do some paddlers detest rafters? Well, if you've ever dipped your kayak in a feisty surfing wave or artfully grabbed a tight eddy with your canoe and then had a herd of commercial rafts descend upon you like blubbery aquatic elephants, you found out why—real quick. These days, just about every good river that's runnable in summer is serviced by commercial armadas of the bumper boats. Screaming amateurs who've never held a paddle in their life come bounc-

ing down the river you're so expertly paddling—making a mockery of the danger and challenge of *your* sport.

That's the kayak or canoe paddler's point of view. For the beginner or total nonpaddler, rafting a river on a commercial, guided trip makes a lot of sense. You get to enjoy much of the thrill of whitewater (riding rafts is fun). Yet you don't need any experience or expensive equipment. It's safe, too. Rafts are very forgiving craft—they bounce off most rocks. They're also great for long trips (plenty of room for gear). And rafting with three or five other people in the boat offers a team camaraderie that you just don't get from solo paddling.

Interestingly, rafting is the victim of an internal controversy—should you use a paddle or an oar raft? Everybody gets to wield a single-bladed paddle in the first, so a paddle-raft crew needs some chief Indian (or commercial guide) to bark commands and coordinate the teamwork. Oar rafts, though, are controlled by one person who handles two massive oars from near the back of the boat. All other hands are just along for the ride.

Actually, this is to a large degree an East-West squabble. Back East, the whitewater rivers are generally small and rocky. Maneuverable paddle rafts are in order on these tight, "technical" runs. The West prides itself on massive, wave-filled rivers, and those powerful currents are best handled by the powerful strokes of one experienced oar paddler.

Should you start out as a rafter? Sure, if you just want to try river running once or twice or if you'd like an easy way to get your whitewater feet wet. You may even find that rafting is the river sport for you. More likely, though, if you stick with paddling, you'll eventually move on to the more personal and intimate experience offered by canoeing or kayaking.

Happy Rivers To You

If you do get the paddling bug, you'll work hard in your chosen boat, develop your skills and run more and more difficult rivers. When that happens, please consider this last piece of advice. Never *ever* decide you've become a hotshot paddler. Treat whitewater magic with humble respect, or you'll find yourself learning wet lessons—fast.

Tubing

Inner tubing is the black sheep of river running. None of the whitewater books talk about riding rapids in a car or truck inner tube. And the official paddling organizations don't want to even mention the topic.

Tubing won't go away just because the paddling establishment wishes it would, but there are some good reasons for its low esteem. Tubing is definitely the most unsafe way of riding whitewater. An inner tube is not particularly maneuverable, flips quite easily and is very vulnerable to getting trapped in hydraulic waves. People have died tubing hydraulics.

But don't write whitewater tubing off completely. It can be a lot of fun. Sit on your duff, keep your feet downstream to push off rocks, and back-paddle with your hands to steer. It's a bit like "baby rafting."

So since nobody else will even address the issue—yet people are going to tube—here now is a minicourse in tubing safety. Basically, these rules consist of using the same common sense and respect for the river that *real* paddlers always follow. It's downright insane to run a river in the most vulnerable "vessel" of all without heeding basic river-safety rules.

● Always wear a good, Coast Guard–approved life jacket.

● Don't tube in cold weather. Tubers stay continually wet, and cold water can suck the strength—and life—out of you.

● Don't ride any really big rivers. Stick to the small and medium ones (rated class II or an easy III on the I–VI international scale). You'll still have a whole lot of fun; small waves feel like big ones in an inner tube. And you'll be a lot less likely to risk your life.

● Know the river. Research how difficult it is, and scout any bad sections from the shore to see if there are any "keeper" hydraulics or damlike drops. Avoid—i.e., walk around—those potential killers.

● Don't tube in high water. A friendly river can quickly change to a dangerous one when it's flooded. (Particularly dangerous are "strainers," fallen tree limbs that let water, but not people, through.)

● If you're dumped out in the middle of a rapid, swim down it feet first just like you tubed it. Don't try to stand up in a strong current—your foot may get trapped by a rock and your body thrown forward. Many people have drowned in shallow water this way.

● And, of course, of course, of course, don't drink while tubing.

FOUR 1" X 8'
NYLON STRAPS

ATTACH TWO BUCKLES TO EACH STRAP
EQUIDISTANT FROM THE CENTER RIVET,
AT A DISTANCE OF 1/2 THE TUBE'S
INTERIOR DIAMETER.

RIVET

CENTER RIVET

OPTIONAL
GROMMET

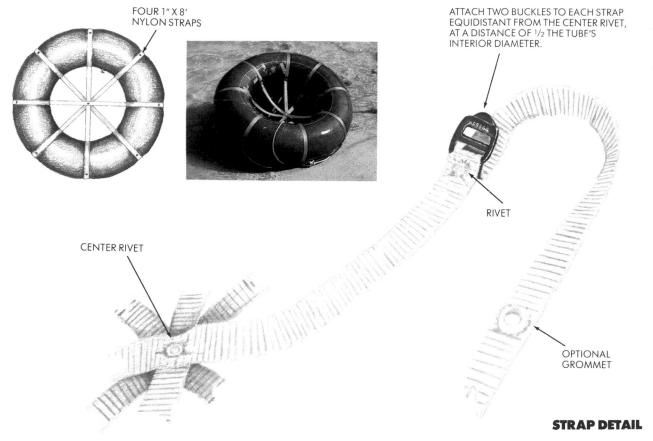

STRAP DETAIL

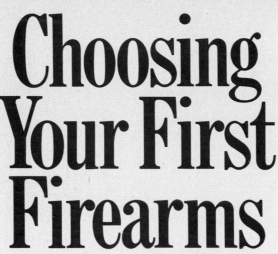

Choosing Your First Firearms

A carefully chosen rifle or shotgun can be a valuable tool. Here's what to look for.

It's in the full glory of summer that we begin to glimpse the season's death. Perhaps a small cool breeze blows through the still-bright evening, eclipsing the scent of iris with something recognized but unidentifiable, a faint aroma of regret. Or maybe a black walnut or hickory tree, last to green, first to bare, drops one precocious leaf. In the great cities, these whispers of change would probably not be heard, but to one raised in the country, or even one whose blood has only begun to ebb and flow to rural rhythm, the hint of fall sends the body into a flush composed of equal parts of a vague loneliness and a delicious anticipation. Autumn is the season of the field and forest; inside some of us an ancient ancestor anticipates the hunt.

For those new to country life, though, this eagerness may be blasted apart by a decidedly modern uncertainty. "Hell," he or she might mutter. "I don't even know what sort of gun I *should* have."

Fortunately, this problem is far from difficult to solve. The selection of basic hunting arms, for the beginner, is a much simpler matter than it is for the more experienced hunter who may be stricken by the equipment mania that seems to infect just about every sport nowadays. Of course, there are a great many models among even the few firearm types discussed here, but the parameters are relatively easy to deal with. For the beginning nimrod (or for any hunter, as many with years in the field sometimes forget), the important consideration isn't necessarily to have a weapon specifically designed for each and every situation, but rather to have one or more reliable, well-made guns and—here's the key—to learn to be able to get something approaching their built-in potential from them.

Paying for a Plinker

For a great many aging country kids, one Christmas day in late childhood or early adolescence will be forever burned into the memory because of a long box propped against the wall behind the tree; that first .22 rifle was a symbol of responsibility and trust, a first sweet taste of independence, the thin edge of the wedge into a door that would one day open to adulthood.

The .22 is probably the ideal first gun, both for a youngster and for an adult whose interest in hunting has just surfaced. It can be used to take squirrels (a delicious and common game animal) and, under the right circumstances, rabbits. More important, though, this small-caliber rifle is inexpensive to shoot and neither too loud nor too physically punishing.

Of the several varieties of .22s available, you'll want, first, a rifle chambered to accept the .22 *long rifle* cartridge rather than the underpowered .22 short or the relatively expensive .22 magnum. From there, you can choose among a variety of types of firearms. The most common of these are the single-shot, the bolt action, the semiautomatic and the pump. Each has its purposes and its devotees, but many believe the bolt action does the best job of developing, and then serving, the serious hunter.

There are several reasons for this. The most important is the fact that a good bolt-action .22 can effectively mimic the larger-caliber deer rifle that the same owner will most likely later acquire, and will thus give him or her counterfeit experience with the bigger gun at much less expense.

The bolt action, forcing the shooter to manually eject the spent shell and insert a live cartridge by manipulating the bolt after each shot, also encourages better field habits than does the semiautomatic, which allows the shooter to keep on firing as quickly as the trigger can be pulled. Don't misunderstand; there are many fine and conscientious marksmen who prefer the semiautomatic. Unfortunately, there are also some beginning shooters who've been seduced by the awesome rate of fire possible with these weapons

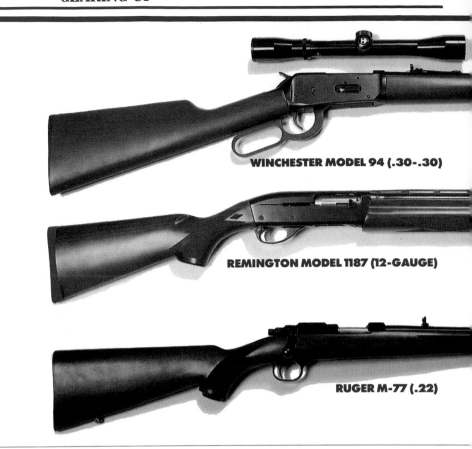

WINCHESTER MODEL 94 (.30-.30)

REMINGTON MODEL 1187 (12-GAUGE)

RUGER M-77 (.22)

and who tend to substitute quantity of shots for quality.

The Shell Game: 1

Since .22 cartridges are inexpensive, it pays to spend a little more for premium ammunition. Quality cartridges offer greater muzzle velocity (the speed at which they exit the gun) and thus greater accuracy, since a faster shell will drop less over distance. Use the same shells for hunting that you practice with, stick with hollowpoints for squirrels (the small animals are surprisingly difficult to kill, and hollowpoints expand when they hit, thus improving your chances of dropping the game cleanly and humanely), and avoid mixing brands of shells in a semiautomatic firearm.

Searching for a Scattergun

If the first .22 provides a novice hunter with a ticket to the world of outdoor sport, owning a shotgun is the equivalent of a full-season pass. In fact, there are few animals in the continental U.S. that can't be hunted with one of these versatile weapons. Squirrel, rabbit, waterfowl and such upland game birds as grouse, dove, quail, woodcock and pheasant are probably the first to come to mind when one thinks of shotgunning, but load that firearm with a single rifled slug rather than small shot, and you have a very effective short-range weapon for deer or even black bear. In fact, in some parts of the country the shotgun is the only legal deer weapon.

Scatterguns are available in most of the varieties offered by .22 manufacturers (pump, single-shot, bolt action, semiautomatic) and also in side-by-side and over/under double-barreled configurations. And, to meet the challenge of multiple usage, some manufacturers now offer single-barreled scatterguns with interchangeable barrels; one suited to firing shot and the other designed to efficiently throw a rifled slug at big game.

Your first decision will concern gauge. (Gauge is to shotguns as caliber is to rifles, and reflects the number of balls, should the shell be loaded with one large ball, to the pound. Thus a dozen 12-gauge slugs would weigh approximately one pound.) The most common options are .410 (which, perverse-

ly, is not a gauge but a caliber, which refers to the diameter of the bore of the firearm), 20-gauge, 16-gauge (which has been in a popularity slump in recent years, so you may find it difficult to locate shells) and 12-gauge.

Each of these has advantages and disadvantages, and a shotgun enthusiast will most likely own several gauges. The .410 is light and doesn't "kick" much when shot, so it's often recommended to young or physically small shooters. It's also by far the least effective game-taker, a fact which would suggest that you start with nothing smaller than a 20-gauge. The 20 is also a compromise, trading its easy handling for limited knockdown power. Still, in capable hands this is a very effective hunting weapon. If you fear that the weight and kick of a larger gun would interfere with your ability to enjoy it, the 20 is a worthwhile first choice. Do be sure, though, to purchase a gun capable of handling 3-inch magnum shells, which give the little gun a lot more punch.

With the 16-gauge in limbo of sorts, the 12-gauge stands out as the most versatile of the bunch, and probably the most versatile all-around hunting weapon. Choose a single-shot if price is a major concern; a pump or semiautomatic, preferably with interchangeable barrels, if you plan to mix small-game hunting with the pursuit of deer; and a double—either side-by-side or over/under—if

you plan to concentrate on birds and are susceptible to the romance and nostalgia that surround these "classic" shotguns. Such recommendations are, of course, quite subjective. If possible, try to shoot a variety of guns before making a decision.

Finally, you'll have to select the appropriate choke for your gun. This term refers to the degree of restriction in the muzzle of the barrel, which controls the spread of the shot. Many guns offer interchangeable choke tubes, to allow you to select an open pattern for, say, close-flushing grouse in tight woods, or a tighter, more distance-stable pattern for fast-flying, long-range waterfowl. If you don't have hunting friends to turn to, let the seller know the uses you intend to put your gun to. And it's always a good idea to get more than one recommendation.

From left to right, a .30-.30, a .270 and a .30-06 shell. These are the most popular deer cartridges in North America, and for good reason.

4X SCOPE

The classic lever-action carbine is still among the most popular eastern deer rifles.

A semiautomatic shotgun with interchangeable barrels may be the most versatile hunting tool.

A fine bolt-action .22 will train the beginning hunter as well as it will serve the expert.

The Optics Option

Most hunters eventually fit their .22s and deer rifles with scopes. (A shotgun used for big-game hunting will perform well enough, within its accurate range, with open iron sights. These will be standard on the slug barrel of an interchangeable-barrel gun and can be fitted by a gunsmith to others.) Open sights have their place on rifles, of course, and many prefer them for the snap-shooting that's commonly called for in the eastern brush. However, others prefer a scope to iron in almost any situation. As should be the case when buying a firearm (or any tool), purchase the best scope that your budget will allow. For general-purpose work, try a non-adjustable 4-power. Be sure it's mounted securely, and sighted in carefully, and *check* that sighting after long travel, a day in rough terrain or after long periods of disuse. You can't shoot what you can't see, and a good scope will give your poor human eyes the chance to come a little closer to competing with the optical equipment of the game you pursue.

The Shell Game: 2

Selecting shells for your shotgun requires almost as many decisions as does purchasing the gun in the first place. You'll have to determine whether you want standard 2¾-inch shells or the more potent 3-inch magnums. As noted above, the latter is best for most 20-gauge work, while the former should be adequate for most 12-gauge situations, with big game, wild turkeys and waterfowl being the exceptions. As a general rule, you'll want to stick with "high brass" shells; the "low brass" variety have less powder behind the shot and are thus less powerful.

The shot itself also demands a decision. Shot sizes are given in numbers, the larger designations referring to smaller pellets. The appropriate shot size will be determined by the game hunted, the terrain, the question of whether, in the case of birds, your game will usually be just flushed or free-flying, and so forth.

If you plan to hunt waterfowl, use steel, rather than lead, shot, and select a shotgun-choke combination to suit such shells. Lead entering the food chain when ducks and geese mistake spent shot for grain has become a serious enough problem to cause its use to be prohibited in some areas.

Buying "The Big Gun"

The high-powered firearms often referred to as deer rifles are used for pronghorn antelope, black bear and even elk in addition to whitetail or mule deer. Again, there are a number of actions available, including bolt action, semiautomatic, lever-action, single-shot and pump. As with the .22s, a good first choice is the bolt action.

Of the many calibers available, the first-time buyer should probably stick to either the .30-30, the .270 (for long-range hunting in the open country of the West) or the .30-06 (probably the best choice for a do-it-all cartridge). There are any number of other fine calibers, but any of these three should be available at any sporting-goods shop and at many country stores, while a more exotic cartridge may be difficult to find should you run short on shells while hunting.

Whichever deer rifle you choose, though, remember that the marksman, not the rifle, makes the shot. One of the worst possible endings to a hunt is to be left haunted with the memory of a poorly hit animal that escaped to suffer and probably die. As noted above, having a .22 similar to your deer rifle will increase your familiarity with the bigger gun at minimal cost. Take advantage of that technique, but be willing to spend the money and time it takes to become comfortable and proficient with the larger caliber, too, before you set your sights on living muscle.

The Shell Game: 3

High-powered rifle cartridges vary in both type and weight, though not so widely as do shotgun shells. Still, the variety is large enough, and the suitability of the various choices determined enough by locale and species of game, to suggest you seek local advice when selecting your ammunition. As a rule of thumb, you'll get satisfactory performance from a .270 bullet in the 130-grain weight range, while a .30-30 will find a 150-grain bullet adequate for most situations, and the .30-06 will happily throw bullets of 150 grains or larger.

And Practice Makes . . .

Put yourself a few months into the future. The last sip of coffee still smoky on your palate, you leave your car and enter the foggy mystery of a predawn field. Your coat hangs warm and comfortable on your shoulders, broken-in boots hiss satisfyingly through the dew, and each step feels more purposeful, stronger, than usual. Your day pack waddles a bit across your back as you step, bringing visions of a lunch to be enjoyed while snuggled up to a stump, with sunlight stroking its tree-limb tattoos across your face. On your shoulder is a firearm that long practice has decorated with the golden familiarity of all good tools. You know what it can do and what you can do with it. You may not raise it to fire all day, but a hunt that begins with a morning like this, and feelings like this, can never be considered less than a great success.

Scattergun shells. The 12-gauge (left) shown is a low-brass shell, not recommended for most hunting. The 20-gauge (center) and .410 (right) shown are high-brass shells.

Fabrics for the Outdoors

Unraveling common "mythinformation" concerning fabrics

If you've shopped for outdoor clothing lately, then you know that new synthetic fabrics with space age names (Thermax, Capilene, Prolon) are breeding like mosquitoes and claim to do everything short of physically transporting you into the wilds and back out again.

Whatever happened to the good old days when you wore cotton in summer, down and wool in winter, and silk if you could afford it? Well, in the eyes of many natural-fiber purists, those days are still around. For others, only the newest, highest-tech, flashiest-hued synthetics will do, even for weekend outings under halcyon skies.

What you wear into the woods, of course, is nobody's business but your own. But to help you get the most for your outdoor-clothing dollar, here's a review of some of the leading fibers and fills available today, detailing the strengths and weaknesses of each.

The Naturals

Cotton was being grown in India 5,000 years ago, and evidence exists of its cultivation in Mexico perhaps 2,000 years before that. Today, cotton is the number one textile fiber worldwide.

Save silk, cotton is the most comfortable of natural materials against the skin. Its durability-to-cost ratio is attractive, it looks good, and laundering a cotton garment is as easy as tossing it into the washer and dryer. For outdoors folk, cotton's most important quality is its absorbency: Cotton sops up moisture from the surface of the skin and releases it grudgingly to evaporation. This can be good—or very bad.

For summertime wear it's good. When the weather's hot, cotton's not. It's lightweight, is cool when dry and becomes a personal swamp cooler when damp with perspiration and a breeze is blowing (or when you're creating your own wind by walking or running).

But that same swamp-cooling quality makes cotton hypothermia-bait in chilly weather. A hiker dressed in cotton who works up a sweat climbing a hill on a mild fall afternoon is fair game for hypothermia upon reaching the top. If the walker sits down to rest in the refreshing breeze, that damp, clinging cotton begins cooling the body. Have you ever tried shaking off a chill once it bites you when you're dressed in damp cotton? Two choices: Build a fire, or get moving.

The ticket for wearing cotton in the out-of-doors is to enjoy its comfortable coolness in summer but to leave it at home in cool weather, or in *any* weather when heading back of beyond.

Wool, too, has been in use as a clothing fiber for a long time, at least since the Neolithic period in Asia. Wool and cotton—the two oldest fiber favorites—are functional opposites. While even the best cotton is relatively inexpensive, top-grade virgin wool can flatten your pocketbook quicker than you can say *baaah*. While cotton is light, airy and soft, wool is heavy, dense and stiff. While cotton is pleasant to the touch, wool's harsh scratchiness puts rashes on sensitive skin. While cotton can be laundered just about any old way, wool demands cold water, special detergents and a gentle machine cycle or hand washing, and it must be air-dried flat. Finally—important to backcountry travelers—while cotton is cool when dry and chilling when wet, wool is toasty when dry and almost as warm when sopped.

Thus, wool is a wise choice for cold-

Above: Tenzing and Hillary show styles after climbing Everest. Left: William La Varre outfitted to recapture ex-slaves. Far left: Teddy Roosevelt models the latest in full buckskins.

weather activities where a little extra weight and bulk matter not (say, sitting in a duck blind or ice fishing) and for mild-weather outings that pose a possibility of getting wet. Wool is commonly used in the manufacture of virtually every type of outdoor clothing, caps to socks, underwear to capotes.

Silk production was well established in China during the Shang dynasty (circa 1523 to 1027 B.C.), and legend has it that the wormy technology was known 1,000 years earlier. That's impressive when you consider the complex processes involved in silk's manufacture, which accounts for its scarcity, which, in turn, accounts for its sky-high price.

But no fabric feels more luxurious against bare skin than silk. And top-quality silk is strong and durable and stretchy and light and breathable and warm. It's also attractive,

wind-resistant and almost frictionless. However, silk absorbs and holds odors and requires either dry cleaning or careful hand laundering.

Silk's primary use in outdoor clothing is in liners—socks, gloves, underwear. The "queen of fabrics" is also popular for balaclavas and scarves. Obviously, silk is a cool-weather-only fabric. Its biggest fans are people seriously committed to active wintertime sports, such as skiing, who demand warm, light, flexible, comfortable underclothing, and can afford it.

Down, the last of the big four naturals, is the soft subfeather fluff from the breasts of geese and ducks. Most down is produced in China, where domestic waterfowl are an important meat source and down is a profitable by-product. Dry down is the warmest of all insulators, natural or otherwise. Down-filled garments can be stuffed into incredibly compact bundles and will spring back to full loft when released, time and time again. Down can be machine laundered and dried. And down is, well, light as feathers.

But down has two big drawbacks: It's expensive, and it's worthless when wet. Therefore, while down is one of the best choices for casual outdoor wear, it's risky protection for prolonged backcountry ventures.

The Synthetics

Polypropylene represents the most significant innovation in synthetic outdoor fibers in decades. It is, in effect, woven plastic, and its primary use is in sock liners and long underwear. Polypro is light, thin, stretchy, comfortable against the skin, warm when dry *or* wet, and specializes in absorbing moisture from the skin and wicking it to outer layers of clothing for evaporation without noticeable cooling. These qualities, combined with midrange pricing, have made polypro *the* favored cool-weather liner fabric among outdoor activists, including the U.S. Army.

Drawbacks? Oh yes: Polypropylene requires cold-water washing and drip-drying; it will melt in a hot dryer. And polypro has a widespread reputation for absorbing and retaining body odors. That proclivity, it is said, abetted by the limited deodorizing capabilities of cold-water washing, can lead to perennial pong.

Fills, many of them polyesters, are available in a plethora of brand names—including Hollofil, Quallofil, PolarGuard, Thinsulate and Thermolite. All are less efficient than *dry* down, but all will keep you warm when wet; none are as light and compressible as down, but all cost less; and synthetic fills, like down, can be machine laundered. Of the five products named above, the first three are used as lofty fill in shell garments and sleeping bags, while the latter two are produced in thin sheets for lining gloves, boots and other close-fitting items.

What's Best for the Great Outdoors?

With fibers and fills, "best" can be defined only in relation to circumstance. For serious backcountry travel—when you have no place to run to for shelter, no place to hide from the storm, and your clothes are the only things between you and the elements—heed the experts: Two of America's largest and most respected wilderness skills schools, Outward Bound and the National Outdoor Leadership School, *dictate* the types of clothing to be taken on their serious backcountry treks. For all but summertime desert courses, both schools require wool and polypropylene clothing, or blends thereof, and synthetic fills for shell garments and sleeping bags. Cotton and down are *verboten*.

It seems the instructors at these schools don't enjoy evacuating hypothermia casualties. It's even less fun to evacuate yourself when you're numb with cold or suffering from heat exhaustion because you failed to choose outdoor clothing of the appropriate fabrics. In the great outdoors, being "well dressed" involves more than fashion.

PART TWO

Backcountry How-To

Basic information
to help even the most
inexperienced
novice avoid beginners'
mistakes

The Essential Art of Tracking

A skill that's unknown to all too many modern hunters

There are two great sins in hunting. The first is to attempt a shot beyond your abilities and by doing so allow the escape of a wounded animal. Of course, even the most conscientious outdoorsman can't always guarantee a quick, clean kill. There are simply too many things that can go wrong in the fraction of a second between the final tightening of the trigger finger and the bullet's impact. The second transgression, though, can be avoided and is thus unforgivable: It is the failure, through laziness or lack of preparation, to make a good effort to find, end the suffering of and recover wounded game. The skill required, of course, is tracking, and it's unknown to all too many modern hunters.

It Starts With the Shot

Many tracking problems can be avoided by simply using all of your powers of observation at the moment you pull the trigger. When shooting at long range, listen for the sound of the bullet striking. This distinctive "thunk" can be heard for a good distance on a quiet day. Even more important, don't take your eyes off the animal until it's either clearly dead or out of sight. Watch for indications of a hit: a stumble, a humping of the back, a quick kick of the front or rear legs (often indicating a heart shot) or a flicking of the tail or head.

If the animal is down, stay calm, and keep your weapon ready for a few minutes before approaching. More than one hunter who has excitedly run up to even such a timid animal as a white-tailed deer has received serious injuries when the stunned creature recovered. At the least, a careless approach could leave you unprepared to shoot at a badly wounded, but suddenly up-and-running, target.

Should you be sure you've hit the animal but not downed it, try to maintain your calm as best you can, and continue to shoot. Once a creature is wounded, you've effectively entered into a contract to finish the job. If you can do it before the beast clears the next ridge or disappears into the brush, your day will be shorter and far more rewarding.

Let's say that you've made your best effort, only to have the animal run off. First and foremost, never simply assume that you've missed. "Missed" shots account for innumerable dead and wasted game animals every year. Instead, make sure your gun or bow is ready, and—keeping your eyes on the area where the animal was last seen—*stalk* slowly to the spot where it stood when the shot was fired. Once there, search the area thoroughly for evidence of a hit. An archer should first look for his or her arrow; often a seemingly missed shot will have actually passed through the animal and will provide ample evidence of having done so. A gun hunter should look for bits of clipped hair or traces of blood.

There's been a good bit written about analyzing the blood trail in order to determine where an animal has been hit. According to the accepted wisdom, bright, frothy blood is evidence of a lung hit (which will usually down the animal within 100 yards), a dark spoor with bits of food in it indicates a gut shot (and a *long* tracking job), while a heavy trail of bright blood indicates a hit in an artery (which will most likely make for easy, and relatively brief, tracking). Try to notice those telltale clues. If nothing else, by doing so you'll be tuning your powers of observation for the job at hand.

If no blood is evident at the site of the shot, move slowly along the path that the animal followed after you fired. Look for tracks; if any are available, take careful note of their size and shape, and memorize any peculiarities (if you're lucky enough to be dealing with a distinctive track). You may have to pick out your animal's trail from others as the day goes on. Continue to look for any sign of blood. And don't limit your search to the ground. High grass, the leaves and stems of brush and the like will often pick up spoor from the animal's coat, even if the bleeding isn't heavy enough to drip freely.

Should you find no blood by searching up to the spot where your quarry disappeared, but feel that you did hit the animal, go on to cover the surrounding area. Mark the point where you lost sight of the beast (a scrap of tissue paper is good for this purpose), and then scan out from that spot, looking for dense cover, fallen logs and anything else that might shelter a wounded creature. Once you've made a thorough search of the terrain without picking up any evidence of a hit, you'll have done about all you can do, other than hope that you did, indeed, miss, and perhaps check the area after 24 hours for signs of crows, turkey buzzards, magpies or other predatory birds that might lead you to a well-hidden animal.

More often than not, though, if you did score a hit, a careful search will turn up sign. Once that happens, your responsibilities multiply and real tracking begins. The first question you'll have to answer is when to start on the trail. Many authorities say it's advisable to wait before following a blood trail in order to "let the animal stiffen up." Advice on exactly how long to wait, however, can range from 15 minutes to 12 hours, depending upon which source you consult. Frankly, hard and fast rules don't apply here. Factors such as weather, terrain, time of day and—when it's known—the type of injury sustained by the animal must be taken into account before making a decision.

Should you be faced with a tracking job during a rain- or snowstorm, for example, get to the task immediately, before blood spoor is covered or washed away. A shot made at twilight, too, should be followed up quickly, as tracking by flashlight is extremely

Note the size and distinguishing features of your animal's track.

difficult (and could result in your being accused of illegal jacklighting). An animal wounded in open country will tend to travel farther before holing up than will one in thick brush, and—especially if you're hunting with a rifle—you might want to begin tracking immediately, moving slowly and scanning ahead for the chance to end the stalk with a well-placed long-range shot. If none of these other factors apply, and you're certain that your hit was in the heart/lung area, wait 15 minutes or so, as much to allow yourself to calm down as anything else,

then stalk slowly along the trail, marking each piece of evidence with tissue paper and stopping at regular intervals to scan your surroundings for the animal. In this case, you'll seldom have to travel more than 100 yards before collecting your game. Should you be less sure of the quality of your hit, and, again, if none of the other factors are in play, you might want to wait a bit longer, say a half-hour to 45 minutes, but more important than waiting is to follow the trail *slowly* and stay alert. Your aim is to see a wounded animal before it sees you.

So move along, constantly checking ahead, to the side and behind you (game will often circle back when hit); look for blood on the ground, on grass, brush, etc., and mark every piece of sign you find. In between blood spots, follow tracks if possible, or even get down close to the ground to scan ahead for a pattern of brushed-aside grass or broken plants.

Tracking is best done by a two-person team, one of whom remains at the last sign and scans the area while the other looks for spoor. If you lose the trail, cast ahead in increasing arcs along the animal's suspected line of travel. (Don't be afraid to get down on your hands and knees.) If you don't have a partner to help you track, make sure to leave an obvious mark on the last piece of sign you've found. Should you fail to turn up any blood or tracks after a thorough search, range out from the last spoor to check any terrain feature that might attract, or give evidence of, a fleeing animal. Game or foot trails, especially those leading downhill, appeal to a creature trying to follow the path of least resistance, and are often clear enough to take tracks. (Here's where the ability to identify *your* animal's footprint might come into play.) Brush, deadfalls and the like offer shelter, while water seems to attract wounded game, and damp stream banks are often composed of sand or mud, giving the hunter a chance to find a clear track.

If you conscientiously perform every task described so far, you'll be dressing out meat at least nine times out of 10. However, if this effort still doesn't end your hunt, go back to the last sign, and, walking in gradually increasing circles, cover the area, working slowly and keeping alert to your surroundings, until you either find the animal, locate a fresh blood trail or run out of daylight. And if the latter happens without your finding your trophy (which is unlikely), come back the following day to pick up any trail markers you've left and to give scavengers a chance to lead you to the kill.

Careful, conscientious, *stubborn* tracking will recover a badly wounded animal almost every time and will usually allow you to bring in game that was hit but would have otherwise survived. More than that, it fulfills the contract you signed with the pulling of the trigger and can replace the horror of a flubbed shot with the satisfaction of bringing in game that a less-committed hunter would have abandoned to suffering and a wasted death.

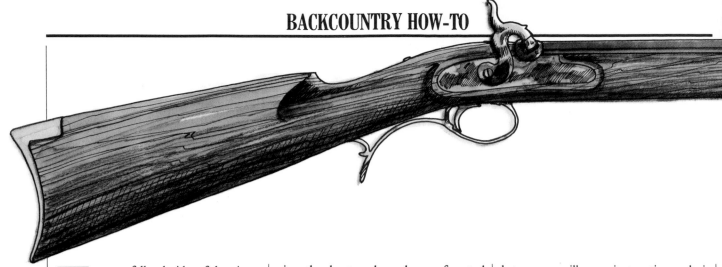

To many folks, the idea of shooting a black-powder gun is, at first, a bit frightening. After all, the primitive explosive used (producing, upon detonation, clouds of smoke the likes of which you'll never see when firing a contemporary cartridge) must actually be *handled* by the shooter. The powder is measured, and then poured directly down the barrel of the gun, and that barrel, if the weapon is one of the popular larger-bore muzzleloaders, looks almost big enough to accommodate a Ping-Pong ball! It's understandable, then, that this collection of factors sometimes brings to mind images of accidental overcharges, of barrels peeled back banana-skin fashion and of shoulder-breaking kicks.

However, when people first fire the old-timey rifles (or pistols), they're generally surprised by the *civility* of the weapons. Black-powder guns don't kick back excessively. In fact, as a result of the slow-burning nature of the explosive (when compared to modern gunpowder), the firearm tends to shove, rather than slam against, your shoulder when it goes off.

Of course, there's a lot more to recommend today's crop of muzzleloaders than their relative gentleness. For one thing, such guns provide an opportunity to experiment with the various components of the charge—amount of powder, kind of projectile, thickness of patch (if a ball is used), type of lubricant and so on—and to learn, through such trial-and-error research, the full range of the gun's capabilities. To duplicate that educational experience with a later style of gun, you'd have to have access to a good bit of reloading equipment and a whole passel of additional know-how.

Furthermore, the black-powder firearms are practical. Most modern muzzleloaders will do almost anything that a cartridge-firing rifle will do, and even make up for their one disadvantage (the time required to prepare for a second shot) with pluses of their own. Consider: When used for recreational target shooting, a muzzleloader, as noted above,

gives the shooter a large degree of control over his or her load, and that extra involvement can't help but increase the satisfaction that results from firing a tight grouping into a target's bull's eye.

If providing a supply of good—*not* pesticide/antibiotic/hormone–saturated—meat for your family is the goal uppermost in your mind, you'll be pleased to know that many states allow shooters with "primitive weapons" to enter the deer woods in search of venison before the crowds of "regular" gunners come in.

And folks who like to be prepared for any eventuality know that, especially when kept in conjunction with more up-to-date firearms, a black-powder weapon can provide a real feeling of security. After all, bullets are as close as the nearest scrap of lead (tire-rim weights, fishing sinkers and the like can all be melted down and molded) and, should worst come to worst, a back-yard chemist very likely could—with little more than pig manure, sulfur and charcoal—actually brew up a batch of crude black powder!

Perhaps the muzzleloader's chief virtue, though, is its ability to demystify today's firearms, providing, in effect, the missing link

between a recoilless semiautomatic assault rifle and the hunk of pipe, rock and firecracker contraptions that many of us either built or heard stories about in our childhood. After all, a gun is a tool—no more and no less—and an implement that's understood tends to be an implement that's operated safely.

Take a Powder

As is the case with almost any piece of equipment imaginable, it's best to spend time (loading, firing and cleaning) with as many types of muzzleloaders as you can before you actually purchase a gun. Unfortunately, few people actually have the opportunity to do that, so enough basic information will be provided here to at least allow the firearm shopper to know, in advance, the kinds of choices available.

First of all, that would-be gun owner must decide whether to buy a *flintlock* or a *percussion* (also called *caplock*) firearm. Your choice will most likely be determined by the uses to which you hope to put the gun.

The flintlock firing mechanism is by far the older of the two. Developed around the

Basic muzzleloading gear; mountain men called it "possibles."

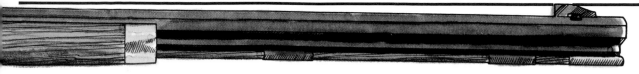

The Modern Muzzleloader

Whether for target shooting or
hunting, there's life in the old-time
"smoke poles" yet.

end of the sixteenth century, this ingenious ignition system depends solely upon a piece of flint and some powder (both a fine and a coarser grade). Real back-to-basics shooters often prefer it to the more modern caplock, which requires one additional manufactured component. On the other hand, the flintlock is generally considered to be more difficult for a beginner to master and—in the hands of all but the most expert muzzleloader enthusiasts—is somewhat more likely to misfire, because of the relative inefficiency of the flint-and-powder priming technique.

Yet the procedure for firing the flintlock is really quite straightforward. With the flint—padded by a cushioning strip of leather or lead—in place and the hammer down, fill the pan with a fine (3F or 4F grade) black powder, and use a vent pick (or any appropriate pointed object) to work a few grains down into the touchhole. Then draw the hammer back, and shut the elongated cap (called the *frizzen*) over the powder-filled pan. After making sure, once again, that the flint is securely in place, you're ready to take aim and fire.

While the percussion lock is newer than the flint-fired mechanism, it still goes a long

way back, probably to the latter part of the eighteenth century. It's generally considered more reliable than its predecessor, largely because it doesn't depend upon a pan of loose powder, somewhat exposed to wind and moisture, for its priming charge.

To prepare a percussion gun for firing (after it's loaded), you draw the hammer to full cock, and slip a "cap"—a small copper cup with a bit of explosive fulminate inside—down over the now exposed nipple. The hammer can then be put in the "safe" half-cocked position until it's ready to be drawn back to full cock again prior to shooting.

The Muzzleloader Marketplace

Not too long ago, prospective muzzle-loading-firearm buyers were often hard put to find much of a selection of available guns and even worse off when it came time to purchase shooting and cleaning supplies for their chosen weapons. Nowadays, however, most sporting goods stores have at least a few black-powder guns (in finished or kit form) hanging on the wall, and anyone who lives in an area with a sizable population of hunters can almost count on the fact that a shop

specializing in muzzleloaders and related paraphernalia can be found within a couple of hours' drive.

If you live in a region where considerable deer hunting goes on, winter's the time to begin scanning local shopper's guides for used muzzleloaders. It seems that a number of folks buy the black-powder guns every year—in the hopes of extending the hunting season—only to sell them as fall draws to a close, probably because the inconvenience of the weapons, compared to modern hunting rifles, turned out to be more than the new owners had bargained for. At times it's possible to get a gun that's been fired only a few times for about half its new price.

If you do plan to buy a muzzleloader from an individual rather than from a store or catalogue, your best bet—before you make the purchase—is to talk the owner into going out with you and firing the piece a few times. Pay special attention to the ease with which the first loaded ball is rammed down the barrel. It should take some pressure, but if the owner has to struggle with a ball that seems to be jamming on its way down, there's a good chance that he or she didn't bother to clean the weapon after its last firing. Such a sign

THE FLINTLOCK

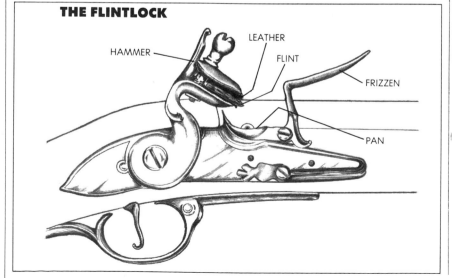

HAMMER · LEATHER · FLINT · FRIZZEN · PAN

Pour powder from the flask or horn into a measure, *never* directly into the rifle barrel.

of carelessness doesn't necessarily mean you shouldn't purchase the gun, but it—or a suspicious succession of misfires—would make it advisable for you to ask the owner to clean the gun after a few shots; then try it out yourself. If the just-swabbed muzzleloader still misfires often, or doesn't load more easily, it's quite likely that neglect has resulted in some internal corrosion.

You may also, in your search for a primitive weapon, come across an actual antique. While such a gun can represent a good investment (and many of them, after restoration, shoot very nicely), *don't* attempt to fire the gun without having a competent gunsmith go over it and recommend an appropriate ball size and maximum powder load. (This course of action is one that you'd do well to follow with any used gun, especially if the manufacturer's load recommendations aren't available.)

Muzzle Ode

Should the information presented here convince you to make the acquaintance of a black-powder firearm—and should you approach the matter with reasonable expectations—you're apt to acquire both a lifetime tool and a long-lasting enthusiasm. Many people have discovered that shooting black-powder guns is one of those rare activities that bridge the gap between practicality and pleasure. In fact, if you're the least bit impressionable, you'll find it difficult to do so much as stroll out in the back field to ventilate a couple of old tin cans without conjuring up images of early Americans who—with horns of powder and a few dozen lead balls strung from their belts—shouldered similar weapons and, turning their backs on the cities, set out into a wilderness that they knew only as borderless, unpredictable and strange.

The Loading Lowdown

When the time comes to push a projectile into the barrel of your new firearm, you'll be faced with yet another choice: whether to shoot the traditional patch-and-ball load, or the more modern—and somewhat more accurate, under most circumstances—conical minié ball (named for Claude Minié, the French army officer who invented it in the nineteenth century).

Of course, before you load *anything*, you'll have to determine the amount of powder, as measured in grains, to charge your gun with. As mentioned before, if you don't know the manufacturer's recommended maximum load, consult a gunsmith to experiment with various loads. You might consider settling on one that produces a somewhat flat bullet trajectory at about 50 yards; it will then be a relatively easy matter to adjust your aim to compensate for drop at greater ranges.

If you choose to use a patched ball, you'll need patches, of course. It's probably best to *buy* a package of them at first, then cut your own to size from cotton or other *nonsynthetic* cloth. The next step is to grease the patch. There are a number of lubricants on the market, but lard works quite well, and even saliva will do if you plan to shoot the gun before the moisture has a chance to start rusting the bore. Pour the powder from your large container (the can the explosive came in or a powder horn) into a measure. *Never* pour directly from a large container into the barrel, since a lingering spark (from a previous shot) could ignite the charge and flash back to turn that flask or can into a bomb. Pour the measure of powder into the muzzle (keep the opening angled away from your body),

then smack the barrel with the heel of your hand a few times, moving from top to bottom, to settle the explosive in the breech.

With that done, place the patch, lubricant down, across the barrel, and center the bullet, with the molding mark *up*, on top of it. Use a mushroom-shaped ball starter (shown in the loading equipment photo) to seat the projectile in the muzzle. If necessary, take a knife and trim away any excess patch. Then, turning the ball starter around, use its short rod to push the bullet partway down the barrel.

The ramrod comes into play next, and this is as good a time as any to recommend that you purchase a fiberglass rod. The wooden units supplied with many modern muzzleloaders seem to break fairly easily. Use the rod to seat the ball and patch on top of the powder with a smooth, uninterrupted movement. It's a good idea to mark the stick at the point where it leaves the barrel when the ball is fully rammed home, as this will help you avoid firing the gun without seating the ball on top of the powder—a mistake that could result in a ruined barrel, or worse. At this point your gun is charged and, after you prime it in the appropriate flintlock or percussion manner, will be ready to fire.

The procedure for loading the minié ball—which is detailed in the accompanying photos—is identical to that used with the ball and patch except that 1) no patch is required, but the grooves in the side of the shell should be filled with lubricant, and 2) you can probably insert the minié into the muzzle without a ball starter.

Step 2: The measured powder is then poured into the barrel of the firearm. Use your hand as a funnel.

Step 3: Now place the greased patch, lubed side down, across the muzzle, taking care to center it.

Step 4: The ball is centered upon the patch. If the ball has a sprue from casting, center it on the bottom.

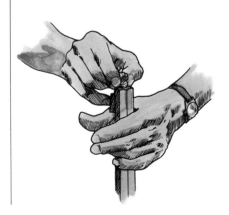

A Clean Shot

Because of the particularly corrosive nature of black powder, you'll have to clean your muzzleloader thoroughly after each shooting session. (In fact, it's often necessary to swab out the barrel with a black-powder solvent—followed by a few clean patches to soak up the residue—after every three to six shots.)

Here's the traditional method of cleaning a black-powder gun: 1) Wash the bore, using a brush on the end of your ramrod, with a strong solution of very hot, soapy water. At the same time, use the liquid to wipe any powder smudges from the hammer area, etc. 2) Rinse the barrel several times with the *hottest* water you dare pour. In addition to removing the soap residue from the bore, this hot bath actually warms the metal of the barrel to the point where it will cause any remaining moisture to begin to evaporate. 3) Using clean cloth patches and your ramrod, dry the bore, and use a cloth to wipe any moisture from the gun's exterior. 4) Swab all cleaned areas with a coating of gun oil.

Thanks to the growing popularity of muzzleloading firearms, there are now a number of black-powder solvents available. To clean your gun with one of these, simply 1) scrub out the bore with the liquid, using first a brass brush and then a number of patches (keep using them until one comes out showing no dissolved powder residue); 2) put solvent on a clean cloth to wipe down and dry all exterior metal parts; 3) again, being generous with your supply of patches, swab the bore dry; 4) coat the inside of the barrel and all other metal components with gun oil.

Remember that a black-powder firearm won't hold up under the kind of neglect that a more modern weapon can tolerate. If you give the gun the care you'd bestow on any quality tool, however, it should serve you, and your children after you, faithfully. After all, there are a lot of century-old—or older—black-powder firearms still shooting today, and most contemporary muzzleloaders are fashioned from better materials than were available when their "ancestors" were crafted.

Some Words of Caution

- All black-powder revolvers, pistols and rifles are intended for use with black powder only. Use of any other propellant may cause serious injury to the shooter and damage to the firearm. Never use smokeless powder.
- Guard against overcharges.
- Wear safety glasses when shooting black-powder firearms. Shatterproof shooting glasses will protect the eyes from sparks, broken percussion caps, hot gases and lead fragments.
- Protect your hearing. Use ear plugs or muffs when firing any firearm.
- Be certain the projectile is seated firmly against the powder charge. Any gap between the projectile and the powder charge could cause serious damage to the firearm and injury to the shooter. Hunters, in particular, should check the position of the projectile in the barrel at regular intervals when they are in the field.
- Use only nonsynthetic cloth patching of suitable thickness when loading round balls.
- Never charge a muzzleloader directly from a powder flask. A sudden powder ignition from a lingering spark could cause the entire flask to explode. Instead, use an individual charge from a powder measure when loading your gun.
- Never smoke when handling black powder.
- Before each shooting session, be sure to check your black-powder firearm carefully.
- Before relying on the half-cocked position, make certain the hammer will not fall when the trigger is pulled.
- While on the firing line, keep all black-powder canisters closed.
- Keep spectators to the rear of the shooter. Standing beside a muzzleloader is not safe enough. Flames, hot gases and percussion cap fragments may fly from the side of the firearm, causing injury.
- Keep clear of the muzzle, particularly during loading.
- If the gun misfires, keep the muzzle pointed down range for at least a minute before attempting to reprime it. There is always the chance a spark is smoldering in the powder charge, and the gun could fire at any second.
- Treat unprimed flintlocks as loaded weapons. Sometimes the sparks of an unprimed flintlock can fire the gun.
- Use a nonflammable material to hold the flint in place. Cloth, cardboard or canvas could hold a lingering spark, which might set off the next priming charge unexpectedly.
- Store black powder and percussion caps in separate locations. Use their original containers when possible. Caps are sensitive to static electricity, percussion, heat and flame. Powder is sensitive to static electricity, heat and flame. Check local fire regulations before storing black powder in the home.
- Follow the basic rules of firearm safety (see "Safe Shooting," page 58) when handling any black-powder firearm.

Step 5: Use the short ramrod, or "ball starter," to force the patch and ball partway down the barrel.

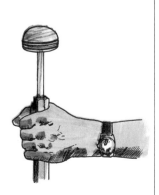

Step 6: The ramrod is now used, with a slow, steady push to seat the ball and patch firmly atop the powder charge.

Step 7: Drawing the hammer back to "full-cocked," place the percussion cap on the nipple.

Sighting In

No scope is fool*proof.*

The hunter, curled fetuslike, presses down into the Space Blanket that serves to separate him from the damp depression overlooking the field. It's two hours into his third and final day. The expectation that once helped keep him still and silent, the absolute *belief* in deer, has long gone. Nothing supports him in the face of stiffness and cold, nothing fights off the nagging whispers that say "quit," or "for God's sake, at least stand and stretch"—nothing but the grim determination to go out doing this right, to give no aid to an unfriendly fate.

Three hours. His body heat has melted the snow; wet fingers stretch over the lip of the ground cover. He closes his eyes against the internal taunts. When he opens them, three bucks are walking stiff-legged into the field, a scant 100 yards distant.

No trouble with control now. The gun comes up to rest on bent knees. A deep breath as the scope fills with deer, a half breath out; the cross hairs drop and hold behind the shoulder of the biggest, rest steady as the trigger creeps toward the always surprising shot. *There!*

But the buck isn't down. The trio mill about in brief confusion and then stretch toward a windrow of trees. He sweeps the scope with them, less steady now, but still vacillating within the area of clean kill. A second shot. No tail drop, no sudden stumble or twitch, no sound of a bullet strike.

He's on his feet now, aiming only at the middle of the big buck's body. Shot. Shot. Shot. And the snick of a firing pin on an empty chamber. Loading on the run, he finds the deep-driven tracks of panic, follows them to the woods. No blood, no hair. *Five misses?*

A shell in the chamber, past believing anything now, he takes a careful rest and aims at a stump-center knot 30 yards off. Steady, squeeze, and bark jumps a full six inches high, three to the right. He looks down at the expensive rifle, feeling betrayal and the slow spread of guilt.

It was spot-on last season.

Inciting a Sight-In

Missed shots or, worse yet, poor shots that result in the escape of a badly wounded animal can often be traced to either improperly sighted rifles or firearms that have had their sights jarred out of adjustment. Of course, the *major* cause of poor shooting is a shortage of hunter ability; no scope, regardless of how well it's sighted-in, will compensate for a lack of familiarity with the gun. The answer here is to practice, and then practice some more.

On the other hand, a scope that's out of adjustment can frustrate the most experienced marksman. So take the time to check a sighted-in rifle before each hunting season (and then practice with it); do the same after traveling to a distant hunt, or after a day in steep or brushy country that could leave your rifle feeling the same sort of knocks that can make a quiet evening in camp seem like a little bit of heaven. More important still, never assume that a newly purchased gun is right, whether bought used or set up by sporting-goods store staff. You owe it to yourself, and to the game you intend to hunt, to burn enough powder to assure yourself that the job has been done correctly.

Begin With a Bore Sighter

Although it's possible to do the job without a bore sighter, most hunters come to consider this tool (Fig. 1) indispensable when setting up a scoped firearm. This device allows the rifleman, without even loading a shell, to align the scope with the bore of the rifle. A bore-sighted firearm will typically be "on the paper"—that is, it should hit *somewhere* on a standard-sized rifle target—at 100 yards. This can save a number of spent shells during the adjustment process. It is, however, only a preparation for final zeroing in.

To use a bore sighter, simply insert the appropriate rod (several will come with the tool) into the muzzle of your firearm, adjust the device until the calibrated lens is centered in front of the rifle scope, then secure the bore sighter in position by turning the knurled-head fitting to expand the rod within the bore. Now look through the scope toward a

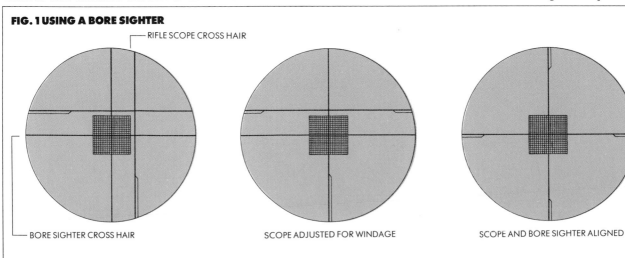

FIG. 1 USING A BORE SIGHTER

RIFLE SCOPE CROSS HAIR

BORE SIGHTER CROSS HAIR

SCOPE ADJUSTED FOR WINDAGE

SCOPE AND BORE SIGHTER ALIGNED

Use a rest when sighting-in, to lower the risk of shooter error.

bright window or other source of light. The calibrations on the bore sighter will be superimposed over the cross hairs of the scope (Fig. 2). Simply adjust the scope until its cross hairs are centered on the bore sighter's checkerboard, and you'll have taken a giant step toward straighter shooting.

Punching Paper

The final stage of the sighting-in process can best be accomplished at a rifle range equipped with benches and good gun rests. Failing that, make up a few small cloth bags (about six inches square), stuff them with sand, and use them to rest the rifle on while shooting.

Set up a target at 100 yards if you're sighting-in a deer rifle, or at 50 yards if you're using a .22. (If you're not at a range, make absolutely certain that you've got a *completely safe* backdrop behind your target, such as a high, thick dirt bank.) Then—wearing ear and eye protection—rest the gun securely, and squeeze off three careful shots at the center of the target. The bullet holes should group at some point on the target paper (Fig.

3). Measure the distance from the middle of your grouping to the bull's eye, figuring first the distance to the right or left of the target center (windage) and then that above or below the bull (elevation). Now adjust your sight or scope to compensate for the error. To do so, you'll have to know how the calibrations on the sight work. Many scopes adjust in clicks, each one equaling a change in point of impact of one inch at 100 yards. With the adjustment made, take another three careful shots. Your group should now be closer to the bull's eye. If it's not close enough to suit you, repeat the measurement, adjustment and three-shot-group process.

(Note: Many hunters sight-in deer rifles to shoot about two inches high at 100 yards, thus enabling the shooter to keep the impact point within a clean kill zone at longer ranges without having to aim high to account for bullet drop. Before doing this, check the ballistics of your rifle-and-cartridge combination—most any gun-shop owner will have a chart—to determine how far you can expect the point of impact to change over a given distance.)

Once carefully sighted-in, your rifle will give you the best it's capable of. Your next step is to get in enough shooting time with the firearm, at various distances and from sitting, prone and offhand (standing) positions, to make sure that you're able to contribute an equal (well, nearly so) ability. With that done, you can take to the field with calm confidence, which is probably the most important hunting tool of all.

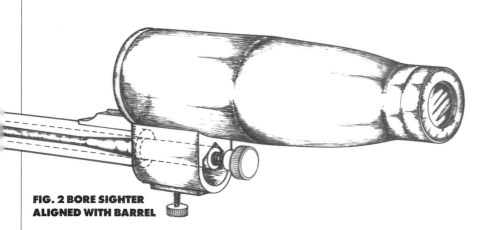

FIG. 2 BORE SIGHTER ALIGNED WITH BARREL

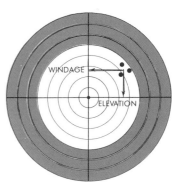

FIG.3 ZEROING IN

A Beginner's Guide to Fishing

It's as peaceful as the
contemplation of philosophy,
and a lot more fun.

Terminal Tackle

Once upon a time, American boys (and many girls) spent more hours staring at red and white bobbers than watching TV. Well, not just bobbers. They also watched the tips of propped-up rods in the white glare of Coleman lamps while bottom-fishing at night. They stared at trolling rods bent with the rhythmic, wobbling pull of a Dardevle spoon. And they followed surface plugs dimpling the skin of evening-smoothed ponds. In short, youngsters of a generation or so ago kept their eyes on just about anything that involved the pursuit of fish.

Most of these children, you see, were lucky to grow up guided by relatives who had long decades of outdoor living to call upon, and who seemingly couldn't think of anything better to do with their free time than spend it on the water with fish-crazy kids. A lot of people today haven't had that kind of childhood, though, and—especially after moving to the country—find themselves hungry to learn the joys of open-air sport but unable to find a teacher.

There's no way that anything written here will take the place of the patience and love of a wise family elder, but this section will attempt to pass along some good basic fishing information without making the subject seem more complicated, or less magical, than it really is. Whether your aim is to catch a panful of small bream for a family meal, to increase the satisfaction of your streamside outings or eventually to pursue the more challenging course of trophy fishing, sit back, glass in hand and gleam in eye, and let's talk fishing.

Gearing Up

All sports attract their share of equipment freaks, but it's hard to imagine one that befuddles the beginner with a wider range of gimmicks and doodads than fishing. It's possible to buy a separate rod and reel combination for just about any stretch of water that you're ever likely to fish, artificial lures for any possible combination of quarry and water conditions and everything else from self-warming streamside seats to electric hook sharpeners. And, as your pursuit of flashing fins takes you down differing trails, a lot of those things might well become must-haves. For now, though, it's best to set yourself up with a versatile, do-most-anything rig, without slashing too deeply into your food budget.

The core of your outfit, of course, will be the rod and reel. And, since the aim is a simple, versatile, more or less foolproof rig, your best bets are probably 1) a bait-casting outfit, 2) a spin-casting set or 3) an open-faced spinning reel and matching rod. There are enthusiastic fans of each option, and any of the choices would do the job, but you won't go wrong if you buy a medium-sized, open-faced spinning reel (one suitable for line in the six- to 10-pound test range; have the salesperson load it with as much as it will hold when you buy it) and a medium action, six- to seven-foot fiberglass spinning rod. (The action, sometimes called power, should appear on a label somewhere on the rod.) With this rig, a few lures and a selection of hooks and sinkers, which will be described below, you should be able to go for most freshwater fish, in most types of water, and will even be well enough equipped to catch a good number of the smaller saltwater species.

Though many recommend a closed-faced, or spin-casting, reel for the beginner, most come to prefer the open-faced because it's simple to operate and, well, open. When the line tangles during a cast (it will), you'll be able to get at that bird's nest without disassembling the reel itself. And, though an open-faced spinning outfit may take a little more practice than the closed-faced variety, it ultimately offers more casting distance and control.

Of course, you will have to practice. Fortunately, all you need to complete your training is an open field or large back yard and a small (1/4- to 1/2-ounce) lead sinker. Just tie the weight to the end of your line, and follow the instructions on page 55. Don't be discouraged when your first attempts at casting misfire. The correct rhythm and touch will come quickly, and in a short time you should develop enough casting range and accuracy to allow you to continue to perfect your skills while you're fishing.

Terminal Tackle

Though the term sounds imposing (and you'll be hoping your gear does prove terminal to numerous dinners' worth of fillets),

MEPPS SPINNERS
1/8–1/4 OZ.

DARDEVLE SPOONS
1/4–3/5 OZ.

JITTERBUG
1/4 OZ.

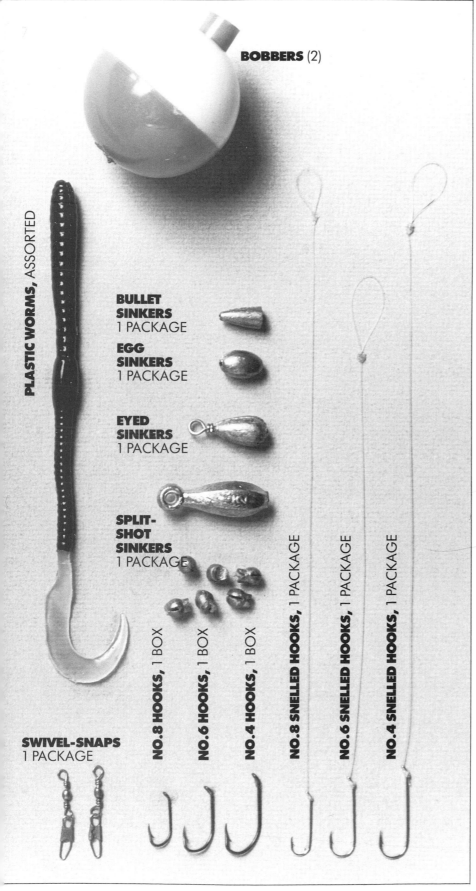

BOBBERS (2)

PLASTIC WORMS, ASSORTED

BULLET SINKERS 1 PACKAGE

EGG SINKERS 1 PACKAGE

EYED SINKERS 1 PACKAGE

SPLIT-SHOT SINKERS 1 PACKAGE

NO.8 HOOKS, 1 BOX

NO.6 HOOKS, 1 BOX

NO.4 HOOKS, 1 BOX

NO.8 SNELLED HOOKS, 1 PACKAGE

NO.6 SNELLED HOOKS, 1 PACKAGE

NO.4 SNELLED HOOKS, 1 PACKAGE

SWIVEL-SNAPS 1 PACKAGE

terminal tackle simply means the hooks, sinkers, bobbers and artificial lures that you'll be fastening to the end of your line before you cast in search of fish. Once again, the choices are wide enough to be overwhelming, but a few basic purchases should get you under way.

A Bit About Bait

Artificial lures catch fish and don't smell when you leave them in the refrigerator too long, but in many instances it's hard to beat live bait. For freshwater fishing, there's no more versatile bait than the earthworm (it ain't called angleworm for nothing). Minnows are another good choice (make sure the ones you use are native to the water you're fishing; "imports" may catch fish, but they may disturb the environmental balance if several escape). Crayfish (also called crawdads) are effective, too, particularly in the spring and early summer, when they've shed one exoskeleton and not yet fully formed another. ("Softshells" are one of the all-time best baits for smallmouth bass.) Other choices for freshwater angling include, but aren't limited to, frogs, crickets, grasshoppers, various salamanders, hellgrammites, grubs and virtually anything else that fish routinely eat.

Saltwater baits also come in a wide variety. If you decide to do ocean angling, ask around at your local bait shop or pier, and find out what's hot and what's not. (Cut mullet, sandworms, bloodworms, squid and shrimp are a few favorites.)

Wetting the Line

The fishing tactics you'll use will vary with the water you're angling in and the species you hope to catch. We'll deal, therefore, with specific strategies and techniques in a series of situations. Just choose the one that's closest to the setting in which you'll be fishing, and the advice should provide a reliable starting point. But don't let anyone's advice keep you from watching and learning from the fisherfolk around you. Every lake, stream, pond and river has its own idiosyncracies. You could fish one area for a lifetime and not uncover all of its secrets, so you're certainly not going to pick up everything you need to know here.

Basic Bobber & Bottom Rigs

The Farm Pond

It's hard to imagine a more congenial setting for "jist sittin' an' fishin'." The air will probably carry the aroma of tilled soil and wildflowers (along with, perhaps, a hint of cow). Swallows will spin their hunting dances overhead, and the surface of the water may swell occasionally with the magical bulge of a surfacing turtle. Better still, farm ponds can be rich with fish. You'll commonly find bream, catfish of one sort or another, largemouth bass and such "trash" fish as carp or suckers. If the pond is deep enough to stay cold and oxygen-rich year-round, it may even be stocked with trout. (It goes without saying that you'd better get permission before fishing anyone else's pond. A well-maintained, stocked pond represents a big investment in time, money and work, and the trespasser is as likely to catch a load of birdshot as a string of bream.)

The most common way to fish a farm pond, or any other small, still body of water, is with a bobber, hook, worms (either red worms or night crawlers) and a small split-shot sinker. Keep in mind that, as the old-timers used to say, "You can catch a big fish on a small hook easier than you can catch a small fish on a big one." Start with a number six or eight. Now simply thread the worm on the hook—leave enough hanging loose to get an enticing wiggle, but make sure the point of the hook is covered—clamp the split-shot a few inches to a foot or so above the bait, fix the bobber to the line at a point where it will float the worm just above the bottom or over any underwater foliage, and flip the assembly into a likely-looking spot. It's a good bet to fish near cover of some sort: a dock, lily pads, a fallen tree, a submerged fence line, etc.

Keep the line relatively tight, but not enough to drag the bobber along. An interested fish will probably first show itself by "nibbling," causing the float to tremble, jerk back and forth or bob up and down. That's your signal to pay attention. But don't *do* anything yet. When the fish drags the bobber along the surface of the water with determination or pulls it under, give a short, sharp jerk of the rod to set the hook, and reel your prize on in.

If you plan to release the fish, wet your hands before touching it, and handle it gent-

Bobber fishing is probably the most relaxing form of angling.

It's best to secure the float to the line with its top and bottom pinch clamps.

Sinkers can be crimped on or tied. The improved clinch knot is used with bobber rigs and when bottom fishing (below).

ly. (In fact, if you're planning to release your day's catch, it's best to bend down the barbs on your hooks with a pair of pliers to make hook removal easy.) Whether you aim to let the fish go or not, take a few seconds to savor its delicacy of color and beauty of line. Few things look as alive as a living fish, and appreciating that beauty is one of your rewards for skillful angling. Enjoy it.

Then, after unhooking the fish and putting it on a stringer or in a water-filled pail, rebait, and cast back to the same spot. Chances are there are more where that one came from.

If, however, a while passes with your bobber doing little more than serving as an aircraft carrier for tired dragonflies, reel it in, check the bait (to make sure you weren't dozing or distracted when a fish hit), and try another spot on the pond. Or vary the depth of your bait by moving the bobber up or down. You might even make a relatively long cast and move the float a foot or so every minute or two until you find fish. In a reasonably productive pond, a few hours of this sort of relaxation ought to provide you with the makings of a nice family dinner.

There are, of course, less passive ways to tackle the same body of water. And, though bobber fishing can yield some huge fish, the techniques described above are far more likely to bring you bream than hefty bass or trout.

If largemouth bass are what you're after, you'll probably do well with a variation of the bobber technique. Just try a bigger float and a bigger hook (size two or larger) and a two-inch-long (or longer) minnow or shiner, hooked either through the lips or just under the back (dorsal) fin so it can swim freely. The small baitfish will pull the bobber around, but you shouldn't have any trouble spotting the difference in the action of the float when a bass grabs the bait and tries to make off with it.

With that "hawg" (bass-fishin' talk for a big one) in mind, this is probably a good time to talk about drag. Either on top of your reel's spool or by the handle (see the owner's manual) will be a dial you can loosen or tighten to make it easier or harder to pull line off the closed spool. Set this to allow line to be taken when the pull is just over half the line's breaking strength (you can guesstimate accurately enough). Then, when a real hawg takes off on a run, he'll simply pull off line

Steps to Simple Spinning

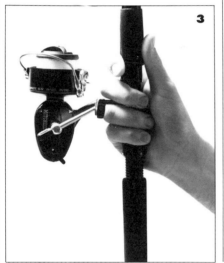

1. With the rod held in your right hand as shown, hook the line just above the reel, with your index finger, and pinch it against the rod handle.

2. Open the bail on the reel (the wire ring that keeps the line from coming out). Now, face in the direction you want to cast, with the rod in front of you and the sinker (or lure, etc.) just inches below its tip.

3. Lift the rod sharply until the tip is just behind your head. The weight of the sinker will bow the rod and add to the power of the cast.

4. Snap the rod forward to just past vertical (about 11 o'clock on an imaginary watch face).

As the sinker starts moving forward, release the line held by your index finger, and the line should uncoil smoothly from the reel.

Casting is all a matter of timing and rhythm. Should the sinker fly straight up in the air, you've released the line too early. If it strikes the ground in front of you or snaps the line, you've held on too long. Keep your casts gentle at first; there's no need to whip the rod back and forth. A spinning reel releases its line with very little friction, so the weight of the moving sinker can carry it a great distance with no more than a smooth, easy flip of the rod.

Once you're casting comfortably, try setting up a target—a paper plate works well, or an old automobile tire will do the job—and attempt to land the sinker near, or on, it. An hour or so of that sort of exercise should have you more than ready to start going after fish (you can continue to perfect your technique while on the water).

against the drag, tiring himself all the while, instead of breaking free. Once you have him on and fighting, keep the rod tip high. Try to reel only when the fish isn't pulling against the drag. If the bass explodes upward in a rainbow-spraying leap, drop the rod tip a foot or so each time the fish breaks water. Try to make your movements smooth, gradual but relentless. With a little luck, you'll soon grab the bass's lower lip (watch that hook) and hoist your prize ashore.

You can also go after pond bass (or trout) with the lures recommended elsewhere in this book. Just cast the spoons and weighted spinners toward a likely-looking spot, and reel in. Vary the depth of your retrieve by letting the lure sink to different depths before you begin to reel. Try fast, slow and jerky retrieves. Again, pay special attention to possible cover, and fish as close to it as you can. You'll lose a few lures to snags this way, but, to quote a little ancestral angling wisdom again, "If you aren't getting hung up, you probably aren't catching anything."

There are many ways to fish plastic worms (in fact, there are books on the subject). One of the easiest and most effective is to rig the worm with a large hook and egg or bullet sinker, cast it out, and bounce it across the bottom by raising and lowering the rod tip while reeling slowly. Try to develop a feel for what the worm is doing. A strike may not be violent. Often, a bass will simply take a worm in its mouth as the bait is dropping (when you lower your rod tip) and hold it. Whenever the lure seems to stop unnaturally, respond by lifting the rod tip sharply to set the hook.

The Jitterbug is a surface lure, and probably most effective at dusk, or even after dark. Cast it near cover, let it sit till the ripples caused by its splashing-down disappear, and try different rates of retrieval. It's often effective just to "pop" the 'bug in with short jerks of the rod, letting the bait rest after each hop. A striking fish will usually hook itself. Just raise the rod tip when you feel the hit, and fight the lunker to shore.

Lakes, Slow Rivers and Ocean Shores

Any tactics that work in a farm pond will work in larger bodies of water—if the artificial lures are suited to the fish available or if you use an appropriate bait. There's

114723356

Five Freshwater Fish

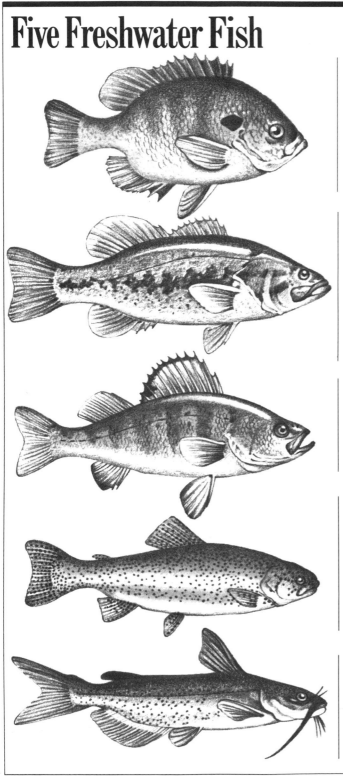

SUNFISH

Lepomis species; includes bluegill
Habitat: Ponds, lakes, rivers
Bait: Night crawlers, red worms, small minnows, crickets, small spinners, artificial flies

BASS

Micropterus species; includes largemouth and smallmouth bass
Habitat: Ponds, lakes, rivers
Baits: Night crawlers, red worms, larger minnows, frogs, salamanders, midsized artificial lures

YELLOW PERCH

Perca flavescens;
Habitat: Ponds, lakes
Bait: Night crawlers, red worms, small minnows

TROUT

Salmo species; includes brown and rainbow trout
Habitat: Stocked ponds, rivers, streams
Bait: Red worms, small minnows, canned corn, salmon eggs, small artificial lures

CATFISH

Ictalurus species; includes the bullheads
Habitat: Ponds, rivers, lakes
Bait: Night crawlers, red worms, minnows, "stink baits"

another form of still-fishing commonly used on big water, though, and it can be very effective. Known as bottom fishing, it calls for a heavier sinker and one or more hooks to hold the bait on, or just above, the bottom, following a (usually) long cast.

Bottom fishing typically calls for live bait and one of the terminal rigs illustrated here. Watch what other fisherfolk, especially the successful ones, are using. In general, it's best to keep a tight line so you can see the sharp rapping on the rod tip that signals a feeding fish, or feel that electric jerking on a fingertip. (To do so, pinch the line, just above the reel, between your thumb and index finger.)

If you have access to a boat, you can cover a lot of water by trolling an artificial lure behind the moving craft. Match the boat's speed to the "action" (flash, spin or wobble) of your lure (usually a comfortable rowing speed or very slow motoring will do). Let out some line (say, 20 yards), and wait for the action. Once you have a strike, you can anchor in the spot and cast lures (or try live bait, *or* troll back and forth over the area a few more times) to see if your first catch was part of a school.

Streams and Fast Rivers

All sorts of fish abound in streams and rapidly moving rivers, but when this kind of water comes to mind, we think trout. And, frankly, when *trout* come to mind, most anglers think fly-fishing, a wonderful and artful sport that's in "Freshwater Game Fish" on page 68. You can, however, experiment with dry (floating) and wet (sinking) flies with your spinning outfit. To do so, just buy a "casting bubble," which is a clear bobber that provides the mass necessary to flip a nearly weightless fly on spinning tackle, then use this rig to fish the water exactly as you would with live bait.

When trout are the quarry, the worm is the most commonly used live bait. In fact, a great many trout are caught by still-fishing—either on the bottom or with a bobber, in the deep, slow-moving pools of streams and rivers. Night crawlers are the common still-fishing bait, but a healthy garden-dug red worm will often outperform a crawler in still-fishing, and is almost a must if you want to "work" a stream like a fly-fisherman.

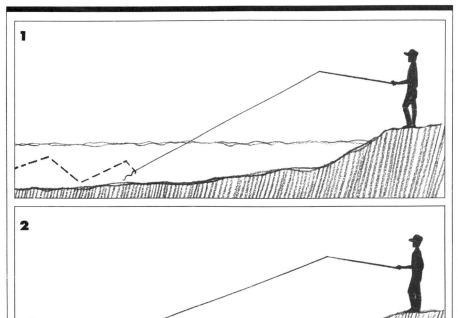

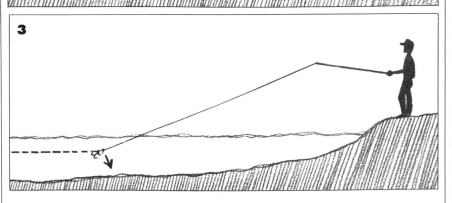

Make Your Lures Alluring

1. The classic method of fishing a plastic worm is to walk it along the bottom by raising the rod tip, then reeling as it's lowered. Work slowly; try to *feel* the surface that the worm crawls along.

2. The Jitterbug is also worked slowly, but waddles its way across the surface. At times, you might simply "pop" the plug in by jerking the rod, then waiting till any ripples fade. At other times, a steady retrieve works best.

3. Spinners and spoons provide their own action. Vary the depth and speed of the retrieve, and also try letting them "scallop" their way in, in a faster version of the plastic worm retrieve.

For this technique, a proven fish catcher as well as a wonderful excuse to explore the tumbling, shade- and sunlight-dappled staircases of a mountain stream, you'll need your smallest hooks, a few tiny split-shot sinkers and a *leader*. Simply a length of line of different strength from what's on the reel's spool, a leader—for our purposes here—consists of a four- to six-foot section of two- to four-pound test line that will be less visible to trout in gin-clear water than the "working" line on the reel. Tie this leader on, then, with the small hook and a worm in place (hook the worm only through the head, so most of its length dangles freely), experiment with different weights of split-shot by dropping the worm, with the weight fixed six inches above it, into the current in front of you. Your aim is to pick a weight that will allow the worm to sink against the current at about a 45° angle, then let it roll along the bottom naturally.

Once your rig is correct, proceed upstream, walking in the water (blue jeans and sneakers should suffice in all but the coldest streams), flipping the bait ahead of you, usually at an angle toward the bank, in such a way that it will drift beneath undercut banks, into the whirlpool washes formed by boulders, under tree limbs projecting into the stream and—in general—anyplace the combination of current-supplied food and slower-than-normal water presents a logical resting place for a hungry trout. This will all take practice, of course. Keep in mind that the water around you is clear, and that trout are flighty. Move slowly. Wait a minute or more after getting into position before flipping your bait to a promising spot, and—as when fishing lakes with plastic worms—consider any unnatural hesitation in the drift of your bait to be a striking fish.

On waters big enough to allow longer casting, your weighted spinners can also be effective. Again, work from a position in the stream itself, either casting upstream, *past* promising hiding places, then reeling fast enough to move the lure ahead of the current, or downstream, casting toward the bank at an angle so the moving water sweeps the lure out toward midstream as you reel. In either case, remember where strikes occur, and be observant. The key to stream fishing is developing a sense of what's going on *under* the water by watching its surface.

When guns and shooting are mentioned, certain images spring to mind. For many Americans, especially those who live away from the land-starved megamesses we call cities, the images are of recreation, competition, personal challenges and family fun. Unseen and unreported by the mass media, millions of people enjoy guns and shoot billions of rounds of ammunition every year in complete safety. And they do it primarily for one reason—shooting is one heck of a lot of fun!

Shooting is traditionally taught by fathers. Many women shoot, but it seems fair to say that in most cases the teaching is done by the menfolk. If your father didn't teach you to shoot, you might be frightened by the thought of learning by yourself. After all, you don't know anything about it and you might do something stupid, or worse. I mean, guns are *dangerous,* right?

Before you have an anxiety attack, though, take some time to consider just how dangerous guns are, or are not. Put a firearm on the table, don't let anyone touch it for 100 years, and I guarantee it will do nothing but slowly rust. Guns don't *do* anything by themselves. The plain fact is that firearms are not dangerous when handled and stored properly. Same as a car, right? You wouldn't presume to be able to drive a car safely if you had never been taught, so don't expect to be able to shoot well or handle a gun safely without instruction and practice.

Fortunately, help is nearby. No matter where you live, there are surely shooters in your area. And as is the case with people avid in any sport, most shooters like to bring others into the fold. Talk with your neighbors. If you live out of the city, you'll find that some of them have guns and like to shoot. Your best bet is a local shooting range or gun club.

No shooting range nearby? Call the police. Someone on the force or in the sheriff's department will be able to teach you. Even if it's not a formal class, just ask if anyone can spare enough time to show you the basics. It's pretty unlikely you'll strike out.

Perhaps you do have some experience with guns. Now you want to teach your family to shoot. How old should children be before you start them off? Some are ready at six, and some still aren't ready at 16. Chances are you'll know when the time comes. First thing, a child must be ready to *obey*. Gun safety is not a matter to be approached democratically. Instructions must be followed exactly, and immediately. At about age six many children are able to handle the smallest air rifles (BB guns, if you will). Of course, they should not be allowed to shoot without direct adult supervision. That

Safe Shooting

Self-control and a sense of responsibility are the primary lessons for the new shooter.

Instruction and practice, with safety a constant concern, will develop responsible and enthusiastic shooters.

means an adult standing right beside them.

Whether you're teaching someone in your family, or you're receiving instruction and practicing on your own, you must develop safe gun-handling habits. Just as you do with everything else, you *will* develop habits in your gun handling. The goal is to start out with safe practices and never deviate from them. Shooting accidents are completely preventable, and a constant awareness of and adherence to accepted safe gun-handling practices are the keys. You must develop an attitude of safety.

There are several basic safety rules in handling guns, but only a couple will be stressed here. The first and most important one is this: Never point a gun at anything you aren't willing to shoot. Simple? Yes. Effective? Undoubtedly. Easy? No doubt about it. The corollary to this is never to let anyone point a gun at you. Not for an instant. If everyone followed this basic rule, even if a gun were to fire unexpectedly, it would be frightening and embarrassing, but not tragic.

The other rule to keep in mind, and it really just reinforces the first, is to treat every gun as if it's loaded. That way, you'll never find yourself thinking "It's OK, it's not loaded." That phrase has too often preceded tragedy.

With your developing attitude of safety firmly in place, it's time to select a gun. Your choice depends on several factors: intended use, experience of shooters, space available for shooting, and cost. With hundreds of models that vary in size, caliber, gauge and configuration, the task is to pick one that is right for you.

The first gun for many of us was the air rifle, and it might be the right gun for your purposes. Available models shoot BBs or pellets, and power comes from a spring, compressed air or a cartridge of carbon dioxide. You can find an air rifle to fit anyone from about age six and up. And the adult air rifles are excellent tools. In fact, there's an air rifle competition in the Olympics, and the guns used there may be the most sophisticated and the most accurate rifles in the world. If you want to shoot targets, knock over tin cans and just have fun, an air rifle is a good choice. Advantages include no recoil (kick), no noise, the option to shoot almost anywhere without the need for wide open spaces (even indoors), and inexpensive ammunition, which allows lots of practice.

Next up the line in terms of power and utility is the .22 rimfire rifle. This is the best choice for a first firearm for many people. There's no noticeable kick, it can be extremely accurate, ammunition is inexpensive, its greater range lets you hit targets 100 yards away (though that's a long shot), and, properly cared for, it will last forever.

A Secure Gun Is a Safe Gun

A common concern of those thinking of buying a first gun is safe storage, particularly if there are children in the house. It's an important consideration.

Children have an unbelievable ability to find what you've hidden, so don't hide your guns. That's not a safe way to prevent children from getting them. Instead, if the children are old enough to accept instructions, explain that the guns are not to be touched, ever, without your permission. With some children, that would be enough. You may, however, want to take other steps to prevent anyone from being able to get access to your guns, or to render the guns inoperable.

Of course, you won't keep loaded guns in the house. Even a gun kept for defense can be loaded quickly, if necessary.

A number of companies make trigger locks that block the trigger completely. The lock can be removed only with a key. This certainly is an effective way to prevent accidents.

You also can buy a gun safe. This is exactly what it sounds like—a very heavy steel cabinet, upright or chest type, that holds a number of guns, as well as other valuables. Safes are expensive, but might be worth the price in peace of mind. Of course, a gun safe also protects your firearms from theft. Check your gun store for trigger locks and gun safes.

A simple way to prevent someone from accidentally firing your gun is to keep it disassembled, with the parts stored in separate locations. This is effective and costs nothing.

Shooting and gun ownership bring with them a responsibility. Not only must you handle your gun safely when you are shooting, but you must store it safely. Give it some thought, and you'll find the method that's right for your situation.

Safety check: Don't let yourself think, "It's only a .22." The ammunition you'll probably be shooting is called .22 Long Rifle. It has an extreme range of a mile and a half. It will kill. Be careful with it, and you'll find your .22 a delight to shoot.

Several types of rifle actions are popular: single shot, bolt action, pump and autoloading. Leave the autoloaders for later, when you're quite comfortable with guns. A bolt-

action or single-shot rifle is perfect, and there are a number of them on the market.

An innovative approach to the question of how to fit everyone with a single gun has been put forward by Daisy, the BB gun people. A new .22 rifle from Daisy has an adjustable stock which will fit youngsters, petite women and full-sized adults. If the public responds well to this new rifle, you can expect to see other gun makers offering this feature.

If your interest runs to wing shooting, you'll need a shotgun. The 10-gauge and 12-gauge shotguns are too heavy for many beginners, and the big shotshells kick too much to make them ideal for learning. Get a double-barreled 20-gauge shotgun, pump or autoloading action. You might hear someone advise using a .410-gauge shotgun because of the reduced recoil. Forget it. The .410 is an expert's gun because the shotshell contains so few pellets. When you can hit targets consistently with a 20-gauge, then try the .410.

Again, some basic instruction will go a long way. The shotgun is used to shoot flying targets, and throwing clay pigeons for each other is a wonderful way to spend an afternoon.

You can throw the pigeons with a hand thrower, available at almost any gun store, or you can opt for the small, spring-powered "trap." For learning, the trap (Trius is the standard brand) is better because you can send the target flying on the same course each time, allowing the "student" to concentrate on shooting, not on finding the target.

Now you have your gun and you're ready to go. Well, not quite. There are two pieces of protective equipment you need. Don't shoot without wearing shooting glasses and hearing protection. Just don't do it. The glasses protect you from tiny flecks of unburned gunpowder which might fly back at you. They also protect your eyes should there be an accident. Some very experienced shooters have had accidents caused by getting an obstruction (mud is the most common) stuck in the barrel. When fired in that condition, it's possible that a gun could burst the barrel. Very unlikely, but wear glasses just in case. Prescription eyeglasses with tempered lenses work fine.

With your eyes covered, you now need to protect your ears. Guns are loud, and repeated exposure to the noise of gunfire will permanently damage your hearing. Earmuffs for shooting look like the big-style stereo headphones without the wires. They work great. If you need to protect several pairs of ears, though (remember, everyone *near* the shooter needs ear protection, too), you might opt for inexpensive foam earplugs. They cost about a dollar a pair and can be used many times. Any gun store will have them.

Before you begin shooting, you also need to do something that's going to sound stupid. You need to see if you should shoot right-handed or left-handed. That's determined by your master eye.

Master eye? Almost everyone has one eye that is dominant. It's the one you usually use in looking through a telescope. If you, for example, are right-handed and left-eyed, you should be shooting left-handed. You can find out by taking this quick test.

With both arms outstretched, bring your hands together, thumbs down and palms out, making a hole by touching your thumbs and index fingers. Close up the hole until it's about the size of a quarter. Keep both eyes open and sight through the hole at someone. That person will see your master eye through the hole. If your left eye is the master eye, you should shoot left-handed. The right eye means you shoot from the right shoulder. Don't fight this! It's important that you learn to shoot with both eyes open, and you can't do that unless you sight with your dominant eye.

When you head out to find a place to shoot,

keep safety firmly in mind. If you aren't going to use an established shooting range, make sure you have a safe backstop. That means you can see where the bullets are hitting behind the target. A hill or pushed-up berm of dirt is perfect. Remember that bullets can ricochet off flat surfaces—that includes dirt and water. Put your targets right in front of the backstop to ensure your bullets stop in the dirt.

Start with the target at close range. Ten feet is about right. The object is to make it easy. Nothing breeds success like success.

What kind of targets? You can buy printed bull's-eye targets, and you'll want to have some of them to "record" your successes, but tin cans, big ones, are hard to beat for just plinking—fun shooting. Be sure to pick them up after you're finished.

You're going to put the targets up close and use big targets so you can hit them. You also should shoot from a position that helps you hit the target.

Holding a rifle puts you in an unnatural position which strains your arm, shoulder and back muscles. Straining muscles quiver, so shooting from a standing position is the

least steady method. Begin shooting from the prone, or lying, position. For right-handed shooters, lie facing the target with your body angling out slightly to the left. Spread your legs slightly so you feel comfortable and steady. Your right hand will grab the stock near the trigger; your left will be farther forward, holding the rifle. Make sure your left elbow is directly under the stock so the gun weight pushes straight down on your arm.

A lot of folks are happy just shooting cans and targets behind the farmhouse, but others heed the call to compete. There are a number of different types of matches available for you. Again, the local gun club is the place to start.

It won't take long for you to realize that shooting is a mental game. You must be in adequate physical condition, but matches are won by those with self-discipline and those who can concentrate fiercely. Jim Clark, a national pistol champion, put it this way, "The most important six inches in shooting is between your ears."

For an exciting informal shoot, tape a round piece of cardboard to an old tire and have someone roll it down a hill (make sure the person gets back behind the hill and that your bullets go into a safe backstop). As the tire builds speed and bounces as it rolls, hitting that cardboard will be all the challenge you'll want.

Another game is to let a breeze blow balloons along the ground while you try to pop them.

For many, owning a gun means hunting. You should match the weapon to the game being hunted. Check the local regulations for restrictions on gauges and calibers for various game animals. Many books offer advice and instruction on hunting, and every state has hunter safety instructors who can help. Call the state game department.

Another reason for owning a gun is protection. Whether you are protecting your livestock from four-legged varmints, or yourself and your family from the two-legged kind, owning a gun for protection is a personal choice you should consider carefully. If you do decide to take this step, there's probably no better choice than the double-barreled shotgun. It's relatively easy to shoot well. While lethal at close range, when loaded with bird shot it will cause pain but usually not kill at distances past 30 yards. You can also store it unloaded, yet slip two shotshells into the barrels quickly should the need arise.

Most people own guns simply because they enjoy shooting. It's a safe sport that can be enjoyed by anyone. If you've considered taking up shooting, or if you've thought about teaching your family to shoot, go ahead. More than likely you'll find it to be more fun than you imagined.

Keep It Clean

1. Check to make sure the gun is not loaded—even though you unloaded it at the range.

2. Dip the cleaning brush in bore solvent, and run it down the barrel several times.

3. Run cloth cleaning patches down the bore until they come out clean. Lightly oil another patch, and run it through the bore.

4. Clean exterior working parts with a toothbrush dipped in bore solvent. Then wipe down all metal (not wooden) parts of the gun with a lightly oiled cloth.

Well, the days went along, and the river went down between its banks again, and about the first thing we done was bait one of the big hooks with a skinned rabbit and set it and catch a catfish that was as big as a man, being six foot two inches long, and weighed over two hundred pounds. We couldn't handle him, of course; he would 'a' flung us into Illinois. We just set there and watched him rip and tear around till he drownded."

That's Mark Twain, of course, and while it might seem that he's wildly exaggerating the size of Huck and Jim's big catfish for literary effect, the old master was in fact merely pushing the limits of reality. For Twain's Mississippi was, and remains, an exceptionally fertile environment for the growth of giants among the two largest catfish species native to North America, the blue and the flathead.

The International Game Fish Association's rod-and-reel record for the blue is 97 pounds; for the flathead, 98. But larger, *much* larger, cats have been taken by non-IGFA-sanctioned methods such as trotlines, bank poles and hand lines.

The heaviest verified weight for a blue is for a behemoth that weighed 150 pounds taken (method unknown) from the Mississippi in 1879. In this century, a 130-pound blue hauled from Tennessee's Ft. Loudon Reservoir in 1976 remains king. And a five-foot-long, 106-pound flathead fell to a trotline in Oklahoma's Lake Wister in 1977. There are even bigger cats still out there, no doubt.

"It was as big a fish as was ever catched in the Mississippi, I reckon. Jim said he hadn't ever seen a bigger one. He would 'a' been worth a good deal over at the village. They peddle out such a fish as that by the pound in the market-house there; everybody buys some of him; his meat's as white as snow and makes a good fry."

And that it does. Sadly, the catfish has long suffered a lowly image, branded by snob anglers as a "trash" or "rough" fish simply because it lives and feeds near the bottom and scavenges as well as hunts. Consequently, Americans have long been lured into viewing the catfish as an undesirable, if not unclean, food.

But oh, the awakening of late!

Today, both catfishing and catfish dining are enjoying a surge in popularity, while catfish farming—reflecting America's expanding appetites—is one of the fastest-growing agricultural industries in the nation. According to Bill Allen, Jr., of the American Catfish Institute (down in friendly little Belzoni, Mississippi), cat growers in 1987 produced and sold 280 million liveweight pounds of fish. With processed meat averaging about 54% of liveweight and selling wholesale for $2.05 a pound, catfish farming last year was a $310 million industry.

While the warm-water South remains the catfish capital of the world, decades of transplanting have established respectable populations nationwide. Wherever you happen to live in the contiguous 48 states, you won't have to travel too far to find lucrative angling for one or more of the five primary (of 26 total) North American freshwater species—blue, white, channel, flathead and bullhead. While each has its own preferred habitat and foods, all can be taken with similar tackle, techniques and baits.

Though few cats approach human size, the *potential* for hooking into a catfish as big as a man is always waiting there at the business end of any properly rigged line dangled in catty water, lending a special mystery and excitement to the sport.

Whether you're after Moby Cat or mere-

Greg Smith's 79-pound blue catfish holds the current world record in the 20-pound-test-line class.

ly want some wholesome fun and a panful of first-class fillets, here's how it's done.

Tackle

The traditional American catfishing tool, immortalized in Norman Rockwell paintings, is the cane pole. Even today it's a good rig for youngsters and anyone fishing for bullheads from shore. At the opposite extreme, trophy catfishers—those who concentrate on the really big boys—prefer light saltwater trolling or surfcasting gear. Another popular rig among die-hards is a stiff fiberglass or graphite "boat" rod mounted with a beefy bait-casting reel with star (adjustable) drag, braided line and a level-wind mechanism.

Such big-gun outfits will turn the trick, all right, but are overkill for everyday catfishing. Any sturdy, inexpensive fiberglass rod and medium-sized bait-casting or spinning reel wound with heavy line (12- to 30-pound test is common) will handle the majority of cats with aplomb, and won't leave you "outgunned" for smaller species.

Rigging

Untold thousands of catfish have been taken on standard, single-point hooks. But due to the large, globular nature of some of the best catfish baits and the size of the quarry's maw, you'll generally do better using a treble, or three-point, hook. Anything from a big No. 2 down to a No. 8 is appropriate, depending on the bait you're using and the size of catfish you're after.

If you get nudges and nibbles but no solid strikes, or miss the strikes you do get, try switching to a smaller hook. Remember, you can catch a big fish on a small hook more easily than you can catch a small fish on a big hook.

Since the upper jaw of a catfish is filled with tiny, sharp teeth, you'll need a short length of tough, abrasion-resistant leader just above the hook. You can make your own from fine copper wire with a double-barreled swivel at one end and a snap-swivel at the other, but it's easier simply to buy commercial vinyl-coated steel leaders already made up. They're cheap.

To save knot tying, wasted line and lost fish, use swivels at all connecting points—hook to leader, leader to line, sinker to line, dropper(s) to main line.

Sinkers come in a myriad of shapes—including round, flat, bell, egg and pyramid—but only three basic styles. Most common are those with embedded metal eyes for attaching line or swivels. Instead of an eye, the slip sinker has a generous tunnel bored through its center so that the line can slip freely back and forth. The third basic sinker type friction-clamps directly onto the leader or line (the smaller sizes of this style are called split-shot) and has little use in catfishing.

Baits

Catfish will eat just about anything, dead or alive, moving or inanimate. Stench is no obstacle. Still, when considering baits, it's a mistake to operate on the assumption that cats are exclusively scavengers, for above all they are active and efficient predators.

A Catfish as Big as a Man

These freshwater monsters can provide fine sport and great eating.

Nice catfish are regularly taken on worms, grasshoppers, crickets, crayfish, frogs and toads, minnows, doughballs, cheese, shrimp, chicken entrails (especially livers), coagulated beef blood, liver, whole perch, cut fish, chunks of Ivory and Castile bar soap, commercial stink baits, artificial lures and combinations of the above. Whatever your choices, always bring along a couple of back-up baits, so that if one doesn't raise any action, you can try another, and another.

Doughballs are a clean, inoffensive, inexpensive and effective form of catfish bait. You can make up a batch yourself by dipping (not soaking) a few slices of whole-wheat bread in water, then kneading the soggy mess until it firms up to the consistency of modeling clay.

Should your doughballs catch more carp than catfish, work a little beef blood, Limburger cheese or other stinkum into the dough to increase its attractiveness to cats and discourage sweet-toothed rough fish. (Since chunks of cut fish of any kind make excellent catfish bait, consider sacrificing one of your accidental carp to that end.)

Live minnows can be impaled through both lips on a single-barbed hook, or you can beg a bucket of corpses from a bait shop and gob as many as possible onto a large treble or single-barbed hook. This is an especially effective bait for big cats.

The grandfather of commercial stink baits is Catfish Charlie, a puttylike blend of blood and who-knows-what. Today, Catfish Charlie comes in a host of colorfully named flavors, including Full Stringer, Pole Cracker, Super Cat and Blood Grubbies.

The trouble with stink baits is that, well,

Here's an example of a one-fish family fish fry!

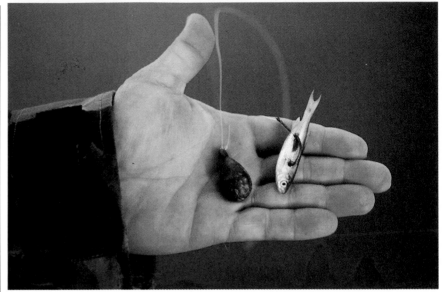

Minnows, alive (preferably) or dead, are prime catfish bait.

they *stink*. They're also messy and often difficult to keep on a hook. That's why the innovative Katfish Lure, marketed by the Little Stinker Bait Company of Lexington, Oklahoma, is finding an eager and growing market. The Katfish Lure is a teardrop-shaped soft plastic balloon rigged with a double hook and an eyed barrel swivel. The hook's two barbs face inward, making the lure weedless, and when the balloon is injected with Little Stinker Kat Katcher (kute, eh?) from its no-mess squeeze tube, you have a deadly catfish lure that "looks real, feels real, smells real." And, if you're careful, your hands stay clean and odorless.

As you still-fish, drift, or work the Katfish Lure slowly along the bottom, as you would when fishing a plastic worm for bass, the Kat Katcher stinkum oozes slowly from pinhole perforations in the lure and creates a scent trail to tempt 'em in. This setup is not only clean and easy to use, it can be deadly in practiced hands.

Technique

Big cats like to hang out near stumps, rocks, sunken logs and other underwater cover. You'll do well, during daylight hours, to locate and fish near such submerged structures in the deepest holes you can find, and over or just off shallower shoals and weed beds at night. If you fish for a while in one spot with no luck, move on a bit, and try again. Keep moving until you find fish.

If it's legal in your state, you can chum. Chumming involves tossing small bits of odoriferous bait into the water to lure in the lunkers and entice them into feeding heedlessly. Dead minnows chopped or squished, blood, and rough fish cut into tiny bits all answer the purpose. The cat's eight "whiskers" are in fact highly developed olfactory sensors

capable of detecting food from a distance in even the muddiest water.

Although cats of all species are primarily bottom dwellers, they don't, as the uppity mongers of the catfish-as-trash-fish myths would have us believe, spend their lives scavenging in mud and muck. Rather, they invest most of their time patrolling lazily a foot or two above the bottom and occasionally even rise to feed in the middle depths or at the surface. Thus, you'll do well to start by positioning your bait near the bottom and fishing with a tight line (no bobber, no slack).

The most straightforward way to accomplish this is to fasten a bell sinker to the end of your line, then attach the hook to a foot-long dropper leader two or three feet or so up from the sinker. Cast out as far as you can, allow time for the sinker to bottom out, then reel in slowly until the line becomes mildly taut. This will position the bait just about the right distance above the bottom. As a bonus, since the bait is dangling from a dropper attached to a tight line, you'll see or feel the line move at even the slightest nibble. If you're alert.

The only significant problem with this setup is that larger and wiser cats aren't blind to the resistance offered by a tight-lined bait, frequently prompting them to drop your offering and leave. A variant rigging technique beats this problem by placing the leader and hook at the end of the line and using a slip sinker above the leader. The swivel attaching line to leader will keep the sinker from riding down onto the bait, and since the line can move freely without having to drag the weight of the sinker, a fish will meet less resistance when it tests the bait. But then, your bait will be lying on, rather than float-

A Fine Kettle of Fish

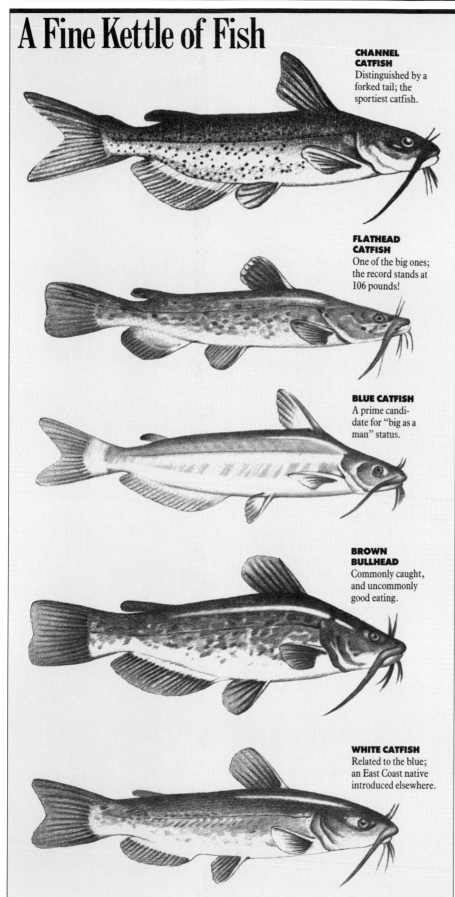

CHANNEL CATFISH
Distinguished by a forked tail; the sportiest catfish.

FLATHEAD CATFISH
One of the big ones; the record stands at 106 pounds!

BLUE CATFISH
A prime candidate for "big as a man" status.

BROWN BULLHEAD
Commonly caught, and uncommonly good eating.

WHITE CATFISH
Related to the blue; an East Coast native introduced elsewhere.

ing above, the bottom. Nothing's easy.

Possibly the most effective rod-and-reel catfishing method of all requires a boat or a tube float. Set your rig to fish near the bottom, and allow the current or breeze to move your craft (be it ever so humble) ever so slowly along. You'll cover a lot of water this way, actively advertising your bait.

One of the most agreeable character traits of catfish is persistence. If you get a strike and, for whatever reason, fail to connect, don't immediately reel in to check your bait. Wait awhile, at least five minutes. More often than not, the cat will come back.

Cleaning Your Catch

Take care when handling catfish, big or small, alive or dead, for all species have needlelike spines at the fronts of the dorsal and pectoral fins. While a stab won't kill you or even make you sick, a cat-spine puncture burns like hellfire for what seems an eternity and can easily become infected. No-nonsense catters keep wire-cutting pliers in their tackle boxes to clip off the offensive spines and have it done with.

The safest way to handle a catfish, no matter its size, is to stick your thumb bravely into its mouth and grasp the lower jaw. Don't worry about being bitten; you'll not come away with anything worse than a sandpaper-like scrape.

Catfish have no scales and relatively little fishy odor. Still, the skin is rubbery and clings to the meat with tenacity; it must be pulled off with pliers (the same pair you used to clip off those nasty spines). The skinning operation is made cleaner, faster and easier with a skinning board, which need be nothing fancier than a pine plank of a size appropriate to the fish.

First, make certain your cat is dead; some species have nine lives and can survive several hours out of water. A sharp blow on the head should suffice (use those handy pliers), or jab a knife or ice pick smartly into the brain (between and behind the eyes).

After gutting the fish, use a sharp knife to slit the skin all the way around just behind the head. Next, make a shallow incision down the full length of the back, cutting around the fins. Now drive a nail or an ice pick through the cat's head to anchor it to the skinning board, and use your pliers to peel back the skin, working from stem to stern. Finally, remove the head and fins.

Small catfish are usually fried whole, medium-sizers are best filleted, and big honkers can be filleted or cut crosswise into steaks. (Catfish bones are prominent and easy to eat around.)

Southern-fried and served with hushpuppies, coleslaw and iced tea . . . *lordy.*

PROPERTY OF
PIKES PEAK LIBRARY DISTRICT
P.O. BOX 1579
COLORADO SPRINGS, CO 80901

Backpacking is queer sport. Your goal is lofty: to escape the boundaries and trappings of civilization and travel by honest sweat and simple foot-power out in God's own country. But to do so you have to lug a complex array of technology—in the form of shelter, clothing, food and more—as part of your attempt to escape it.

It's a biting irony, but, for most of us, a reasonable and necessary one. You simply *can't* enjoy a wilderness experience when you're suffering—if your tent doesn't keep you dry or your clothing doesn't hold in warmth, or if all your gear is so primitively heavy that you become a beast of burden for your possessions. The vast advances in lightening and improving backpacking gear over the past two decades have made the sport safer and more enjoyable.

Yet the central contradiction comes to a head the day before your trip, when you're frantically, finally, assembling a pile of high-tech necessities in one place. There they all are—cookstove, vapor-breathing rain gear, matches, first-aid kit, canteen, nylon rope, spare matches, packets of freeze-dried food, tent, sleeping mat, extra socks, down vest, binoculars, camera, compass, spices, utensils, pots, toilet paper, bug spray, spare spare matches . . . *arrgggh*!

Two worries prey at you as you stare at this disheveled heap of food and gear: Do you have enough equipment (or too much)? And how can you carry it all without breaking your poor overloaded back?

Oh No, I Forgot the . . .

There's only one way to answer the first question: Make a check list. An example is shown on the opposite page, but use someone else's list only as a starting point. As soon as possible, make your own. You can then create one that will reflect your personal preferences and can modify it to fit your experiences ("No, I didn't need that extra pot, but I wish I'd brought pot mitts for cooking. Better add those to the list . . . as soon as the blisters heal.")

A good check list will help you recognize the things you've gathered that are unnecessary (and why lug something if you don't have to?). Most important, it will keep you from forgetting items crucial to your safety or comfort. So even if paperwork trip preparations seem a bit antithetical to the spirit of hiking, make and use a check list.

Distributing the Load

Once you've got all the essentials (and as little more gear as possible), it's time to pack that pack. There are two basic guidelines, and the first is simply this: If you need it, put it where you can get at it. First-aid kit, the day's trail food, sunscreen, water bottle, map, toilet paper and feces-burying trowel, warmer clothes or rain gear in case the weather changes—these things need to be in the top of the pack or in its side pockets. Sleeping bag, tent, tomorrow night's supper, spare fuel, etc., can be stashed deep in the bowels of your bag.

The other basic principle: Pack the heavy items close to your back. The greatest innovation in modern backpack design was the addition of a hip belt. That wide, tight strap should support 80% to 90% of the pack's weight, leaving only a modest 10% to 20% to bear on your shoulders and back. What a world of difference it is to have a pack's weight pushing straight down on your strong hips and legs instead of tugging backward on your spine and tormenting your shoulders.

For a hip belt to work, most of the pack's weight needs to be close to your back and thus pushing down, not away from your spine and pulling backward. Most authorities also recommend placing heavy items up high so their weight is more directly over the hips. (Some say that if you'll be scrabbling across boulder fields or crossing slick-rocked creeks, you should stow your gear low for a lower center of gravity. Take your pick.)

After that, it's all common sense and personal preference. Make sure the weight load is balanced, left and right, so it's not pulling more on one side. Don't put anything with a sharp edge right next to your back. Consider using stuff sacks to help keep batches of similar equipment together. Make sure you've protected your gear (wrapping it in trash bags, if necessary) so it won't get wet in a sudden rainstorm. And fiddle with all the adjustment straps as much and as often as necessary to get that pack fitting as comfortably as possible. (For instance, the back bands that hold the pack off your spine should always be tight. The frame itself should not touch your back.)

Home, Sweet Mobile Home

Finally, all check-list items are checked. Every spare nook of the pack is occupied. The ounce-paring, meticulous, tedious preparations are over. One more hassle—the drive to the trail head—and then you can take off. Hoist that pack on your back, tighten up the hip belt, and head out.

Each fall of a boot takes you one step farther from civilization, one thought further from your normal work-life worries. And since the portable home you're carrying is fully (but not overly) loaded, you're confident, prepared—free to enjoy the adventures that lie ahead.

UPPER LEFT POCKET

LOWER LEFT POCKET

UPPER THIRD OF PACK

UPPER RIGHT POCKET

CENTER OF PACK

LOWER THIRD OF PACK

LOWER RIGHT POCKET

Packing the Pack

The first, worst, but nigh onto most important part of a hiking trip

A BACKPACKER'S CHECK LIST

UPPER THIRD OF PACK
Rain gear
Wool pants
Wind pants
Warm shirt
Food (prepare your own list)

CENTER OF PACK
Tent
Tent fly
Poles and pegs
Ground cloth
Stove
Fuel bottle
Stove accessories
Spare socks
Camp shoes
Long johns
Jacket
Shorts
Pot(s) or pan(s)
Cooking spoon
Eating spoon
Fork
Pot mitt
Plastic water jug
Scouring pad
Nylon cord

Emergency money
Spare pack parts
Repair kit
Flashlight
Batteries
Candle
Soap
Towel
Toothbrush
Toothpaste
Dental floss
Signal mirror
Emergency flare
Whistle
Fishing tackle
Book
Plastic bags

LOWER THIRD OF PACK
Sleeping bag
Stuff sack
Foam pad

UPPER LEFT POCKET
Trail snacks
Pocketknife
Sunglasses
Bandanna
Wool hat
Mittens

LOWER LEFT POCKET
Matches
Water purification tablets
Map
Compass
Toilet paper
Plastic trowel
Lip balm
Insect repellent
Sunscreen

UPPER RIGHT POCKET
Canteen
Cup

LOWER RIGHT POCKET
Snakebite kit
Gauze pads
Moleskin and molefoam
Foot powder
Ace bandage
Antibiotic cream
Aspirin
Adhesive tape
Adhesive bandages

WEIGHT DISTRIBUTION

▨▨▨▨ = Light

▨▨▨▨ = Light/Medium

▨▨▨▨ = Heavy

Pack heavy items high and close. Remember, this is a suggested packing order; adjust to suit your personal needs and preferences.

Freshwater Game Fish

Understanding your
quarry is the key to
satisfying and
successful fishing.

Some 60 million Americans enjoy fishing, making it our nation's most popular sport. Angling attracts a diversity of people because the sport itself is so diverse. It can be athletic or sedentary, social or solitary, competitive or contemplative, highly technical or utterly simple.

Some enthusiasts fish primarily for food; their pleasure comes from the practice of an ancient survival skill. Others, the catch-and-release purists, almost never kill the fish they catch; rather, they approach their sport as an art form. Most of us fall somewhere between these two extremes. Improvement of your fishing skills and enjoyment of the outdoors go hand in hand. The more you know about the natural world, the more likely you are to succeed in catching fish. Of course, the fish themselves are the focus of the angler's natural world, but it's surprising how many people take to the water with no precise idea of what they're trying to catch.

There are nearly 800 species of fish inhabiting the freshwater streams, lakes and reservoirs of North America. Of these, only a relative handful are classified as major "game fish," a term which refers to those species that will take an artificial lure with fair regularity and put up an enthusiastic fight when hooked. This doesn't mean that game fish can't be caught with live bait or that you can't have fun pursuing fish that don't take artificial lures—only that it's generally conceded that the highest recreational experience to be had from angling is in the capture of game fish using artificial lures.

Volumes have been written on the topic of sport fishing. Many think of Izaak Walton's classic, *The Compleat Angler*, as the first treatment of the theme, but angling was the subject of a much earlier book, one of the first to be printed in English, which predated Walton by almost two centuries. This was *A Treatyse of Fysshynge With an Angle*, published in 1486 (and written still earlier, before the invention of the printing press) by Dame Juliana Berners, prioress of a Benedictine nunnery.

It stands to reason that everything that has been learned about fishing—from Dame Juliana's day to Walton's and beyond—has been learned by observing fish in their natural settings. If you have some idea of what to look for and a basic knowledge of tackle and techniques, you too can learn by watching and doing; you can catch fish and reap a bounteous harvest of outdoor recreation while you're about it. After mastering the basics, you can proceed, through practice and study, to any level of sophistication. Or you can keep it simple and still have fun.

Let's examine the primary game-fish species, one at a time, and the tackle and techniques commonly used to challenge them.

RAINBOW TROUT
Trout fishing suggests a
sparkling clear, small to
medium-sized river or
creek flowing over
rocks and gravel.

Trout

Dame Juliana was primarily concerned with trout, and to this day the trout is considered one of the most prestigious of freshwater fish. No quarry can surpass the trout for grace and beauty, and the ambiance of typical trout habitat adds greatly to the enjoyment of the sport. Trout will live in most waters that are cold (below 70°F at all times) and well oxygenated, but the term *trout stream* conjures up a particular image.

A trout stream suggests a sparkling clear, small to medium-sized river or creek flowing over rocks and gravel, usually through a forested watershed, with alternating patches of flat water and riffles, occasional deep holes and maybe a small waterfall here and there. It's in this sort of environment that trout fishing reaches its aesthetic peak.

The image becomes complete by the ad-

dition of an angler casting a fly. Fly-fishing can be raised to the level of art, and it does require investment in high-quality tackle, but the fact is that fly-fishing is not nearly so arcane a craft as is often portrayed. You *can* purchase a fly-fishing outfit and be catching trout within a week; even within a day.

There are four basic categories of trout flies: *Dry flies* are designed to float, in imitation of mayflies and other flying insects that trout eagerly feed on during the summer months. Conventional *wet flies* sink, as do the related *nymphs* and *streamers*. These three lures imitate adult underwater insects, insect larvae and small fish, respectively.

For many, the greatest pleasure in trout fishing comes from dry-fly angling. This is also the easiest fly-fishing method to learn and, at times, the most effective. The trick is to spot trout rising to insects without being seen yourself, to choose an artificial that looks like the insects on which the fish are

feeding, then to present the lure delicately enough to fool the trout. For this you'll need some knowledge of aquatic insects and a modest assortment of flies. Even the names of the flies—Ginger Quill, Whirling Blue Dun, Royal Coachman—figure in the pleasure of this form of angling.

Trout can also be taken on spinning lures or live bait, especially worms. These methods come into their own just about anytime on big waters, in all waters during early spring when trout are loath to rise to the surface, and in streams muddied by rain or snowmelt. Except when fishing big waters, you should stick to small lures of $^3/_{16}$ ounce or less. You'll need an assortment of wobbling spoons and spinner lures, in red and white combinations and in a variety of metallic finishes. Also be sure your collection is assorted as to the gauge of the metal used—heavy gauge for fast, deep water and thinner metal for working the shallows.

Catching Trout

Stream trout fishing, by any method, is a lifetime study. Still, there are two basic rules:

1. Look for current edges, or seams. Trout are masters at conserving energy, wisely preferring to relax as much as possible in still water rather than constantly fighting a stiff current. It's the current, however, that brings them their food. You'll catch more trout by using these two bits of knowledge and by fishing the seams where flowing and still waters meet.

2. Work upstream, and be quiet and inconspicuous. Stream trout rest facing into the current, so are less likely to see you if you fish from below. Avoid heavy footsteps when approaching a fishing spot, and dress in colors that blend with your surroundings (more and more serious fly-fishers are turning to camouflage waders and clothing). When wading, try to avoid kicking stream-bottom rocks and stumbling or other sudden movements.

Trout weighing up to 40 pounds are taken from large lakes, from the tail waters below hydro dams and from streams flowing into an ocean or the Great Lakes, where the fish can fatten on the abundant feed. But most trout fishing is done in small to medium-sized waters, and the quarry are relatively small fish. The primary pleasures arise not from the quest for a trophy, but from the aesthetics of the activity and the skills required to be consistently successful.

Unfortunately, it's the smaller trout streams which have suffered most from human abuse. Due to their very size, they are easily fished out. And even a little industrial pollution or soil erosion—insults that might cause only minor damage to a larger body of water—can ruin a small, delicate trout stream. The sad fact is that most trout angling exists in America today only because state wildlife agencies raise trout in hatcheries and stock them for put-and-take fishing in streams and lakes that can no longer support breeding populations of these sensitive fish.

Catching stocked trout is fun, but still, they're not the genuine article. In brilliance of color, vigor of fight and texture and excellence of flavor, they fall short of wild trout. More important, stocked trout don't "act right." Hatchery trout are bred to be caught, and often it's just too easy to catch them.

You may want to develop your skills on

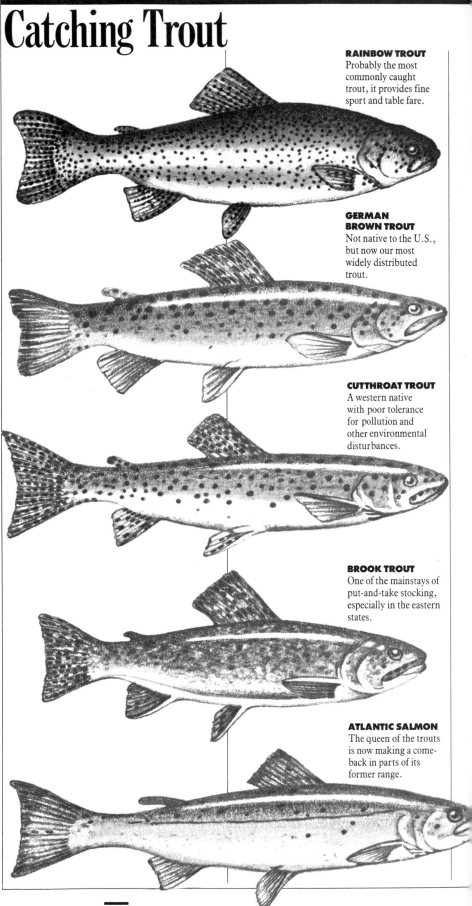

RAINBOW TROUT
Probably the most commonly caught trout, it provides fine sport and table fare.

GERMAN BROWN TROUT
Not native to the U.S., but now our most widely distributed trout.

CUTTHROAT TROUT
A western native with poor tolerance for pollution and other environmental disturbances.

BROOK TROUT
One of the mainstays of put-and-take stocking, especially in the eastern states.

ATLANTIC SALMON
The queen of the trouts is now making a comeback in parts of its former range.

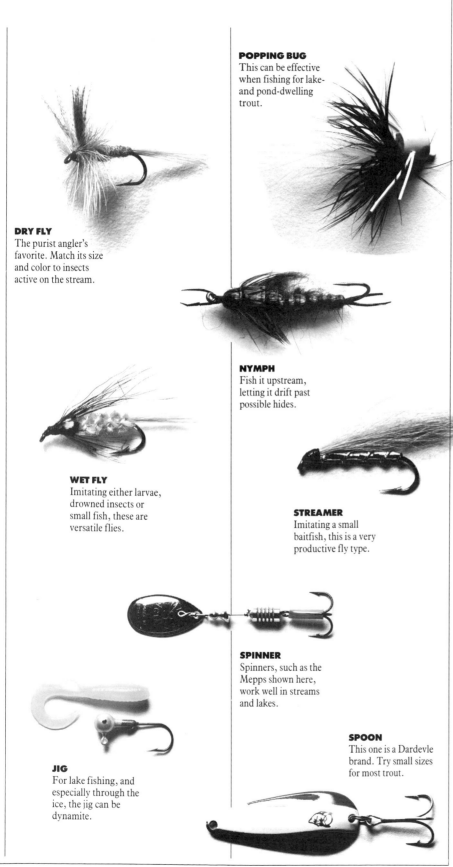

DRY FLY
The purist angler's favorite. Match its size and color to insects active on the stream.

POPPING BUG
This can be effective when fishing for lake- and pond-dwelling trout.

NYMPH
Fish it upstream, letting it drift past possible hides.

WET FLY
Imitating either larvae, drowned insects or small fish, these are versatile flies.

STREAMER
Imitating a small baitfish, this is a very productive fly type.

SPINNER
Spinners, such as the Mepps shown here, work well in streams and lakes.

SPOON
This one is a Dardevle brand. Try small sizes for most trout.

JIG
For lake fishing, and especially through the ice, the jig can be dynamite.

hatchery trout, but if you have access to wild trout, don't pass up a shot at the real thing. A nationwide organization dedicated to the restoration of natural trout habitat and self-supporting fisheries, as opposed to stocking, is Trout Unlimited (501 Church St. N.E., Vienna, VA 22180). Local Trout Unlimited chapters might be willing to help you locate good wild-fish waters, especially if you're willing to get involved in their good causes, which include stream restoration projects.

Scientists currently recognize 14 North American species in the genera *Salmo* and *Salvelinus*, popularly referred to as trout. Some of these species are of extremely localized distribution, but three may be found in streams from coast to coast.

The most widely distributed trout, the German brown (*Salmo trutta*), is, as its name indicates, not a native here, but was introduced from Europe beginning in 1883. The brown is often considered the most difficult of the 14 species of trout to catch. Use smaller, less colorful flies for browns than you would for other species. If you locate a lunker, try fishing for it at night. The brown is more tolerant of environmental degradation than our native species, and so has been the salvation of trout fishing in many damaged waters across the country.

The native trout of eastern North America is the brook trout (*Salvelinus fontinalis*), also called speckled trout and squaretail. Far easier to catch than the German brown, the brookie is one of the mainstays of put-and-take stocking, especially in the eastern states. Environmentally, however, it's among the most delicate of the trout. In most parts of the country, naturally reproducing brook trout populations have been pushed back into small headwater streams.

A wild brook trout is arguably the most beautiful of North American fish. Even though in many streams a nine-incher is a whopper, it's worth bushwhacking up into the headwaters just to get a glimpse of these lovely creatures.

The rainbow trout (*Salmo gairdneri*) has made the opposite journey from that of the brookie. Native to the Pacific slope, the rainbow is now found in many eastern waters. Among all the trout species, the rainbow has been selected for breeding as a food fish. So you'll find it in commercial catch-your-own

PIKE
The star of the Canadian fishing lodge circuit, the pike preys on everything from minnows to ducklings.

fisheries. In nature, rainbows occupy a variety of habitats; don't neglect to look for them in powerful currents that would be avoided by other trout species. Rainbows usually put up a terrific fight when hooked; they're unexcelled as jumpers.

When it gets a chance, the rainbow will go to sea, returning to its home river to spawn. These sea-going rainbows are known as steelheads and support a specialized fishery on the Pacific Coast. Steelhead fishing can be a rugged, even dangerous sport, often carried out in the dead of winter. Seek local advice before attempting it.

In the West, the niche of the native brook trout is filled by the cutthroat (*Salmo clarki*). Unfortunately, the cutthroat has a low tolerance for pollution or other disturbances to its pristine natural environment and so is becoming increasingly rare—restricted these days primarily to small, clear streams at high altitudes. Additionally, cutthroats readily interbreed with planted rainbows, creating hybrids and hastening the demise of the pure form of this beautiful, scrappy and delicious species. Cutthroats are less likely to take a dry fly than most other trout species, so fish deep.

From Washington State north along the Pacific Coast, you'll find the Dolly Varden (*Salvelinus malma*), named after a pink-spotted calico cloth popular in the West in the midnineteenth century. Dollies prefer to eat other fish, so go after them with streamer flies or silvery spoons.

Two important trout species remain. The lake trout (*Salvelinus namaycush*) has been left until now because it's so atypical. As its name implies, this fish is almost totally confined to deep lakes. Except in the very early spring (or in the Arctic), fishing for lake trout necessitates trolling with wire line and other devices designed to take large, shiny spoons to the depths lake trout frequent.

The royalty of the trout family isn't even called a trout. The Atlantic salmon (*Salmo salar*) originally was native to both sides of the Atlantic, from Spain north and on around at least to the Connecticut River. Today, this species has been eliminated from much of its natural range by dams, pollution, deforestation and overfishing. In Europe and Canada, the degree of protection necessary to preserve the species has contributed to its elevation to elite status.

Traditional Atlantic salmon fishing involves the use of incredibly complex and colorful flies and techniques that can fairly be described as ritual. Unfortunately, most American anglers can't afford to jet to Europe to fish for Atlantic salmon, much less rent a "beat" on one of the better salmon rivers of Scotland or New Brunswick.

In the U.S., although sea-run populations of Atlantic salmon have been sadly depleted, landlocked populations are found in several lakes in Maine, and these fish have been introduced to other lakes in New England. They are usually taken by trolling special streamer flies with a trailer-hook attached. The prime season is immediately after ice-out.

The good news about Atlantic salmon is that in recent years U.S. fishery biologists and conservationists have succeeded in bringing salmon runs back to such rivers as the Connecticut and Maine's Penobscot. This ranks as one of the great environmental success stories and eventually may mean that the average angler can get a chance at what many consider to be the greatest of all freshwater game fish.

Pacific Salmon

The Pacific salmons are members of the same family (Salmonidae) as are the various trout species but are typically saltwater fish that enter freshwater rivers only to spawn. These fish generally don't feed while in fresh water, so the idea is to stimulate anger or curiosity with your lure. This often means relying on fluorescent pink or red spoons. These husky (20 pounds and more), vigorous fish are tremendous fighters, so have plenty of strong line (15-pound-test or better) on your reel.

Two species of salmon have adapted well to spending their entire lives in fresh water. The largest is the coho or silver salmon (*Oncorhynchus kisutch*). Native to the Pacific Coast, the coho has been introduced to the Great Lakes and a few Atlantic Coast rivers.

The kokanee salmon are in fact landlocked sockeyes (*Oncorhynchus nerka*) that have been successfully stocked into many western lakes and reservoirs. By planting fingerlings in a

Purists pursue trout and salmon with flies—a fascinating challenge.

YELLOW PERCH
A favorite of commercial fisheries and young anglers alike, the yellow perch readily takes minnows and is usually superb eating.

lake at the mouth of its feeder stream, the infant fish imprint on that stream and will return to it as mature adults to spawn, creating a miniature late-fall salmon run and providing fast-paced sport for snagging enthusiasts and a feast for bald eagles and carnivorous mammals. (Salmon die after spawning, and if not taken by snaggers, eagles or animals, go to waste.)

Pike

While trout and salmon are cold-water fish and the majority of our freshwater food and game fish are warm-water dwellers, there are a few in-between groups that can be loosely categorized as cool-water fish. All our important cool-water species are in the pike or perch families (Esocidae and Percidae, respectively).

The angler can choose to fish for small, medium or large pike. Apart from some very small species of negligible sporting interest, the smallest pike is the chain pickerel (*Esox niger*). This fish occasionally reaches a maximum weight of around 10 pounds, but most pickerel caught are 14 to 18 inches long and weigh less than two pounds.

The top of the line among the pikes is the muskellunge (*Esox masquinongy*). The current record musky falls just an ounce short of 70 pounds, and the average fish caught weighs eight to 10 pounds.

In between the chain pickerel and the muskellunge is the northern pike (*Esox lucius*). Northerns usually run three to four pounds. A 15-pounder is cause for bragging. The northern pike is the most widely distributed of freshwater game fishes, occurring north of latitude 40° around the world. Most plug or spoon lures, cast or trolled around weed beds, logs or rocks, will catch northern pike, but the classic lure is a red and white spoon in the ³/₄-ounce size.

In good pike waters, one can count on catching northerns with fair frequency. The same can't be said for the muskellunge. Musky fishing calls for a certain fanaticism. In western New York, for example, anglers are allowed to keep five muskies annually, and only a dedicated and expert minority manage to land their limit of five 30-inch-or-

Young anglers will grow to respect and protect our fish and waters.

better legal keeper-sized fish.

Muskellunge aren't widely distributed; in addition to western New York and Pennsylvania, prime musky fishing is to be had only in the St. Lawrence River, Lake St. Clair, numerous waters in Wisconsin, Minnesota and Ontario, and some rivers on the western slope of the Appalachians.

If you want to have a go at musky fishing, equip yourself with a heavy bait-casting outfit wound with 20-pound-test line, and stock your tackle box with a variety of plugs and spoons in the ³/₄-ounce size. Fish pretty much as you would for northern pike, but prepare yourself psychologically to have a nice day afield or afloat with not so much as a sign of fish. Or carry lighter tackle, and try for lesser game when the muskies outwait you.

The chain pickerel, found in Atlantic Coast drainages from New Brunswick south to Florida, is an underrated game fish. Temperamentally, it is unlike its moody big cousin, the musky. Pickerel are usually willing to cooperate—in the heat of summer, during storms, under the ice or during midday—when other species take a break. Only darkness stops their feeding.

Most pickerel are taken in or near lily beds or weeds, so use a stouter line than the modest size of the fish would suggest. Eight-pound-test is usually a good choice. The only lure you'll need to take pickerel is a red and white Dardevle, but for added fun try a surface lure, especially on calm fall days. You may be treated to the thrilling sight of a big pickerel charging your lure with its dorsal fin slicing along the surface of the water like a cinema shark.

Please use large lures for pickerel. Small ones will take as many fish, but small pickerel are such enthusiastic predators that they often swallow small lures, forcing the angler to kill them in the process of trying to extract a swallowed lure, wasting fish that could have been released alive had they been hooked in the mouth with a larger lure. Switching from a ³/₁₆-ounce to a ¹/₄-ounce Dardevle makes all the difference.

Here are a few additional tips for going after all the pikes, large or small:

Retrieving: Keep your lure moving. Unlike trout and bass, pike very rarely take a still lure. And stay alert during the *entire* retrieval; pike, unseen, often follow lures

Catching Pike

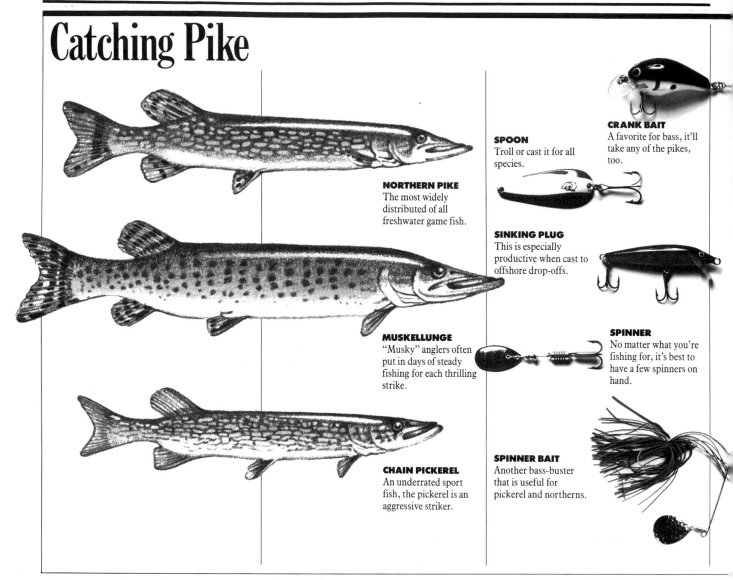

NORTHERN PIKE
The most widely distributed of all freshwater game fish.

MUSKELLUNGE
"Musky" anglers often put in days of steady fishing for each thrilling strike.

CHAIN PICKEREL
An underrated sport fish, the pickerel is an aggressive striker.

SPOON
Troll or cast it for all species.

CRANK BAIT
A favorite for bass, it'll take any of the pikes, too.

SINKING PLUG
This is especially productive when cast to offshore drop-offs.

SPINNER
No matter what you're fishing for, it's best to have a few spinners on hand.

SPINNER BAIT
Another bass-buster that is useful for pickerel and northerns.

right up to the boat or shore, then make an explosive strike at the last moment.

Hooking: Pike have hard, bony mouths. So when one strikes, set the hook by hauling back hard on your rod a couple of times.

Teeth: Pike have numerous long teeth that are sharp on the sides as well as the tips. This necessitates using a wire leader between line and lure so that a hooked fish doesn't cut your line. And don't put your hand in a pike's mouth; carry pliers to remove hooks.

Live bait: Avoid fishing for pike with live bait—except in special situations such as ice fishing, where you can see the fish take the bait. Almost the only way to consistently hook pike on live bait is to let them swallow it. This results in death for most small fish that could otherwise be caught and released.

Perch

The largest member of the perch family, the walleye (*Stizostedion vitreum*), is com-

monly and incorrectly referred to as the walleyed "pike." Its long, slender shape and toothy mouth are reminiscent of the pike, but the two dorsal fins, one of them spiny, set the walleye and its smaller, less well known relative the sauger (*Stizostedion canadense*) apart. A better generic name for these two species, both of which are widely distributed in North America, is the European term *pike perch.*

The main thing to remember in fishing for pike perch is that they like to take their time making up their minds. For this reason, trolling is often better than casting, as the fish get more time to follow the lure. Still-fishing with live minnows is also effective. Whatever method you choose, look for pike perch off ledges, and experiment with various depths. A variety of plugs, spoons and spinners will take these fish, and jigs are becoming increasingly popular. But the classic method is to troll a "June bug" spinner (a type of spinner designed to rotate at the very slow speeds

preferred by these fish) with a night crawler harnessed behind.

When freshwater anglers say "perch," they usually mean the yellow perch (*Perca flavescens*) found almost everywhere in North America outside the Deep South. The perch is one of those species often collectively called *pan fish,* in reference to their convenient frying-pan size. Although the pan fish aren't as dramatic as the larger game fish, they readily take artificials and are every bit as scrappy, ounce for ounce, and so rate discussion here.

Anglers usually rely on live minnows to take yellow perch, but another favorite bait is a $1/16$-ounce jig. Like the larger pike perch, the yellows prefer to take their time, making trolling one of the most effective methods of locating them. Once you find a perch hole, anchor, and jig straight up and down.

The size of perch caught varies greatly from place to place. In one pond, few perch

Catching Perch

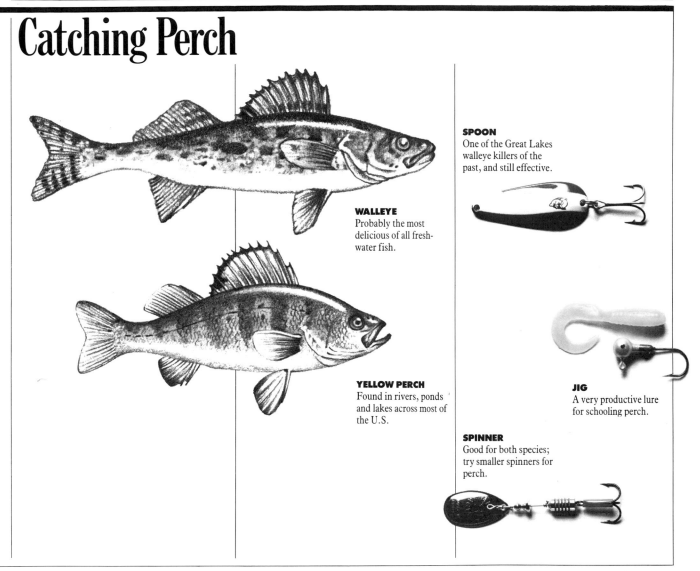

WALLEYE
Probably the most delicious of all fresh-water fish.

YELLOW PERCH
Found in rivers, ponds and lakes across most of the U.S.

SPOON
One of the Great Lakes walleye killers of the past, and still effective.

JIG
A very productive lure for schooling perch.

SPINNER
Good for both species; try smaller spinners for perch.

will be big enough to be worth catching, while a neighboring pond might yield 15-inch "jack" perch. Often, the best perch are taken where the species is relatively scarce. Look for individual big fish in isolated deep holes, in shallow, weedy ponds or in slow, deep rivers and creeks flowing through acidic swamps.

Black Bass

The quintessentially American game fish is the black bass. In particular, the largemouth bass (*Micropterus salmoides*) is by now accessible to virtually all anglers south of the Canadian border. Consequently, the techniques of bass fishing have become nearly as sophisticated as those used for trout; sometimes bordering on the ridiculous.

Bass fishing, as practiced in the bizarre spectacle of bass tournaments, may seem to require not only technique but thousands of dollars' worth of technology and the com-

petitive spirit of an NFL lineman. Still, ordinary anglers catch more largemouth bass than any other freshwater game fish.

The largemouth is an amazingly adaptable fish, and methods of fishing for it are as diverse as the environments it inhabits. Although it had long been thought of as a shallow-water dweller, when dam-building mania struck the South the largemouth made itself at home in the new deep reservoirs. Now anglers search for contest winners as deep as 100 feet.

Most of the lures now on the market, especially the plugs, were created mainly to catch largemouths. Of course, bass can also be taken on streamer flies and a variety of live baits. The assumption is that you're not a trophy seeker, but rather a sensible angler who'll be delighted with a string of two-pound fish.

Casting vs. trolling: Casting for largemouths is usually more effective than trolling, but on a large, unfamiliar body of water

try trolling the shoreline. You'll cover more water and so locate fish more quickly.

Sight and sound: Keep your eyes and ears open. A sudden *kerplunk* or a visible swirl in the shallows may be a bucket-mouth bass having its dinner. If you locate such a fish, cast a little beyond the spot, and retrieve over it.

Lure size: Bass lures come in many sizes. If your goal is to catch *more* bass, try a lure smaller than what you see others using. If you want *big* bass, try a larger lure.

Retrieving: Vary the speed and cadence of your retrieval. Try fast, slow and stop-and-go. Often, the retrieval speed is even more important than the choice of lure.

Crank baits: In deep waters, try crank baits. These are plugs designed to dive at a steep angle when reeled in fast. Then, when the retrieval is slowed, they level out and come in deep. With crank baits you can search for fish along drop-offs and explore a variety of depths without changing lures.

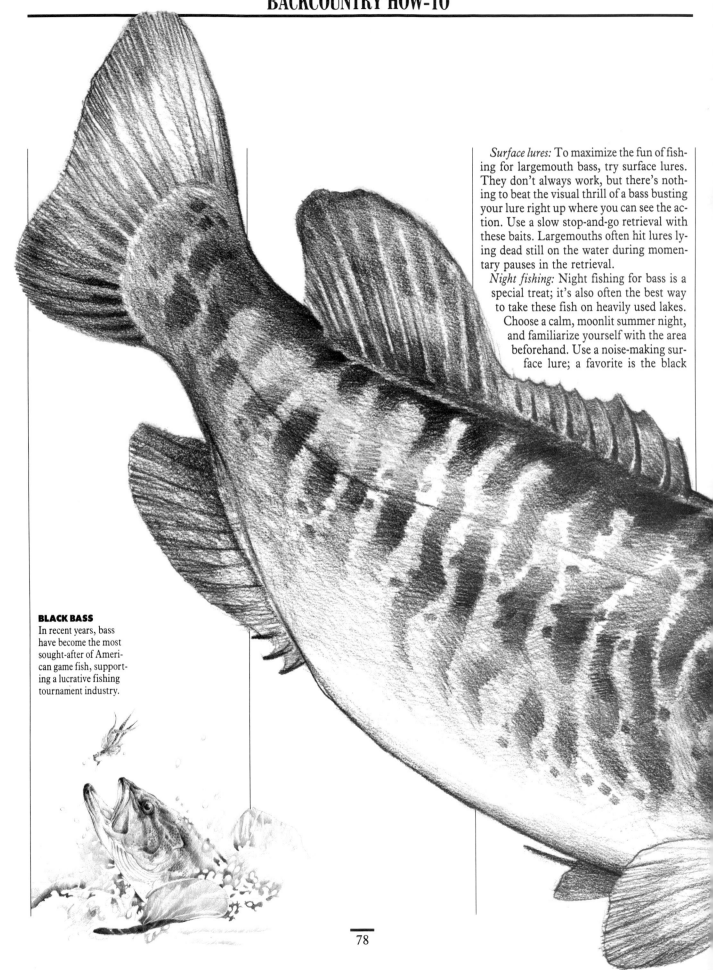

Surface lures: To maximize the fun of fishing for largemouth bass, try surface lures. They don't always work, but there's nothing to beat the visual thrill of a bass busting your lure right up where you can see the action. Use a slow stop-and-go retrieval with these baits. Largemouths often hit lures lying dead still on the water during momentary pauses in the retrieval.

Night fishing: Night fishing for bass is a special treat; it's also often the best way to take these fish on heavily used lakes. Choose a calm, moonlit summer night, and familiarize yourself with the area beforehand. Use a noise-making surface lure; a favorite is the black

BLACK BASS
In recent years, bass have become the most sought-after of American game fish, supporting a lucrative fishing tournament industry.

Jitterbug. Play it by ear, as they say.

Edges: Above all else, think edges. Largemouth bass are rarely found in open water, preferring to lurk in cover and charge out to seize their prey. "Edge" may signify lily pads on one body of water, submerged logs on another and underwater ledges in a third.

The smallmouth bass (*Micropterus dolomieui*) is in some ways an even better game fish than the largemouth. Back in the last century, Dr. James Henshall, the father of modern bass fishing, dubbed this species ". . . inch for inch, and pound for pound, the gamest fish that swims." There's no reason to dispute him today. Although it runs smaller than the largemouth, is less widely distributed and harder to fool with a lure, you'll forget all that when you see what a splendid account of itself the smallmouth gives when hooked.

The smallmouth usually avoids the muddy bottoms frequented by the largemouth. Look for it around rocks. In lakes, it will be found in deeper, cooler waters, while in streams it will tolerate more current.

Most methods used to take largemouth bass will take smallmouths as well, but be more conservative in your choice of size and colors of lures. Often, smallmouths simply can't be persuaded to take an artificial lure at all. Minnows or worms will do as live bait, but the smallmouth bait par excellence is the relatively rare soft-shelled crayfish.

Sunfish

The largemouth and smallmouth bass, with a few obscure relatives, are the largest of the Centrarchidae, but the family also includes most of our pan fishes, the most familiar of which are the sunfish.

Among sunfish, the bluegill (*Lepomis macrochirus*) reigns supreme for size, adaptability, edibility and sporting qualities. An eight- or nine-inch bluegill will give you a real tussle. Bluegills are found in streams, but the best fishing is usually to be had in lakes and ponds. The more than 2 million farm ponds

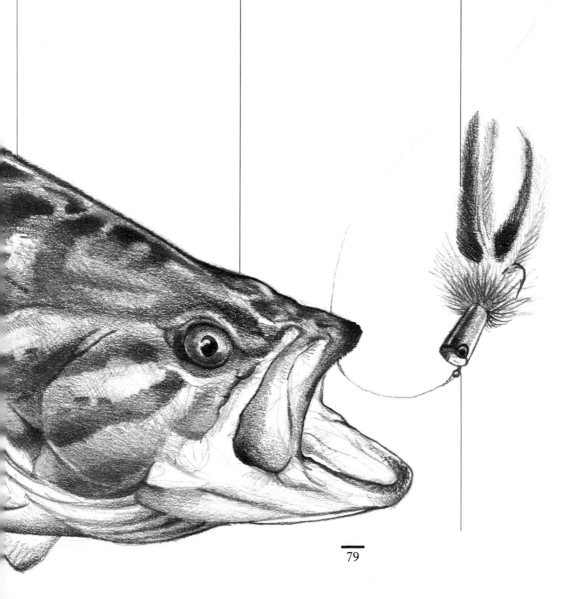

Catching Bass

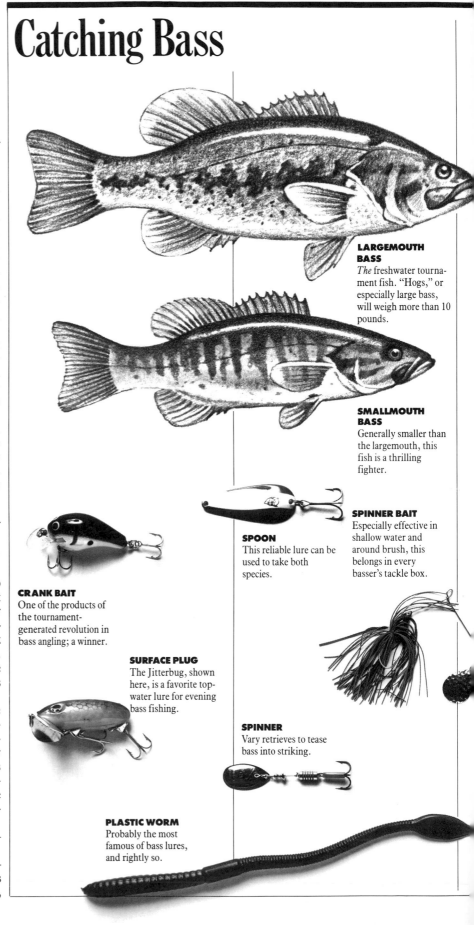

LARGEMOUTH BASS
The freshwater tournament fish. "Hogs," or especially large bass, will weigh more than 10 pounds.

SMALLMOUTH BASS
Generally smaller than the largemouth, this fish is a thrilling fighter.

SPOON
This reliable lure can be used to take both species.

SPINNER BAIT
Especially effective in shallow water and around brush, this belongs in every basser's tackle box.

CRANK BAIT
One of the products of the tournament-generated revolution in bass angling; a winner.

SURFACE PLUG
The Jitterbug, shown here, is a favorite top-water lure for evening bass fishing.

SPINNER
Vary retrieves to tease bass into striking.

PLASTIC WORM
Probably the most famous of bass lures, and rightly so.

built in the U.S. since the late 1930s have traditionally been stocked with a mix of largemouth bass and bluegills.

One point that should be made about sunfish in general goes double for farm-pond bluegills: You needn't be inhibited about keeping all you catch. A common problem in farm-pond management is overpopulation by bluegills, with consequent stunting. The bass are supposed to act as predators and control the bluegill population, but too often anglers fish out the bass and ignore the bluegills, resulting in a pondful of tiny, useless fish. Keeping more bluegills, then, can be good conservation.

Bluegills can be caught year-round, but spring is the prime season. Look for spawning aggregations in shallow water. You can spot them from a distance by the neat circular nests the males make by sweeping the debris from the bottom.

When you find fish, you can offer them live worms or crickets suspended just off the bottom with a bobber. Or cast a $1/16$-ounce jig. If the fish are slow about taking a jig, you can create a killer bluegill lure by tipping the hook of a jig with a small piece of worm.

Fly-fishing is also an effective way to take sunfish, and loads of fun. The most fun of all is to use a dry fly—any pattern will do. Whatever lure or bait you use, remember that sunfish have small mouths.

Some of the other sunfish species are too small to be of interest to adult anglers, but a few do merit mention. The most widely known is the pumpkinseed (*Lepomis gibbosus*), a dazzling little fish that rivals the brook trout as our most beautiful game species. Pumpkinseeds often run small, but in some waters they grow to be every bit as big as bluegills.

In the South, you may encounter the redear sunfish (*Lepomis microlophus*), the redbreast sunfish (*L. auritus*) or the longear sunfish (*L. megalotis*). The redear is a deep-water fish that rarely feeds at the surface. Worms or jigs, therefore, are your best bet for taking it. The redbreast and longear are more typically stream dwellers than the other sunfish species.

Crappie

The look-alike black and white crappies (*Pomoxis nigromaculatus* and *P. annularis*,

Catching Sunfish

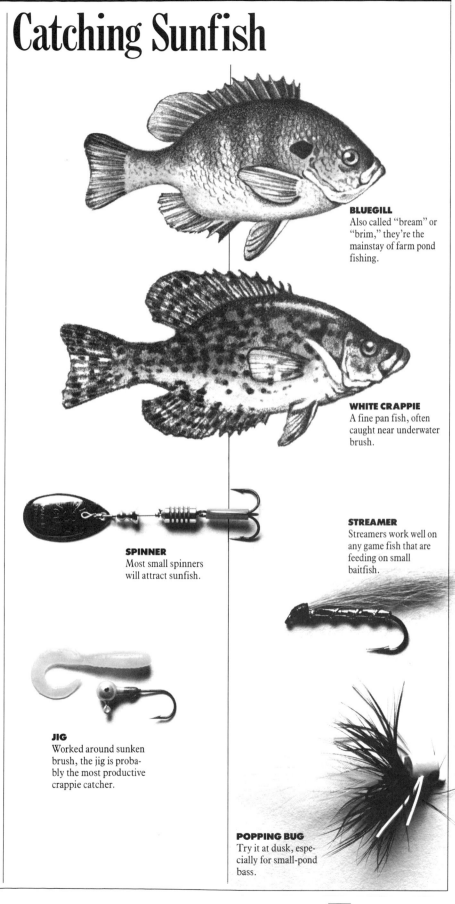

BLUEGILL
Also called "bream" or "brim," they're the mainstay of farm pond fishing.

WHITE CRAPPIE
A fine pan fish, often caught near underwater brush.

SPINNER
Most small spinners will attract sunfish.

STREAMER
Streamers work well on any game fish that are feeding on small baitfish.

JIG
Worked around sunken brush, the jig is probably the most productive crappie catcher.

POPPING BUG
Try it at dusk, especially for small-pond bass.

respectively) are not generally distinguished by anglers and are popular pan fish, particularly in the South. Crappies do best in large bodies of water, and the construction of reservoirs has brought them to the forefront of angling in some areas.

Depending on water temperature and the season of the year, crappies may be found deep or shallow, in stream mouths or well off shore. But the key to good crappie catches is brush. Always try to fish around sunken bushes or treetops. A stout line is necessary to pull off the many snags you'll hook.

Probably the most efficient way to catch crappies is with live minnows fished on double-hooked "crappie rigs." But small streamer flies or lures will also take them. One favorite is a $1/16$-ounce white jig.

Rock Bass

Also in the family Centrarchidae are a miscellany of fish the size of sunfish but with mouths that are more nearly like those of bass. The savvy angler will quickly surmise that this means more small fish and fewer insects in the diets of these species. That translates to larger lures and hooks.

Chief among these fish is the rock bass (*Ambloplites rupestris*), sometimes called the redeye. As its name suggests, the rock bass is usually found around rocks. It's a frequent associate of the smallmouth bass, with which it shares a prominent red eye and a taste for baitfish and crawdads.

If the smallmouths are hitting like crazy, rock bass are nothing but a nuisance. But when the smallmouths aren't cooperating, rock bass can be the salvation of a fishing trip. If you really want a string of rock bass, use the very same methods you would for smallmouths, but use slightly smaller lures and work pockets of quiet water. If "rockies" are around, you won't have to wait long.

The Serranids

A final group of warm-to-cool-water game fish belongs in the mostly marine sea bass family (Serranidae). Of these, the striped bass (*Roccus saxatilis*) is a major freshwater game fish, reaching weights of over 50 pounds. The striper historically was a saltwater species sometimes caught in fresh water when it ascended rivers to spawn. In recent dec-

Catching Serranids

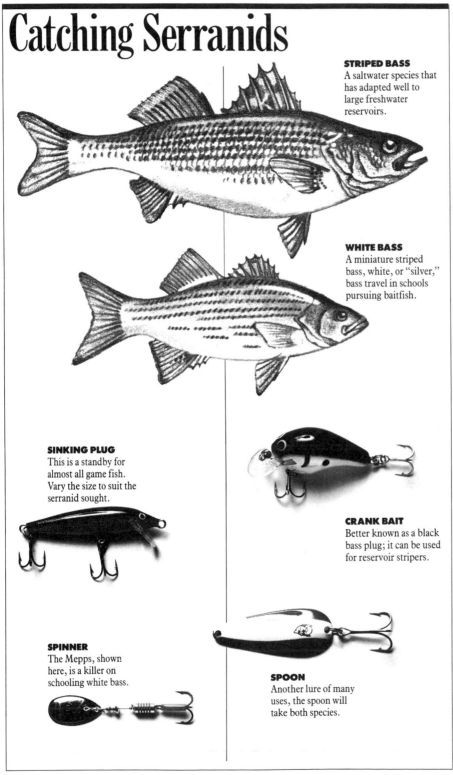

STRIPED BASS
A saltwater species that has adapted well to large freshwater reservoirs.

WHITE BASS
A miniature striped bass, white, or "silver," bass travel in schools pursuing baitfish.

SINKING PLUG
This is a standby for almost all game fish. Vary the size to suit the serranid sought.

CRANK BAIT
Better known as a black bass plug; it can be used for reservoir stripers.

SPINNER
The Mepps, shown here, is a killer on schooling white bass.

SPOON
Another lure of many uses, the spoon will take both species.

ades, however, it has been successfully introduced to many large, deep reservoirs across the country, such as Lake Powell in Arizona and Utah.

The other three serranids are much smaller, verging on pan-fish size. The largest and most widespread of these is the white bass (*R. chrysops*). Unlike most freshwater game fish, white bass should be sought in open water, well away from cover. And when you find them, you'll find plenty.

Trolling, jigging and deep fishing with live bait all work well, but the most exciting way to take white bass is called "fishing the jumps." A pair of binoculars and an outboard motor will help, though neither is absolutely necessary. Early or late on a calm

BLUEGILL
More young anglers get their first lessons from this scrappy sunfish than from any other species.

summer's day, cruise around looking for schools feeding near the surface. You'll know one when you see it: For an area of at least several square yards, the surface of the water will be churned to foam and the silver sides of white bass and leaping, terrified forage fish will be flashing everywhere.

When you find a school, get there as fast as you can. Choose a small, silvery lure made of fairly heavy-gauge metal so that you can cast it a good distance. Cast around the edges or completely across the school—*not* into its midst—and let the lure sink a bit before retrieving. For even more action, tie a fly onto a short dropper line ahead of your lure; you'll often pick up doubles.

In the Mississippi River valley lives the yellow bass (*Morone interrupta*). The fishing technique is similar to that used for white bass.

The pan-sized serranid of the Atlantic coastal plain is the misnamed white perch (*Roccus americanus*). Unlike other serranids, this species may be found in small, weedy or brushy ponds as well as in large, open waters. The conventional wisdom is that the white perch is a mystery fish, taken often enough when fishing for other species, but unpredictable and rarely taken in numbers.

If you go angling and succeed in bringing home a fish dinner, fine. But remember that fishing is meant to be recreation—fresh air, exercise, a test of your angling skills—whether you catch fish or not. We should fish in order to re-create the kind of awareness of and appreciation for nature by which our hunter-gatherer ancestors lived.

But unlike our forebears, you needn't feel compelled to bring home the meat each and every time out. If you don't catch anything, you can still have fun. If you do land a few, realize that killing isn't essential to the sport. A panful of fresh-caught fish frying on the stove creates a satisfying feeling, it's true. But there's another good feeling to be found in gently putting back a little one to grow up and be caught again another day. Or even in releasing a big one, fairly outwitted and battled into your net. Both of *these* rewards have a rightful and increasingly necessary place in modern recreational fishing.

PART THREE

A Naturalist's Guide

Wildlife is the
lure that draws us to the
woods; its ways
keep the fascination
ever fresh.

▲ Long-jawed cisco

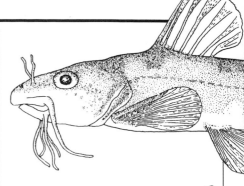

▲ California condor
Gymnogyps californianus
The last wild California condor was taken into captivity on Easter Sunday 1987, officials having determined that the wilderness was a threat to the species' survival. As is the case with many species that have already disappeared, the condor was once common, ranging from Canada to Mexico and from the Rocky Mountains to the Pacific. It has been poisoned, shot and had its lands systematically appropriated by hu-

mans for their purposes. Faced with a population of condors that has plummeted from thousands a century ago to around 30 a decade ago, the FWS and the National Audubon Society embarked on a "condor recovery program" that aimed to restore the species by taking eggs, young birds and adults from the wild and rearing them in captivity. After some 20 years, perhaps, the birds will be returned to the wild. *Estimated population: 0 wild, 28 in two zoos.*

▼ Palila
Loxioides bailleui
This Hawaiian honeycreeper (all native Hawaiian birds are legally endangered) was threatened by competition for food and shelter from feral sheep and goats that had been moved into its only range: the upper slopes of Mauna Kea on the island of Hawaii. Some years ago, the Sierra Club Legal Defense Fund brought a suit with the palila itself as the lead plaintiff—the first time a court had allowed such a case to be prosecuted. After two lawsuits and 10 years, the palila prevailed, and the court ordered the government of Hawaii to remove sheep and goats from the birds' habitat. A promising recovery is under way for the honeycreeper. *Estimated population: 2,000.*

▼ Tecopa pupfish

▲ Black-footed ferret
Mustela nigripes
This weasel was thought extinct until 1984, when a colony was discovered in Wyoming. Black-footed ferrets live exclusively with prairie dogs, their principal food. The ferrets have been nearly exterminated by poisons aimed at the prairie dogs, by epidemics of dog distemper and by a renegade virus that struck them recently. The ferrets' lot, though still tenuous, may be improving. Captive breeding experiments have finally yielded survivors, and there have been confirmed sightings in the wild. *Estimated population: 35-40.*

Farewell, Fellow Travelers

The Endangered Species Act is only a *step* in the right direction.

June 17, 1987, is not a date most people will remember for long. On that day, the last dusky seaside sparrow in the world was found dead of old age in its cage in Florida. His species had fallen victim to the space program, a mosquito-abatement project, fire and Walt Disney World. It is the latest species to be declared officially extinct. And, despite the best efforts of environmentalists and the Endangered Species Act, it won't be the last.

There's nothing quite so final, so irrevocable, as extinction. There's no appeal, no rematch, no instant replay to see who should be penalized. And driving thousands of species from the face of the earth is as big a crime as we could possibly commit against the future. As Harvard professor E.O. Wilson observed: "The worst thing that can happen—will happen—is not energy depletion, economic collapse, limited nuclear war or conquest by a totalitarian government. As terrible as these catastrophes would be for us, they can be repaired within a few generations. The one process ongoing in the 1980s that will take millions of years to correct is the loss of genetic and species diversity by the destruction of natural habitats. This is the folly our descendants least likely to forgive us." Indeed, allowing an extinction is perhaps the most modern of sins.

Besides—and ultimately more important than—the loss of directly exploitable economic benefits when a species becomes extinct, the continuing smooth operation of our planet is threatened. Biologists sometimes liken the diversity of species on earth to the numerous rivets in a piece of equipment. The dispersion of the load through the rivets makes the machine flexible and durable; a few of the rivets can be lost without disaster. Once a certain number pop out, however, massive failure occurs. The diversity of species in the earth's ecosystems provides this flexibility and serves humans by stabilizing the climate, processing wastes and returning nutrients, generating and maintaining soils, controlling pests and diseases, and providing the raw materials for medicine.

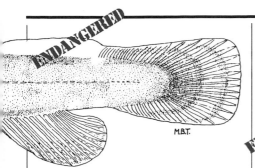

M.B.T.

▲ Sciota mad tom

Noturus trautmani
This small catfish from
the Ohio River may
already be extinct. It
was last seen in 1958 or
'59, though it was very
difficult to find. This is
a good illustration of
how the FWS is loath to
actually declare a
species extinct. The
regulations on this
point read as follows:

"*Extinction:* Unless all
individuals of the listed
species had been
previously identified
and located, and were
later found to be
extirpated from their
previous range, a
sufficient period of time
must be allowed before
delisting to indicate
clearly that the species
is extinct." *Estimated
population: Unknown.*

▲ Perdido Key beach mouse

*Peromyscus polionotus
trissyllepsis*
This species was
discovered during
studies of the environ-

mental impact of
building condominiums
on Perdido Key off the
Alabama coast. Biolo-
gists counted the mice,
determined their
population at about two
dozen, and immediately
added them to the
endangered species list.
Construction of the
condos is halted—
temporarily, at least—
while an attempt is
being made to breed the
beach mice in captivity.
*Estimated population:
24.*

▲ Dusky seaside sparrow

▼ Santa Barbara song sparrow

WARD

▲ Bowhead whale

Balaena mysticetus
Driven to the edge of
extinction in the last
century by Yankee
whalers, the bowhead is
now hunted only by
Inupiat Eskimos in
Alaska. While it's still
in peril, it provides an
interesting example of
the hubris of Western
science. In 1977,
responding to scientific
estimates that the
population had plunged
to between 800 and
1,200 whales, the
International Whaling
Commission voted to
ban all hunting of
bowheads, whether for

commercial or subsist-
ence purposes.
The Eskimos reacted
sharply, saying that
there were far more
than 1,200 bowheads
still alive, and that
native people weren't
stupid enough to kill
the last remnant of a
species vitally impor-
tant to their survival.
The Eskimos were
permitted to hunt, and
as of 1986, owing
entirely to enhanced
counting capability, the
total population of
bowheads is now
considered to be in
excess of 7,000. *Esti-
mated population: 7,000.*

▼ Blue pike

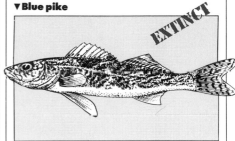

Cataloguing the Morgue

In the last 20 years, several thousand species have been extinguished worldwide. The
number is unknown and unknowable. Estimates vary widely. Norman Myers, an En-
glishman who has spent his life studying the
wildlife in East Africa, estimates that we may
be losing a species a day at present. That rate
could increase to a species per hour by the
year 2000.

We do know some facts about extinction
rates, thanks to the Endangered Species Act
of 1973. That law set up an elaborate system
for listing various species worldwide as endangered or threatened. Species are added to
the list after a review by officials in the Fish
and Wildlife Service's (FWS) Office of Endangered Species.

This is a fiercely political process, and
greed often wins out over biology. The
presence of an endangered species can halt
any development that might threaten that

species' habitat, so there is incentive to
prodevelopment types to keep that list as
short as possible. (During the first three years
of the Reagan administration, for example,
only two species were added to the list,
despite near-unanimous agreement that there
are thousands of as yet unlisted species in
need of protection.)

In addition, it's often impossible to determine precisely when a listed species finally
does vanish: One cannot prove a negative. A
species is removed from the endangered list
only when there is scientific consensus that
the species is gone. There's always the
chance that one last survivor will appear,
much the way Japanese soldiers still appear
now and then on Pacific islands wondering
if World War II has ended yet.

On rare occasions, there *is* good news, as
when on May 5, 1986, ornithologists an-
nounced that they had positively identified
two ivory-billed woodpeckers in Cuba—
birds that had been feared extinct for two
decades.

Official Body Count

Only five species have been declared officially extinct and removed from the endangered species list since it was begun in 1973:
the Tecopa pupfish (1982), the longjaw cisco (a Great Lakes fish, 1983), the blue pike
(1983), the Santa Barbara song sparrow
(1983) and the dusky seaside sparrow. During the same period, three were taken off the
list for the better reason: They had pulled
back from the brink of extinction. These
were all birds that live on Belau (formerly
spelled Palau) in the western Pacific.

The Fish and Wildlife Service's international list of endangered and threatened
animals, fish, amphibians, birds and insects
now numbers around a thousand. (There are
at least 200 endangered plants in the United States alone.) Many of them are teetering
on the brink of extinction, and a variety of
government agencies and citizens' groups are
working to rescue them before it's too late.

The Wash Bear

City or country, the raccoon's right at home.

It would be stretching things to say that raccoons are taking over Washington, D.C. But not by all that much. Dr. John Hadidian, an urban wildlife specialist at the National Park Service's Center for Urban Ecology in Washington, estimates that more than 600 of the ring-tailed creatures make their home in the capital city's 1,700-acre Rock Creek Park alone. And though the city's roving raccoons won't hold still for a head count, their total D.C. population may top 8,000. That's a lot of scurrying things to go bump in the night.

It's not so much that raccoons are enamored of D.C., it's just that the intrepid little beasts are so remarkably adaptable that they don't know when, or where, to quit. In fact, the raccoon is possibly the most adaptable wild mammal in North America, having firmly established itself from southern Canada to Central America, and in all 48 contiguous states between.

The name *raccoon* comes from the Algonquian word *arakun*, meaning "scratcher." And scratchers coons most certainly are. Equipped with five long, nimble, unwebbed fingers on each forepaw, they're extremely touch-oriented creatures. But the German name for the animal is even more descriptive: *wasberen*, or "wash bear." Not only does the raccoon resemble a small bear in appearance, habit, appetite and the humanlike tracks it leaves behind, but it can claim at least a tenuous genetic relationship to the bears in that it belongs to the same family (Procyonidae) as the lesser panda (genus *Ailurus*) of eastern Asia.

The raccoon's scientific title is *Procyon lotor. Procyon* is Latin for "before the dogs." Scientific or no, the term *procyon* is a bit misleading, since coons did not evolve before, but more or less parallel with, the canine, with the two species sharing the same early ancestors. The second part of the raccoon's scientific name, *lotor,* means "washer." That's more apropos, for, as the

German *wasberen* also indicates, the creature has a distinctive habit of dunking its food before eating it.

Which brings us to the Great Coon Quandary.

For many years biologists assumed that raccoons wash their food in the true sense— to tidy it up before tossing it down. But during the early twentieth century, that idea was pushed aside in favor of the theory that raccoons wet their food because their salivary glands don't produce enough saliva to meet their digestive needs. By the early 1960s, though, researchers had decided that raccoons *do* produce sufficient saliva, and another explanation was called for. The third theory postulated that, since the coon so enjoys handling its food before eating it, it wets both its paws and the item being pawed in order to heighten the sense of touch.

Nowadays, the Great Coon Quandary seems to have wandered full circle, for the latest edition of Hall's *Mammals of North America*—a zoological reference many biologists consider the final word—reasserts the idea of washing as cleansing: "Washing the food caught along a stream removes sand and grit, as well as perhaps certain skin secretions of the prey."

Still, there's no solid academic agreement on the subject, leaving the true reason the raccoon washes its food a mystery. But there's no doubt about *what* the coon washes and then gobbles down—just about anything it can get its paws on. In the natural state (that is, beyond the bounds of D.C. and other garbage-rich cities), a raccoon's diet is dictated primarily by the seasons.

The backcountry coon's most important food source in spring is offspring—that is, the young of other wild creatures. A competent swimmer and superb climber, *P. lotor* excels at stealing eggs and chicks from birds' nests, snatching muskrat kits from their islandlike mud-and-stick houses, bagging baby bunnies and generally raising Cain amongst the wild

and young. (But what goes around comes around: Raccoon kits are favored prey of great horned owls and other predators, and even adult coons sometimes fall victim to larger carnivores such as mountain lions, bears, coyotes and coon hunters.)

In summer, the raccoon's diet could be described as a Cajun salad: wild greens supplemented with all the crayfish, frogs and other riparian (streamside) meat items the talented little angler can catch.

Come fall, like a miniature bear, the raccoon goes on an all-out fattening spree, trying to store up enough calories during this annual time of plenty to see it through the coming months of cold, hunger and reproduction. Autumn staples for raccoons are berries and mast (fallen nuts). Before the

Cute as they are, baby raccoons shouldn't be fed or handled.

blight that wiped out the once-abundant American chestnut, the prickly-hulled harvest of this magnificent tree was the raccoon's favored fall food. Nowadays acorns are the coon's primary fall fare, fleshed out with insects and the ever-popular crayfish.

Autumn is also when the coon works hardest to sustain its reputation as a masked bandit. If you've ever had a garden crop of milk-ripe sweet corn wiped out in just a few nights, you know how destructive a few foraging raccoons can be—and that most attempts to protect coon-targeted corn generally come to naught.

Raccoons are also adept hen house raiders,

taking eggs, chicks and layers.

Whether fattened on poultry and produce or not, a raccoon that's well into its average 10-year life span can grow to be a virtual walking tub of lard, with adults averaging 12 to 20 pounds and sometimes porking up to nearly 50. The largest raccoon on record was killed in Wisconsin in 1955, measured 55 inches tongue to tail and weighed a whopping 62 pounds six ounces. The smallest subspecies inhabits the Florida Keys and averages a mere 3.3 pounds fully grown.

With the onset of winter, north-country wash bears retire to dens in standing dead trees, hollow logs or rocky crevices to coonnap through the cold months. While raccoons don't actually hibernate, they doze in their dens for extended periods when tem-

peratures are well below freezing. But on days when a bright sun warms the air to above freezing and the snow isn't so deep that walking (and running) is difficult, they're very likely to venture out in search of food and excitement. Southern sunbelt coons remain active year-round, as do big-city raccoons everywhere.

Between naps, raccoons manage to find the time to breed during winter. A male will mate with as many receptive females as he can find, frequently trekking great distances in his pursuit of love. (Wildlife photographer Leonard Lee Rue III reports snow-tracking one particularly energetic coon Casanova eight miles in a single night.) The ladies of the species are more civilized in their affairs, keeping near home and generally ac-

Raccoons and Rabies: An Eastern Urban Threat

Most people think of dogs, skunks and bats as the primary carriers of rabies (once commonly known as *hydrophobia* because of its victims' apparent fear of water), but this dreaded viral disease can infect most any mammal and, if untreated, guarantees a slow, painful, messy death.

The good news is that the traumatic series of 13 injections in the stomach required for persons bitten by animals suspected of being rabid has been relegated to history along with other medieval tortures. Instead, medical science has recently given us a prophylaxis that's 100% effective when administered promptly and, best of all, requires only five injections (plus one or more shots of serum globulin) in the arm rather than the stomach.

The not-so-good news is that, with the recent and drastic increase in the population of raccoons in Washington and other eastern cities, the threat of rabies has increased dramatically throughout the mid-Atlantic states.

One researcher who has closely monitored this epizootic (an epidemic among animals) of raccoon rabies is Dr. Suzanne Jenkins, assistant state epidemiologist for Virginia and a former veterinarian epidemiologist with the Centers for Disease Control in Atlanta. Dr. Jenkins points out that rabies is always with us—generally dozing, but rousing from time to time to cause a ruckus. The current outbreak among urban raccoons began with a single case in West Virginia in 1977 and spread rapidly to Virginia, Maryland, Pennsylvania and the District of Columbia. During the past decade, the numbers of rabid raccoons found in the mid-Atlantic region look like this:

1977	1	1983	1,608
1978	3	1984	1,439
1979	12	1985	1,079
1980	21	1986	1,193
1981	131	1987	966
1982	837	1988	962

As the numbers show, the epizootic peaked in 1983 and has been more or less decreasing since. However, the outbreak appears to be rolling like a wave northward, and even as the mid-Atlantic epizootic ebbs somewhat in its southern extreme, the incidence of raccoon rabies in Pennsylvania and other northeastern states is on the rise. Meanwhile, Florida is the center of a separate mini-epizootic that's more tenacious (it's been around for a quarter of a century or so) and less urban. In recent years, raccoons have carried the disease across Florida's borders to Georgia, South Carolina and eastern Alabama.

In spite of their numbers, rabid raccoons rarely pose a *direct* threat to humans. Dr. Jenkins and her associates worry most about cats and dogs that haven't been inoculated against rabies contracting the disease from infected raccoons and passing it on to their owners. "It's a real problem for health professionals and animal-control agencies," says Jenkins. "We can't reassure the public that we have things under control, because we don't. As yet there's no direct control method for raccoon rabies. Research teams in several areas are working to find a way to protect wildlife with an oral rabies vaccine placed in bait, but—though preliminary results are encouraging—this approach doesn't promise to provide a remedy in the near future."

What can people living or vacationing in high-risk areas do to protect themselves, their families and their pets from the threat of rabies? "Our current thrust," Dr. Jenkins says, "is to convince people to have their pets vaccinated against rabies and to leave wild animals alone—to avoid feeding raccoons or allowing them to get into garbage containers, and to discourage the animals from nesting in residential areas. But even with all the publicity we've generated concerning this problem, people still find and adopt baby raccoons, or pick up what they think is an injured animal and get bitten and possibly infected with rabies."

If you or a member of your family should be bitten by *any* animal, wash the wound thoroughly and contact a doctor immediately. If the animal is still lurking about, ask your local animal-control authorities to pick it up and examine it for rabies—which just might spare you a lot of worry and needle holes.

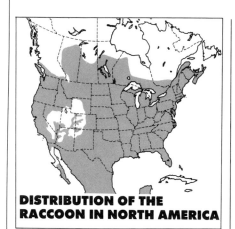

DISTRIBUTION OF THE RACCOON IN NORTH AMERICA

where they grow fat and sassy on human handouts (occasionally biting the very fingers that feed them), raid and scatter garbage, startle light sleepers with their infernal nocturnal racket, invade basements, chimneys and sewers, and spread rabies.

So what's being done to halt the raccoon invasion of D.C. and other eastern cities? The question should probably be, what *can* be done? The answer so far is, not much. Dr. Hadidian and his colleagues are working literally night and day to keep tabs on the furry immigrants while experimenting with methods for mass-vaccinating raccoons against rabies, using smelly baits placed in strategic locations. But metropolitan coon management is a relatively new science which so far offers no immediate reprieve from the current trends of more raccoons and more rabies.

Eventually, of course, humanity—being even more adaptable and occasionally more clever than the raccoon—will get the upper hand. But before passing too harsh a sentence on the fate of urban raccoons, it would be well for us to remember that, for almost 500 years now, we've been gnawing away at the natural domain of the raccoon; appropriating, displacing or destroying many of the animal's traditional foods; clear-cutting the old-growth forests that provide its favored housing; and polluting the waterways near which the creature lives and on which it depends for a major portion of its sustenance.

After all of that, it's understandable why the wash bear is moving to Washington in such numbers. He's undoubtedly decided that—what the heck?—if you can't beat 'em, join 'em.

cepting only one mate in each season.

Gestation requires around 63 days, with litters averaging three or four 2.5-ounce kits. Within three weeks of birth the wee coons have their eyes open; after about 50 days they're able to scamper in and out of the den under their own power, and by 10 weeks are accompanying their mother on her nightly rounds. (As is common among mammals, a mother raccoon receives no child-rearing help from the long-gone father.)

By the following winter, most young coons will have left home to pursue their own adventurous lives in the North American backcountry. Or, of course, they find themselves in some of our biggest cities,

The Fox Next Door

Here's your chance to get to know a red-haired stranger.

If you live in any of the lower 48 states, Canada or Alaska, at least one of the five North American fox species—red, gray, kit, swift or arctic—is your neighbor. And if you reside in Colorado, Utah, Texas or New Mexico, you have four of our continent's five smallest canids as fellow residents—whether you know it or not.

Of the five species, the one with the red hair—*Vulpes vulpes*, the sly antagonist of Aesopian fables, the trickster Reynard of French-Canadian folklore—is far and away the most plentiful and wide-ranging. In short, it's the fox you're most likely to meet someday.

The red fox has made its home in North America for a long time. But in the geologic view, the little dog is a relative newcomer. Like most other creatures that didn't evolve here but were present when Columbus's ship came in, *V. vulpes* hiked over from Asia in relatively recent geologic times, crossing on God's own drawbridge, that ephemeral Ice Age isthmus, the Bering-Chukchi Platform.

It's no mere coincidence, then, that North

The fox is a member of the dog family, but is catlike in its grace.

American and Eurasian red foxes are near-twins (the European version runs a bit larger and evidences minor microchromosomal variances); they haven't been separated long enough to have evolved significant morphological differences. Matter of fact, though the two were long categorized as separate species simply because they inhabit different continents, wildlife taxonomists now lump them under a shared name, *V. vulpes* (Latin for "fox fox").

And thereupon hangs a tale.

Convinced that native American red foxes were both too few and too plebeian to provide their highbred horses and hounds with proper sport, aristocratic European settlers imported, beginning in 1750, substantial numbers of Old World reds to Virginia, Pennsylvania and New England. But the immigrant foxes proved less aloof than their importers and promptly mingled genes with the natives, producing—for a while, at least—a hybrid species. This hybridization, in turn, long confused all attempts at drawing definitive distinctions between the North American and European species.

Today, most authorities agree that the transplants were too restricted in both area and number, and took place too long ago, to have carried through genetically to the present. Thus, while European and American red foxes are closely related, and though a Euro-American hybrid undoubtedly did exist a couple of centuries ago in a few northeastern states, time has probably filtered any Old World genes from the native pool, leaving our fox a true red, white, yellow, gray and brown American—the hues of an adult red fox's many-colored coat.

And occasionally, other shades as well.

Take, for example, the silver fox. This is nothing more than one of three rare color variations, or phases, of the common red fox. The second is melano, or pure black. The third shows up in the "cross" fox, which has the normal red-fox color mix, but is distinguished by two wide, dark brown stripes—one running the length of its back and the other across its shoulders—forming the cross from whence cometh its name. These variant phases occur randomly anywhere *V. vulpes* ranges, but are more common in the North, in particular on northern fox farms, where all three variations—especially the silvers—are bred in captivity for their valuable pelts.

A typical red fox measures about three feet overall, including more than a foot of luxuriant tail; stands 14 to 16 inches at the shoulders; and weighs a mere eight or 10 pounds, with 12 about tops these days. (Turn-of-the-century naturalist Ernest Thompson Seton, in his classic *Lives of Game Animals*, reports a record American red fox weight of 16 3/4 pounds—a male raised on a game farm—and cites a Welsh specimen that went an astonishing 29 pounds.)

Although foxes don't mate for life, neither are they particularly promiscuous. Each winter, the vixen (female) prepares a nursery den, often enlarging a woodchuck burrow in a sandy hillside or renovating a fox den from a previous season. When she's set, she'll send out a scent invitation, then choose a spouse from among the numerous dog foxes (males) that come to call.

Once mated, a fox pair will remain together, sharing the joys and labors of parenthood, until the following autumn. Next season, the same vixen and dog may get together again. Or they may not.

Seven to eight weeks after the honeymoon, the vixen will give birth—usually in late March or early April—to around half-a-dozen quarter-pound pups. Red fox *kinder* resemble fuzzy lumps of charcoal at birth, save for their white-tipped tails. (This marking is unique among North American canids, and remains with red foxes throughout their lives, no matter what color they become when mature.) Born deaf and blind, the pups will remain within the womblike protection of the den for their first few weeks, attended constantly by Mom.

Outside, Papa plays the role of sole family breadwinner during this critical time, hunting almost continuously to feed himself and his nursery-bound mate—for whom he leaves mousy little love offerings at the doorstep to the den.

After about a month, the pups—their fur now faded to sandy gray to better match the earth around the den opening—will begin surfacing from their subterranean nursery. Early forays into the great outdoors are brief and tentative, but will gradually lengthen to several hours at a stretch. These first few weeks under the sun are the most hazardous in the young foxes' lives, since they look just like lunch to a variety of predators—notably big cats, coyotes, great horned owls and golden eagles.

About 40 days after giving birth, Mama Red begins weaning her litter and providing them with solid food. At about 10 weeks, the pups start to evidence adolescent curiosity and begin accompanying their parents on the nightly hunts. By autumn—approximately six months from their birth—the pups, though not fully grown, will have taken on their adult coloration and be capable of fending for themselves. Soon they'll wander away from home to stake out turfs of their own.

That's the way a fox's youth *should* unfold. But life is tough out there in the natural world—survival of the fittest, you know—and more than half of every litter of fox pups before reaching maturity will succumb to the elements, disease, predators or men with guns, traps and poisoned baits. For those making it to adulthood, the average life span is three to seven seasons.

Like all canids, foxes mark the boundaries of their territories with urine, also relying on scent to broadcast other important messages. But the primary means of red fox communication is vocal, with a language that includes yaps, barks, mews, whines, growls, churrs, yurrs, gurrs, squalls and screams. E.T. Seton, though a great admirer of the red fox, nonetheless described the little beast's alarm scream as "probably the most sinister, unearthly wild-animal note that can be heard in North America."

In light of this "unearthly" quality of the fox's scream, it seems safe to postulate that a good many of the eerie nocturnal cries traditionally attributed to "panthers" in fact originate in the narrow throats of pint-sized canines.

Among the most intriguing characteristics of the red fox is the way it conducts business. Whereas wolves, coyotes and most other dogs evolved as pack animals—group hunters, practitioners of the cooperative chase and the open pursuit—the fox is more akin to the cats in its social and hunting habits.

Except during mating and pup season, the red fox prefers to live and hunt alone. And rather than running its prey to ground after the fashion of its larger relatives the coyote and wolf, *V. vulpes* relies on catlike stealth, prowling slowly and quietly along established huntways.

Canadian naturalist J. David Henry has spent years observing the hunting techniques of red foxes in northern Saskatchewan's 1,500-square-mile Prince Albert National Park. Writing in *Natural History*, Henry postulates that the red fox has two good reasons for hunting alone: 1) Its primary prey are meadow mice—hardly meat enough there to share among a whole platoon of hungry hunters; and 2) such a tiny quarry is more easily captured by a pussyfooting loner than by a boisterous pack of brutes.

Henry's observations have shown that the red fox hunts four distinct categories of prey and—this is the sly part—has evolved a specialized technique for taking each.

The smallest red fox prey are bugs, which Reynard hunts in a cavalier fashion, sauntering along until he spots a fat juicy beetle or whatnot, then strolling over and smacking a paw down on the little beastie.

Next up in size—and most important to the red's day-to-day survival—are mice, shrews

**DISTRIBUTION OF
THE RED FOX
IN NORTH AMERICA**

and similar minirodents. These the fox hunts slowly and carefully. After detecting a mouse from a distance and stalking to within pouncing range, the hunter crouches to compress its springs, then uncoils in a leap calculated to land its front paws atop the furry victual.

The third classification is an unlikely pairing: birds and squirrels (lumped together because they're of a size and hunted similarly). According to Henry, the red fox considers these as "targets of opportunity," to be taken as they come rather than hunted deliberately. Upon fortuitously spotting a ground-feeding bird or squirrel, the little red hunter begins an impromptu stalk, moving only when the quarry is looking away, then charges the final distance in a "crouched, dashing run." In most instances, the fox will attempt to grab a bird or squirrel in its mouth rather than risk pinning it with its paws.

Henry's final class of fox prey—and the largest animals these smallest of the wild canids will normally tackle—consists of rabbits and hares. When hunting these alert quarries, the fox is rarely fortunate enough to sneak within pouncing range undetected. More often, the approaching canine flushes the watchful lagomorph and is forced to pursue it in a wild, zigzag chase through the densest brush the bunny can find. If and

when the fox closes on its prey, it will attempt to bring it to ground by snapping at the hindermost portions. With the quarry down, the diner anchors its dinner with its paws and administers the coup de grâce by sinking its needlelike teeth into the victim's neck or head.

Cruel?

No. Merely necessary.

We upright predators do most of our hunting these days at the supermarket, bagging meat that's killed, cut, wrapped, labeled and no longer recognizable (if you don't think about it too hard) as a gentle creature with trusting eyes. The fox must come by its dinner in a more honest fashion.

Inevitably, humans and foxes will occasionally find themselves in competition for the same piece of meat. When prompted by hard times or tempted with easy pickings, old Reynard can be not only an adept hen heister, but a talented duck buster as well—as noted (albeit philosophically) by avocational duckman E.T. Seton:

"Many a duck have they [red foxes] taken from my stock, but I gladly forgive them. It is worth more to me to hear that squalling night cry under my window in the darkness than to be the overfed owner of many fat, stupid table ducks."

He's right to forgive the raiders, you know. It's hardly fair, or logical, to take umbrage at a natural-born hunter for snatching unprotected poultry; to a hungry fox, a chicken (or duck) ain't nothin' but a bird.

Deep within the age-parched pages of *Animals of the World*—an obsolete zoological text published in 1917 by the University Society (whoever they were)—reside some vintage "facts" concerning wild canids. To wit:

"The dog family is not characterized by many admirable traits in its wild state. It is usually cunning, vicious and treacherous, and exhibits no bravery except where there are numbers of its own kind. It is furtive and sneaking, looking for every unfair advantage, and, once in danger, is an arrant coward. From the commercial side, however, the family is entitled to respect. The pelts of both wolves and foxes are of value; those of certain varieties of foxes bringing high prices."

There we have it—the prejudices of the times neatly summarized by the University Society (whoever they were).

But even back then predators had a few friends. Seton, as we've seen, was one. Another was a lanky, bewhiskered mountaineer name of John Muir. In 1916—the year before the University Society published the myopic canid dogma quoted above—Muir penned an eloquent, marvelously iconoclastic little essay entitled "Anthropocentrism and Predation." Therein, the father of the Sierra Club charged:

"The world, we are told, was made especially for man—a presumption not supported by all the facts. A numerous class of men are painfully astonished whenever they find anything, living or dead, in all God's universe, which they cannot eat or render in some way what they call useful to themselves. They have precise dogmatic insight of the intentions of the Creator. . . . Now, it never seems to occur to these farseeing teachers that Nature's object in making animals and plants might possibly be first of all the happiness of each one of them, not the creation of all for the happiness of one."

Someday, perhaps, the tunnel-view contention that any creature not providing direct benefit to humanity is *a priori* useless, even evil, may finally be chased out of our collective consciousness—like a fox on the run.

An Afternoon with the Bears

Strange as it may seem,
a black bear by any other
color is *still* called
a black bear.

In the hardwood forests of eastern North America, almost all black bears are, in fact, black (often with a blaze of white on chest or throat). But in the Rocky Mountain West, a pure licorice black bear is the exception rather than the rule, with chocolate, cinnamon and vanilla being the more common flavors. And somewhere up in the primeval forests of coastal British Columbia roams the ghostlike Kermode's bear, a snow-white black-bear variation.

Another regional difference in this interesting race of bruins is that eastern black bears tend to be larger than their western cousins. While Rocky Mountain males rarely exceed 400 pounds, 600-pound boars occasionally turn up in some northeastern states. (The largest black bear on record, killed in Wisconsin in the late 1800s, crushed the scales at just over 800 pounds—a respectable weight even for a mature male grizzly.) Female black bears average a petite 150 to 230 pounds in the Rockies, while ranging up to as much as 350 pounds in some eastern states.

Wildlife biologists say that *Ursus americanus* is omnivorous—meaning the species consumes both meat and greens. But "opportunistic" might better describe the creature's dietary habits, since a hungry black bear will eat almost anything. (Including, in rare but documented instances, people.)

In the vegetable department, black bears

are partial to berries, forbs, grasses, mast, sedges, herbaceous plants and the cambium of soft-barked trees. In matters of the flesh, they dig gophers, marmots, ground squirrels, voles, mice and grubs, and, when they're very hungry and very lucky, occasionally

A brown-phase black bear cub (below) and a black adult "angler"

take deer and small livestock such as pigs, goats and sheep. Additionally, the rotting carcasses of winter-killed animals—carrion—can play an important nutritional role during early spring when bears are just emerging, quite literally starved, from their winter dens and the spring green-up isn't yet in full swing. Wild honey, of course, is the dessert of choice, with discarded human food—garbage—running a close second.

Black bears almost never pose a serious threat to humans—so long as the bruins are treated with the respect due unto large, fast, well-armed, heavily muscled, unpredictable predatory beasts. In fact, *wild* bears—nonpark animals—are among the most reclusive of all large mammals, want only to be left alone and generally will hightail it out of the neighborhood at the first hint of human presence.

Yet, there have been several dozen people mauled by black bears in North America since the turn of the century—with a score or more of those maulings resulting in the death of the victims. And some of those attacks were determined (by the most grisly evidence imaginable) to have been predacious.

In the southeastern U.S., black bears often den out the winters high above ground in the rot-hollowed trunks of large, standing hardwood snags. In the Rockies, the bruins are more likely to keep to the ground, seeking out natural caves and the bowl-shaped depressions created when trees fall and are uprooted. Throughout their North American range, however, the well-insulated creatures will sometimes simply plop down on a hospitable-looking patch of ground and wait for Mother Nature to cover them with a blanket of snow. Rarely will black bears actually excavate dens; such an exhausting expenditure of energy consumes too many of the fat-stored calories needed to see them through their long winter's slumber.

Black bear progeny begin life at little more than eight near-naked ounces each, and are allowed to enjoy two winters' naps snuggled hard against their mother's warmth before being abandoned to earn their own livings in the world.

Thus rid of her litter of cubs, a Mama bear is free once again to accept the affections of a concupiscent male (or several, bears being joyously promiscuous creatures) during the

ursine courting months of June and July. Then, the January or February following a successful mating, the sow will give birth to another biennial litter of from one to four cubs. (But only if she has enjoyed a bountiful autumn that allowed her to put on sufficient fat to insure the production of enough milk for the babes' survival; otherwise, her pregnancy will self-terminate.)

One of the first lessons a mother bear teaches a fresh litter of cubs, after quitting the nursery den in April or May, is the high art of arboreal acrobatics: tree climbing. Very young cubs are defenseless when away from their mothers, and are filled with youthful temerity. Consequently, infant bears might easily fall prey to predators were it not for their ability to climb.

With the mighty grizzly rare and getting rarer, we can be thankful that we still have the black bear in relatively sound numbers across much of America.

The Bear Facts

Unlike the grizzly, the black bear probably won't become a threatened or endangered species in the lower 48 states within the next few years. Nonetheless, *Ursus americanus* is already extinct on a local basis in many states and is listed as threatened or endangered in others—and more of these spot extinctions can be expected as an ever-increasing human population makes expanding demands on our country's shrinking wilderness and its wildlife.

Still, when compared to the seriously threatened status of grizzlies in the lower 48,

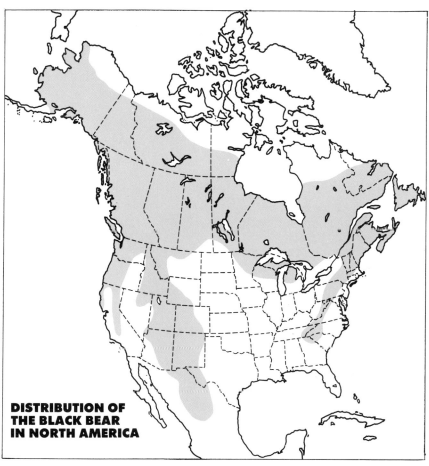

DISTRIBUTION OF THE BLACK BEAR IN NORTH AMERICA

black bears have several survival advantages over their bigger cousins.

For one thing, they enjoy a more rapid rate of reproduction. This is due in part to the differing lengths of time grizzly and black bear mothers keep their cubs before casting them off. While grizzly mothers stay with their young for 30 months or more, black bear matrons typically boot their cubs out after only 16 months. And since mother bears with young in tow don't breed, a black bear female will produce more cubs in her lifetime than will a grizzly.

Another factor working in their favor is that black bears are more tolerant of humans than grizzlies are, and thus can hang on in areas that are too densely settled to make survival realistic for the bigger bruins with their greater needs and visibility. Nevertheless, black bears are often killed when civilization invades the wilds, and the bears—finding ranch, farm, homestead or subdivision where their favorite berry patch used to be—are forced by hunger to prey on the livestock or pets brought by humans into bear country. Some sheepherders are among the worst offenders here, often shooting bears on sight. (One sheepman reportedly killed seven black bears in a single summer.)

In his book *Bear Attacks*, Canadian researcher Steve Herrero reports that he has been able to verify 23 cases in which people were killed by black bears in North America from 1900 through 1980. That's about half the number killed by grizzlies during the same period. Consequently, since black bears aren't perceived as being as dangerous as grizzlies, there has been less pressure to eliminate them in the name of human safety.

The major force working against black bears is dwindling forest habitat. *Ursus americanus* evolved as a forest-dependent species, and rarely ventures into open country. Heavily timbered areas provide black bears with food and protection from inclement weather, hide them when necessary and give them trees to climb in order to escape immediate danger.

But prime forest habitat is rapidly being destroyed for human use via deforestation for subdivisions and urban-suburban sprawl, as well as by the unrelenting advance of the agriculture, mining, livestock and timber industries. And the water and air pollution that follow these scratchings of civilization compound the problem even more.

In short, the continued survival of bears in the wild—both blacks and grizzlies—will depend on how humanity treats not just the animals themselves, but planet earth as well.

Meet Peter Cottontail

Understanding your basic, ubiquitous bunny

Here comes Peter Cottontail . . . yes, indeed. You know it's that springtime of year again when you hear children (and children's TV and radio programs) belting out the old familiar ditty.

"Peter Cottontail" was written by Steve Nelson and Jack Rollins back in 1949. Since then, the loony little tune has become as musically evocative of the nonsectarian aspects of the Easter season as "Here Comes Santa Claus" is of Christmas—with the Easter rabbit now almost (but not quite) as prominent as jolly old Saint Nick himself.

Bringin' ev'ry girl and boy, baskets full of Easter joy, things to make your Easter bright and gay.

How in heaven's name—have you ever wondered?—did a concept as preposterous as an egg-laying rabbit (a *male* rabbit at that) ever manage to become associated with a sacred Western religious observance?

Look at him stop, and listen to him say: "Try to do the things you should." Maybe if you're extra good, he'll roll lots of Easter eggs your way.

The story of Peter Cottontail had its beginnings in the old days—the *very* old days. Back then, centuries before the birth of Christ, the forerunner of the Easter bunny was already a celebrated figure in the springtime fertility rites of the ancient Celts. But this prototypical Easter bunny wasn't a cottontail rabbit at all (they didn't exist in Europe in those days), no sir; he was a European hare. *Rabbit, hare*—so what's it matter, you ask? After all, they're both furry little critters that hop and chew and wiggle their noses. Granted, it's a hare-splitting distinction, but for those interested in the nature of all things natural, it remains a distinction worth clarifying. So—as a brief and relevant sidetrack off the ancestral trail of Peter Cottontail—here's a quick run-down on bunny genealogy:

Both rabbits and hares belong to the order Lagomorpha (literally, "hare-shaped"), which almost certainly had its origins in Asia (like most everything else mammalian) but can be traced back a good 50 million years right here in North America. Lagomorpha is a smallish order, comprising just two families—Ochotonidae, those vociferous little alpine funny-bunnies known as pikas (sometimes called conies), and Leporidae, the rabbits and hares. All lagomorphs have cleft upper lips (giving rise to the unfortunate expression *harelip*) and long, rodentlike incisors that grow constantly to compensate for wear. But, contrary to popular (and until 1912, scientific) belief, lagomorphs are not rodents.

Thus, rabbits and hares belong to the same family but are distinct genera. (In descending rank by size, the scientific classification of living things goes like so: order, suborder, family, genus, species, subspecies.) And how can those who care to do so tell rabbits from hares? It's not always easy, as evidenced by the frequency with which our language confuses the two: In addition to the original Easter beast having been a European hare rather than an American cottontail rabbit, the domestic bunny commonly known as the Belgian "hare" is actually a rabbit, and the jack "rabbit" is really a hare—just as the snowshoe "rabbit" in fact is a snowshoe (also called "varying") hare.

Be all of that as it may, there are a few recognizable distinctions: Most hares are larger than most rabbits and have bigger ears in proportion to body size, and most hares have black-tipped ears, while most rabbits don't. Additionally, rabbit kittens (yes, odd as it seems, that's what baby bunnies are called) are born blind, naked and helpless in nursery nests constructed especially for the occasion by the expectant mother; while hare kits are born in the open, wherever Ma happens to be at the time, and enter the world with vision, a cozy coat of fur and—within a bare few minutes of birth—the ability to scamper out of harm's way.

To bring all of this to bear on our original question, then, Peter Cottontail—technically speaking—should never have been honored in song as the Easter creature, because the prototypical Easter "rabbit" was in fact a hare, and a cottontail technically is a rabbit (which is born without hair while hare kits are hairy).

Quite so.

The cottontail (left) and the white-tailed jack rabbit (above) hold sway in the East and West.

the word *Easter* derives from the Celtic goddess Eostre, whose name means, literally, "fertile."

And so the association of an egg-bearing hare with an important religious holiday comes clear at last (sort of): The springtime fertility rites of pre-Christian Celts, centering around the hare and his lady friend Eostre, provided these ancient folk with an important sense of long-term security—just as the Biblical account of the resurrection decreases angst for Christians today with a promise of eternal life. Difference was, the Celts were petitioning their deities for the renewal of the natural world in the form of children and the replenishment of the crops and creatures critical to the people's sustenance—while the Christian celebration offered (and offers) its followers hope, not for the rebirth of *nature*, but for *personal* immortality in a world above and beyond the natural.

Across the European centuries, these two ideologically divergent springtime observances came to share the same date and name, and somehow survived in parallel, even though one remained stringently religious while the other gradually entered the realm of children's folklore. When German emi-

The question properly becomes, then: How in heaven's name did anything as silly as a male, egg-laying *hare* ever manage to become so closely associated with one of Western religion's most sacred observances?

Here (if you'll pardon the plagiary) is the rest of the story.

Just as Easter for Christians honors a resurrection from death and holds a promise of eternal life, to pre-Christian European ancients the egg and the hare were important symbols of the springtime rebirth of nature following the dead zone of winter. The two traditions, sharing the same season as they did, were bound to cross paths.

To wit: The egg as a symbol of fertility and birth—what could be more appropriate?—has been traced back to the beginnings of history in a great many cultures. The hare, likewise, was a major symbol of fertility for many ancient peoples. In the religious mythology of the Celts, the prolific little creature was the loyal sidekick of Eostre, the goddess of spring. Around the time of the vernal equinox (March 21) each year, this unlikely couple was honored with various pagan (earth-centered) ceremonies, most of which were intended to seek favor and thus assure success in the coming season's agricultural and hunting endeavors.

Thus, the Celts' springtime celebration of life's conquest over death, with the hare and egg as symbols of this triumph, significantly predated the arrival of Christianity in Europe. Additionally—according to the English historian The Venerable Bede (672–735)—

Rabbit Fever: The Wild Bunny's Bane

Tularemia—commonly known as rabbit fever—is an infectious disease caused by a parasitic bacterium with the lilting name *Pasteurella tularensis*. Primary hosts for these nasty little buggers are rodents and lagomorphs, but rabbit fever can be transmitted to humans through physical contact—as in preparing an infected animal for the stewpot. (Thorough cooking kills the bacteria, rendering the meat of infected animals safe to handle and eat.)

In rabbits, the symptoms of tularemia include lethargy and damage to various internal organs; in humans, the primary indications are fever and the swelling of lymph nodes. Although the disease is rare these days and can readily be cured with prompt medical attention, the threat remains: grave illness and the remote possibility of death.

Country wisdom has long held, and correctly so, that rabbit fever can be avoided by not hunting wild bunnies until after autumn's first killing frost; and even then, never handle—dead or alive—an animal that behaves unnaturally. Today, that wisdom has been indirectly incorporated into law in most states, since legal rabbit-hunting seasons almost never open before late fall or early winter, and generally close before the arrival of spring.

So, yes, there is such a thing as rabbit fever, even today. But no, it isn't a great threat and shouldn't keep those who wish to do so from hunting and eating wild lagomorphs. Here are the rules for safety:

1. Hunt wild rabbits only during legal seasons.
2. Avoid handling animals that indicate by their actions (or inaction) that they may be ill.
3. If you have cuts or open sores on your hands, wear rubber gloves when preparing wild rabbits for the pot.
4. Cook all wild meat thoroughly.

The meat of cottontail rabbits and snowshoe hares is tender, tasty and healthful. There's no need to let the remote threat of tularemia keep you from munching bunny. Just be aware.

grants came to North America in the 1700s, they brought the tradition of the Easter hare and his eggs with them. Eventually, through the provincial idiosyncrasies of our language, the hare got transformed into a rabbit, while his eggs were stuffed into a basket for portability.

To summarize the secret life of Peter Cottontail, then, it came to pass that out of the ancient Celtic honoring of Eostre and her pal the hare, hopped our own Easter rabbit with his basketful of eggs. And the Easter rabbit, in turn, provided inspiration for "Peter Cottontail," the giddy little ditty that brings so much joy to the wee folk every spring.

You'll wake up on Easter morning and you'll know that he was there, when you find those chocolate bunnies that he's hiding ev'rywhere.

Of course, it doesn't take a pagan to see how the bunny came to be regarded as one of the ancients' most potent fertility symbols; everyone knows that lagomorphs breed like —well, like rabbits. Consider, as a particularly pregnant example, old Peter's clan, genus *Sylvilagus*, the cottontails (including swamp rabbits, marsh rabbits, brush rabbits, forest rabbits, pygmy rabbits—plus eastern, western, New England, mountain and desert cottontails as well as four other species, for a total of 14).

The cottontail is native to, and ubiquitous across, the Americas, ranging from east coast to west, and from southern Canada on the north to as far south as Argentina and Paraguay. Of the 14 species, the eastern cottontail (*S. floridanus*) is the most plentiful, claims the greatest range (all 48 contiguous states plus) and is the archetypical white-bummed bunny that most of us envision when we say "cottontail."

When you consider that virtually all North American predators—from the tiny least weasel to the gargantuan grizzly bear, plus myriad other hunters both winged and human—hold the cottontail to be one of the most delectable items on nature's menu, the continued survival and even prosperity of the genus is downright amazing. Sure, old Peter is adept at both running away (at up to 20 miles per) and hiding from those who would invite him to dinner, but the real secret of the cottontail's success is its prolificacy:

To get the reproductive ball rolling, nature has endowed cottontails with a randiness rivaling even that of humans. Second, cottontails attain sexual maturity with astonishing rapidity (females of one species are capable of breeding within 80 days of birth). Third, the cottontail's short gestation (26 to 30 days) allows for the production of from two to six litters during the annual half-year breeding season (roughly February through August, peaking in May). Fourth, cottontail litter size is large, with three to six kits common and up to eight not unusual.

Thus, a single Madam Cottontail has the potential of producing some 50 young per year.

And, as if all of that wasn't sufficient to guarantee their survival, nature has equipped rabbits with some of the animal kingdom's finest, and least understood, conceptional shortcuts.

Witness: Through the phenomenon of *induced ovulation*, rabbit does release their eggs, not on a fixed timetable, as do most mammals, but only and always in response to the stimulus of copulation. This assures that every time a female cottontail mates, an egg will be in position for fertilization. A second little-known bunny reproductive aid is *postpartum estrus*, wherein female lagomorphs are capable of conceiving immediately after giving birth, thus achieving continuous pregnancies. (In fact, in a remarkable phenomenon known as *superfetation*, the females of some species apparently can conceive a second litter *before* completing delivery of the first, thus achieving *overlapping* pregnancies.)

In addition to reproducing themselves in wholesale lots, cottontails have an impressive potential longevity for such small mammals, with many species capable of living as long as 10 years under benevolent circumstances. In the wild, of course, this potential is seldom realized; the average life span for adults is just 15 months, with around 90% of each season's crop of kits perishing of natural causes (primarily, disease and inclement weather) or taken by predators. (The hunting of these rabbits by humans seems to alter the death rate only slightly.)

It's no wonder that mortality is so high among cottontail kits, since they enter life

"Ears lookin at ya." A marsh rabbit (right), an antelope jack (above) and a snowshoe hare (far left).

pitifully ill equipped for the many challenges and hardships of the wilds. Newborns weigh only one to two ounces each and are blind, near-naked and totally helpless. But small mammals mature quickly, and after just a week or so of guzzling their mother's nutritious milk, baby cottontails are furred, have opened their eyes and are squirming about in the nest. Another week and the kits have tripled their birth weight and are ready to venture out on short treks. Within a month of birth, young cottontails are weaned and entirely on their own.

Each spring and summer, innumerable "abandoned" cottontail kits are discovered by well-meaning folk and taken home to be saved—where they almost always die within a few days. If you should happen upon a seemingly deserted nest of quivering bunny young, be certain, before "rescuing" the little waifs, that they are, in fact, orphaned. Unless you can locate a dead mother rabbit, assume that she's hiding somewhere nearby and will return as soon as you leave, and *don't touch the young*. If, however, you are absolutely positive that the kits are orphaned, and wish to take them home, you'll have to go out of your way to assure their survival. To begin with, the brood must be provided with a clean, dry nest box housed indoors or at least protected from wind, rain and deep

cold. Nurse cottontail kits on low-fat milk enriched with egg yolks and bunny vitamins (available from feed stores, vets and mail-order houses).

Adult cottontails can and do eat nearly every type of vegetation their home turf offers—including (depending on season and locale) grasses, forbs, bark, leaves, nuts, berries, seeds and cultivated crops (even, in rare but documented instances, insects). In a phenomenon known variously as *refection* and *coprophagy* (use your dictionary, or ask a rabbit rancher to explain), most everything swallowed by a lagomorph is (to word it as politely as possible) run through the animal's digestive system twice to assure maximal absorption of nutrients. This recycling-for-efficiency is especially important in winter, since cottontails neither hibernate nor store food for the hard months, and therefore must make the most of any nourishment that comes their way.

It's no accident of nature, then, that the annual early-summer peak in rabbit population corresponds exactly with the appearance of yummy young green goodies everywhere—including in our gardens. Consequently, in rabbit-rich areas, Peter and his extended family can sometimes become first-class pests.

Of course, being earth's ultimate predators, we human animals have devised a number of ways to combat crop-raiding bunnies, some of which have proven effective, others not. The most certain way to keep hungry rabbits out of small gardens is

chicken-wire fencing. If your veggie patch is too spacious to be economically fenced in, you can experiment with various organic defenses—such as bordering your crops with a ring of unappetizing marigolds, spraying sprouting plants with a solution of hot pepper sauce diluted in water (one tablespoon per gallon), dusting both plants and the earth around them with finely ground cayenne pepper, spraying crops with diluted onion juice (liquefy several onions in a juicer, or set them to soak for several days in a bucket of water) or placing old shoes (the funkier the better) near where the bothersome bunnies have been feeding.

Some folks even create scent barriers by urinating around the borders of their gardens. (A few years back, one adventuresome entrepreneur marketed lion poop as a mammalian-pest repellent. The product proved equally effective at discouraging rabbits, deer and gardeners.)

More direct (and, thus, more certain) robber-rabbit remedies include fast dogs, large cats, live-trapping and—in rural areas, at least—shotguns and well-aimed .22s.

But around Easter, before you take aim on a bunny in your garden with the intent of transmogrifying diner into dinner, look closely to be certain your potential target isn't toting a basketful of odd-colored eggs. Your kids would never forgive you.

Oh! Here comes Peter Cottontail, hoppin' down the bunny trail—hippity hoppity, happy Easter Day!

The Big Stink

When the polecat hops, all the kidding around stops.

America's skunks belong to the subfamily Mephitinae (from the Latin *mephitis*, meaning "poison gas"), which comprises three genera. Between them, the three fairly blanket the lower 48 states, Canada to Mexico and sea to shining sea.

The most numerous of this fetid trio is the striped skunk, a stocky, short-legged, long-haired animal whose jet black coat is trimmed with two wide white stripes running up the back and converging at the nape. A single thin white line descends from forehead to nose. The tail is almost as long as the body and lushly furred, with a blurred white stripe along its top. Since it ranges across all of the U.S. save parts of Utah, Nevada and southern California, this is the skunk you're most likely to see. And, should you be careless, to smell.

A sister species to the striped skunk (they share the same genus) is the hooded skunk, a two-toner with white head, back and tail, and black undercarriage. (There's also a nearly-all-black phase.) Its range in the U.S. is restricted to the southern portions of Arizona, New Mexico and Texas.

Next in abundance is the little spotted skunk, a smaller, slimmer, sleeker animal built much like a weasel—to which family (Mustelidae) all skunks in fact belong. Although commonly called the civet cat, the spotted skunk is no more a civet (which is an inhabitant of Asia and Africa) than the pronghorn is an antelope. For that matter, the spotted skunk isn't truly spotted, either, but marked with a hodgepodge of blurred stripes and splotches, the pattern varying more or less among individuals. The spotted skunk ranges across most of the southern and western United States.

The rarest of our stinkers (though some would say not nearly rare enough) is the hognosed skunk, an emigrant from Mexico. The hog-nose resembles the striped skunk in size and shape, and the hooded skunk in range (portions of Texas, New Mexico, Colorado, Arizona and a tiny bit of Nevada). Its snout looks pretty much like what its name implies. Its back is marked with two wide white or yellowish stripes, or sometimes is solid white.

By and large, all three genera share the same habits, appetites and dispositions, and so can be discussed as one—with the exception that the spotted skunk, with its streamlined build, is far more energetic and athletic than its rotund cousins. (For a couple of examples, it can climb trees, which the others can't, and regularly does a handstand on its front paws just before or while spraying.)

Of course, what makes a skunk a skunk, no matter its genus or species, is the tear-gas musk it can jet, on demand, from twin vents located on either side of the rectum. When the tail comes up, these normally retracted nipples protrude, leaving the striped samurai armed and ready for action.

The comparison of skunk musk to tear gas is no mere metaphor. Both cause extreme irritation to eyes and sinuses. Both interfere with respiration. Both bring on nausea, headache and uncontrollable tearing, nasal drainage and salivation. And both, with a direct hit to the eyes, can cause temporary blindness. Tear gas, however, is far less malodorous, quicker to fade away and easier to wash off than is skunk musk.

For a tailgunner, the skunk's aim is superb. And it always aims for an enemy's eyes. The animal can fire its twin weapons singly or in unison, with an accurate range of eight to 10 feet (less if shooting into a stiff breeze, more if the target is downwind). Several rounds of a few drops each (that's all it takes) can be discharged in rapid succession before the ammunition pouches are depleted.

A popular misconception holds that the skunk can shoot only straight back. In fact, the animal rarely sprays directly to its rear, preferring a slightly angled stance so that it can keep an eye on its target. According to credible reports, in a real pinch the striped skunk can even hump up and fire over its

Skunks and Rabies

The skunk is the primary wildlife carrier of rabies in the contiguous United States (raccoons are second). According to Dr. Thomas Eng of the Centers for Disease Control in Atlanta, during the seven years 1980 through 1986, an average of 2,988 cases of rabies in skunks were confirmed annually. Although most common in the Midwest and West, none of the lower 48 states is completely free of the threat.

Rabid wild animals, skunks or otherwise, rarely pose a direct threat to humans. More often, dogs and cats that haven't been inoculated against the disease contract it when pestering an infected wild animal, then pass it along to humans. Thus, the first line of rabies defense is to have your pets vaccinated in accordance with local law (and see to it that your neighbors follow suit). Do that, and avoid handling or harassing wild animals, and the threat of contracting rabies, which is already minor, can be virtually eliminated.

own back while facing the threat.

A good thing it is, then, that the skunk isn't trigger-happy. Unless surprised at very close range or pushed too hard too fast, the easygoing creature almost always gives you three warnings before resorting to its sole and essential means of self-defense.

So long as a skunk is moving away or paying you no mind, you're safe. But if the animal stops suddenly, turns to face you and stamps its forepaws, consider yourself *cautioned*. If you continue to advance or otherwise behave in a threatening manner (throwing rocks will do it), the skunk will turn away and erect its tail, save for the tip, which will remain drooped. The animal may also hiss. You have now been *warned*. If and when the tip of the tail snaps to attention and spreads, you have received your third and final warning, a *threat*. If you're within range, it's now too late to turn and run or try to back away; rather, freeze in your tracks, try to relax, divert your eyes, turn your face slowly away, say something friendly in a soft tone, and hope the skunk is still in a calm enough frame of mind to accept these gestures of acquiescence.

But it might not, so it's handy to know

When you're eye to eye with a striped skunk, don't blink.

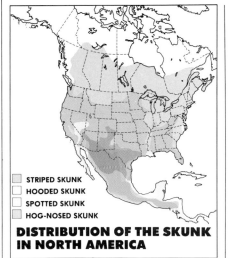

STRIPED SKUNK
HOODED SKUNK
SPOTTED SKUNK
HOG-NOSED SKUNK

DISTRIBUTION OF THE SKUNK IN NORTH AMERICA

what can be done to limit the damage should you, a companion or a pet get hit with the big stink.

First, to minimize contact of the musk with your skin (it's acidic and can burn), remove any sprayed garments. Second, if water is available, wash the affected area (generally the face and eyes) immediately and thoroughly. And third, deodorize.

A tomato-juice rubdown is the best known of the folk "deskunkers," and it works, sort of. For those of us who can chase the tomato scrub with a hot shower, it's OK. But for a dog or cat that you have no intention of taking into the house, much less the shower, tomato juice isn't so wonderful. Other home remedies include mustard, vinegar and diluted chlorine bleach.

But what if you're way off somewhere in the boonies and fresh out of tomato juice, mustard, vinegar and bleach? In that case, build a small fire, and stand (or hold your pet) in the smoke of burning grass, hay, juniper or cedar. Similarly, owners of woodstoves can help freshen a skunked house by building a slow fire of cedar or juniper, then closing the top damper and opening the stove door so that the fragrant smoke fills the room. (Neither of these sister woods contains pitch or other resins, so, unless you drastically overdo it, you needn't worry about smoke damage.)

The obvious problem with most of these home detoxifiers is that the cure can be nearly as unpleasant as the curse. Therefore, anyone whose profession or recreation puts them at high risk of being skunked, or who has children or pets that enjoy running wild in the woods, would do well to purchase and keep at the ready a small squeeze bottle of one of the clean, very effective commercial skunk antidotes, such as Skunk Stuff or Skunk Off.

For good reason, skunks never employ their musk when quarreling amongst themselves, nor to subdue prey. Rather, like their weasel cousins, they go for the necks of rivals and prey with their hunter's teeth.

Skunks are opportunistic feeders, omnivorous and less meat-minded than most other members of the weasel family. While mice, voles, shrews, rats and other small mammals are significant in the skunk's diet, it also consumes a wide variety of vegetable foods. Other favorites, at least during the warm months, are insects. Especially relished are grasshoppers, crickets, beetles and members of the wasp clan. Reports are abundant of individuals devouring several hundred insect pests in a single day.

Concerning reputation: While it's true that a skunk will occasionally pilfer the eggs and young of wild and domestic fowl, it much prefers the eggs of the snapping turtle and will consume all it can sniff out and exhume from the mud in which they're deposited. In the big picture, the skunk is of great benefit to both humankind and nature, and only a minor and occasional nuisance.

Still, while it would be a serious moral and ecological mistake to condemn skunks, a priori, as bad guys and gun down every one we see, it's nevertheless sometimes necessary to eliminate a persistent troublemaker. When hit with a well-placed shot, a skunk will generally die before it has time to muster a reprisal.

If you're not a shooter, you can easily catch a marauding skunk in a live trap; they're pitifully trusting creatures and come readily to baits such as meat or sweets. The capture accomplished, approach slowly, cover the trap and its inmate with an old blanket, and transport the works to a suitable release site several miles distant. Don't worry: Skunks have learned down through the ages that it's unwise to spray while inside a den or other dark, confined space (they have no special defense against their own offense) and seem to extend this instinctive self-restraint to covered traps and cages as well. So long as you handle your prisoner gently, then, there is probably very little to fear.

If it's an egg or poultry thief you're up against, you can skunk-proof your coop by siding it from a foot below the ground up to a height of at least three feet with metal roofing or plywood; while skunks can scoot right up and over a wire fence, they can't climb a hard, smooth surface.

When skunks work their way under a building, they're not looking so much for food as for a dark, secure place to snooze through the day or lay low for the winter (they're not bona fide hibernators but take extended naps between occasional nocturnal outings). Therefore, a quick, easy, inexpensive and almost sure defense against subfloor skunk invaders is an extension cord and a light bulb. If a crawlspace isn't dark, it just doesn't look like home to a skunk. For added protection, you can sprinkle mothballs on the ground around the inside of the foundation. Skunks don't like mothballs. They stink. Finally, avoid using spun fiberglass for crawlspace insulation, since it seems to be an irresistible nest-building material.

Would you believe . . .

The seemingly innocuous little creature we call the weasel is an insatiable killer driven to murderous frenzy by a large parasite residing in its stomach. It sucks the blood of its victims, conceives through its mouth and gives birth through an ear, can squeeze itself through a wedding ring and magically changes from brown to white within hours of the first snowfall each winter.

Each of those beliefs concerning the weasel is recorded in various literature as myth, legend or scientific fact. Of course, there's not a word of truth to any of it. But lack of truth has seldom stopped people from believing what they will about the mysteries of life.

In fact, weasels belong to the family of carnivores known to biologists as Mustelidae—a taxonomic moniker that translates crudely to "mouse stealers" and includes 64 species worldwide. North America's mustelids include weasels, badgers, skunks, otters,

minks, wolverines, fishers, martens and the critically endangered black-footed ferret. The smallest of the lot is the least weasel (imagine a svelte chipmunk), the largest is the sea otter (up to six feet, tongue to tail), and the most powerful is the wolverine.

All mustelids have highly developed anal scent glands, from which they can emit a strong musk more or less on demand. Unlike the skunk, however, most lack the apparatus to spray their musk any distance, instead using droplets or smears of the noxious perfume to mark the boundaries of their territories and for close-range self-defense.

With few exceptions, no matter where in North America you live, you're certain to have one or more of the continent's three weasel species—long-tailed, short-tailed and least—as a secret neighbor. While each species has its distinctive physical and behavioral traits, the three are more alike than different. All can take prey much larger than themselves and move with blurring speed.

All can climb and swim but are primarily terrestrial, making their homes in woodpiles, under rocks or fallen logs, and in burrows appropriated from rodents that were literally eaten out of house and home.

Weasels are primarily nocturnal but often venture out in daylight. All have beady, forward-set eyes with the binocular vision necessary to successful hunters; small, rounded, close-set ears; large brains relative to the size of their bodies (a characteristic shared by all predators, including humans); elongated faces and even longer necks; slender, sleek-furred bodies; short legs; five-toed feet with scimitar claws; and pencil-thin tails. The weasel's average life expectancy in the wild is about six years.

These pint-sized predators feed primarily on rodents—mice, squirrels, pocket gophers, moles, voles, shrews, chipmunks and rats—but also take lagomorphs (rabbits, hares and pikas), birds (including chickens) and their eggs, reptiles, amphibians, insects and fish.

Weasel in the Woodpile

This small carnivore is probably the true better mousetrap!

Young weasels go "pop" in a woodpile (above); short-tailed weasel shows its winter coat (left).

In spite of their lack of size, weasels are ferocious hunters, locating their quarry primarily by scent, and shunning the common tactics of stalk and ambush in favor of flush and chase. The weasel is both sprinter and endurance runner, hinging its back greyhoundlike as it bounds along tirelessly until it has worn down its fleeing prey, then springing forward in a last lightning-fast leap to seize its exhausted dinner. Additionally, the tiny hunter's slim and supple form enables it to weasel through any opening large enough to accommodate its head (which your average wedding ring isn't), easily penetrating the hidey-holes of its quarry—which it dispatches instantly with a powerful bite to the base of the skull.

Weasels need to eat an amount equal to only a quarter to a third of their body weight daily. That means a mouse or two a day will do. Still, when confronted with a particularly happy hunting ground, the little terrors often will continue killing until everything in sight is dead. Studies indicate that movement triggers such massacres: As long as there's a wriggle, jiggle or squirm in an enclosed kill area, the weasel will press its attack, often wiping out an entire colony of mice—numbering in the hundreds—or a coop full of chickens in a few furious moments.

Understandably, the weasel is considered "bloodthirsty"—a term appearing repeatedly in many older biology texts. Today we know that bloodthirstiness is a false charge, that the weasel isn't some vampire guzzler of blood and that its predatory excesses are sparked, not by evil intent (and certainly not by stomach parasites), but by instinct: In the weasel's genes it is programmed that he must lay in food when it's available, against those inevitable times when the pickings will be slim.

105

The once-common belief that weasels, especially the short-tailed (ermine) species, don seasonal camouflage by changing color from dark to white at the time of the first significant snowfall is based, not on myth or legend, but on relatively recent scientific research. Until the late 1800s, biologists believed that weasels shed their brownish summer pelage and replaced it with a thicker white winter coat in response to the lowered temperatures of autumn.

That theory was refuted when researchers noticed that captive weasels caged in heated buildings still molted. The researchers also noted that their mustelid prisoners began molting within 48 hours of the first real snowfall—and thus was born the theory that the seasonal onset of snowfall controls the timing of the weasel's annual change from brown to white.

We now know that the weasel's biannual color change stems not from snowfall but from a decreasing photoperiod: When days become shorter in late fall, the decreasing daylight triggers, via the weasel's pituitary gland, the molting of the summer coat and simultaneously inhibits the production of hormones that produce the pigments coloring the weasel's fur. Come spring with its lengthening days, this phenomenon reverses itself, replacing the white fur with a dark summer coat.

The myth that the weasel conceives through its mouth and gives birth through an ear originated in the fertile imaginations of ancient Greek storytellers. While the truth isn't quite that strange, it's interesting and unusual in a couple of ways.

In a process known as *induced ovulation*, the female weasel releases her egg, not on a regular timetable like most mammals, but only when it's needed—that is, at the instant of copulation. There's good reason for this: Adult weasels are generally loners, so, rather than chancing a mating meeting while the female's egg is not viable, nature invented on-demand ovulation to make certain that an egg will be ready and waiting whenever a male might happen along to fertilize it.

The weasel's second unusual reproductive trait is called *delayed implantation*, and applies to the long-tailed and short-tailed species, but not to the least weasel, which can mate and give birth at any time of the year. This biological anomaly allows mating to

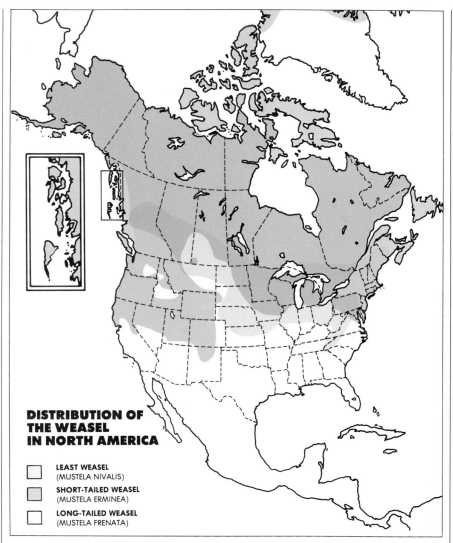

DISTRIBUTION OF THE WEASEL IN NORTH AMERICA

- LEAST WEASEL (MUSTELA NIVALIS)
- SHORT-TAILED WEASEL (MUSTELA ERMINEA)
- LONG-TAILED WEASEL (MUSTELA FRENATA)

take place during summer, when weasels are out and about and the most likely to meet—but the resulting fertilized egg goes on hold, not implanting in the uterus until late winter. This months-long delay assures that the young will be born during spring, when the weather is more favorable, food is plentiful and living is at its easiest.

Weasel kits are born with a strong hunting instinct, but must learn strategy and tactics from their mothers (with some help from the fathers in the long-tailed species). The kits mature rapidly and, by the winter following their birth, are fully grown and fending for themselves.

Despite the many similarities shared by all weasels, each of the three North American species has its own physical and behavioral distinctions.

Least weasels (*Mustela nivalis*), also known as common or pygmy weasels, have been aptly called "cigar-sized," with adults measuring 5.2 inches to a little over 13 inches long (of which about a quarter is tail) and weighing as little as 25 grams (less than an ounce). In addition to being the smallest member of the weasel family, *M. nivalis* also has the distinction of being the smallest carnivore in the world. (A member of this tiny species could, in fact, squeeze through a wedding ring, providing the ring belonged to someone with a finger diameter of an inch or so.)

In summer, this littlest hunter's fur is red-

A least weasel (above) between seasons, and a long-tail (left)

13.4 inches, nose to tip of tail, and, as you might expect, has a shorter tail relative to its overall length than the other two species.

Long-tailed weasels (*M. frenata*), besides being the most plentiful and wide-ranging, are also the largest of the three North American species. Adults weigh 2.9 to 6.9 ounces and measure 8.9 to 10.2 inches, head and body, plus a generous 4 to 5.9 inches of tail for a total length of 13 to 16 inches or so.

Northern long-tails turn white in winter (save for their ink-tipped tails), while the various southern subspecies merely fade to lighter shades of brown. Quite the athlete, the long-tail may jump six feet straight up and take prey 10 times its own size.

While humans are the only animals capable of premeditated murder, you can't argue that weasels don't sometimes indulge in instinctive overkill. Audubon (he watched more then birds) reported a classic example of just such a mustelid massacre, writing that he had "known forty well grown fowls to have been killed in one night by a single Ermine."

If you suspect a weasel of raiding your hen house, search out and plug even the tiniest coop entrances such as knotholes and cracks. If that doesn't work, you'll have to resort to trapping the raider—live or otherwise (as dictated by your conscience or lust for revenge, whichever is the stronger).

Unlike the least and short-tailed species, the long-tail is a notorious chicken killer; it's quite possible that Audubon's "Ermine" was in fact a white-phase long-tail. But even the chicken-stealing long-tail benefits the farmer in the long run, since it destroys rats that would otherwise prey on eggs and newborn chicks, and limits the number of crop-damaging mice.

Just how efficient a mousetrap is the weasel? One field study conducted in a national park netted these hungry statistics: In 37 days of observation, one mother weasel brought to her litter of kits a total of 148 rodents, including two moles, three rats, four ground squirrels, 27 gophers, 34 chipmunks and 78 mice. In all, a single weasel will kill from 500 to 1,000 prey animals—mostly mice—a year.

In the final analysis, then, that weasel hiding in the woodpile is neither monster nor magician, but the original (and still champion) better mousetrap.

ic snowfall (though often fading to a lighter shade), but it molts to white for winter in colder climes. The most reliable field identification feature of the least weasel is the lack of the black-tipped tail of the other two species.

Short-tailed weasels (*M. erminea*) are commonly known as ermines during their all-white winter phase, and as stoats in their darker summer pelage. Lagomorphs are a favored food. This species has a reputation for playfulness, and—when not hunting or holed up in its burrow—is known to gather in groups to frolic in the sunshine.

The short-tailed weasel's summer coat is reddish brown above, with yellowish underparts and a black-tipped tail. In winter throughout its range—except for a strip along the Pacific coast from British Columbia southward—the short-tail turns pure white, save the tip of its tail, which stays black. An adult short-tail will measure 7.5 inches to

dish brown across the back and sides, with a white underbelly. The least weasel keeps this two-toned coloration year-round in the portions of its range that receive only sporad-

Franklin's Eagle

The wild turkey is one of conservation's success stories.

Benjamin Franklin knew that America was full of turkeys, which he considered to be hardy, intelligent and beautiful birds. In fact, he even lobbied to have the wild turkey (*Meleagris gallopavo*) designated as young America's national symbol. Looking back on it now—especially in light of the secondary meaning attached to the word *turkey* in modern usage—it's just as well that Uncle Ben's candidate was soundly defeated by the rival Bald Eagle party.

But in fairness to the good Mr. Franklin, we should keep in mind that beauty is in the eye—however nearsighted or jaundiced that organ may be—of the beholder. And Ben's fine-feathered friend does have a few attributes that should appeal to anyone with good taste, especially when it comes to appreciating art at the dinner table.

Turkey scholars (yes, there are such beings) have estimated that North America's pre-Columbian wilderness supported more than 10 million wild turkeys. Of course (the familiar story), by 1900 the big birds were nearing extinction because of habitat reduction and overhunting. Today, according to the latest estimate released by the National Wild Turkey Federation, the continental U.S. supports a population of between 2 and 2.5 million wild turks. In fact, every state save Alaska is now home to a self-sustaining wild turkey population. That's a remarkable comeback, due almost entirely to strict controls on hunting and the advent of innovative management programs involving restocking depleted areas as well as introducing starter populations to new habitat.

Whether or not the wild turkey is considered beautiful depends, in more ways than one, upon individual point of view. When seen from a distance and in the right light, the wild gobbler glows with iridescent red, green, blue and copper tones painted on a sleek, dark background. But if you single out just the head and neck for inspection, you'll be confronted with a bald, misshapen mess.

Among the most obvious of *M. gallopavo*'s facial beauty problems are the fatty *wattles* dangling from the throat and projecting from above the bill, and the equally unsightly *caruncles* of the neck. However, these gross appendages are also remarkable in their ability to change size, shape and color to reflect the mood of their wearer. A sexually aroused tom might, for instance, alter the coloration of his head and its protuberances from gray-blue to red, then back to blue again, seemingly on command.

In addition to his wattles and caruncles, the adult tom (and the occasional hen) also sports a beard—a collection of primitive black contour feathers that are stiff, straight and up to a foot in length (eight inches or so for bearded females). Double-bearded gobblers are common, triple beards aren't too unusual, and males with five beards or more turn up from time to time.

The wild turkey's bulky body gives a false impression of great weight. In fact, an adult wild tom generally weighs no more than 15 to 18 pounds, with hens averaging a petite nine to 11 pounds. Those 25- and 30-pound gobblers that hunters often brag about bagging are rare almost to the point of being mythical.

Still, nine to 18 pounds is a lot of bird—which makes it rather surprising that the hefty fowl are such strong fliers. Turkeys need no runway for takeoff, and can climb almost vertically from a standing start—much in the manner of their distant relatives the pheasants. They fly low, straight and fast (around 40 miles per hour), and are graceful gliders. But, for all of that, they generally prefer walking and running to winging it.

The wild turkey's dread of raptors and other predators is instinctive and strong—but, strangely, its fear of humans may be an acquired trait. In pre-Columbian times, turkeys seemingly had little aversion to people, which made them easy prey even for hunters equipped only with the most primitive of

DISTRIBUTION OF THE WILD TURKEY IN NORTH AMERICA

weapons. But over the centuries, as hunting pressure mounted and weapons became more and more sophisticated, so also increased *M. gallopavo*'s expertise in avoiding *Homo sap*. These days, a big gobbler is every bit as elusive as a wise old buck deer. Part of the reason for this is that the turkey's vision and hearing are superb. (The big bird's sense of smell, however, stinks.)

A large gobbler will gobble as much as two pounds of food per day, and will down whatever he can scratch up when he's hungry. But when times are good, wild turkeys prefer dining on mast (fallen nuts). They also consume insects (grasshoppers are their candy), crustaceans and small snakes (for protein), and will nibble on various succulent plants (to get their vitamins). In winter, if the snow gets too deep or crusty to scratch through, these cagey fowl just drop in behind a herd of deer, elk or livestock and peck for food in the bare spots where their hooved

In full mating display, a wild turkey is impressive indeed.

predecessors have pawed away the snow.

Sometime after the evening meal and always before dark, wild turkeys seek out tall trees in which to snooze, safe above the world of things that go bump in the night. Preferred roost trees have large, sturdy limbs that project over water or a steep drop-off, providing a degree of added protection against mammalian predators. Several birds may share a particularly desirable tree, or they may sleep in separate "bedrooms." Only after the sun is well up will the rested turkeys leave their roosts and wing their way to breakfast.

The onset of spring mating season is the Big Event in a wild turkey's year, and is sung in with gusto by the suddenly amorous toms. Courtship gobbling is primarily a sunrise activity, engaged in while the birds are still on their roosts. If a tom's mating calls elicit an answer, he'll gobble again, and with greatly increased enthusiasm. When the tom gets sufficiently excited, he'll leave his roost and seek out the respondent to his gobbles—which might be a hen, a rival tom or something else entirely (like a hunter with a turkey call and a shotgun).

When a love-struck tom draws near to the object of his intentions, he'll display his tail feathers in a peacocklike (though more modest) copper-toned fan, spread and lower his wings and commence strutting his stuff. At the same time, the lustful lummox will draw back his head, fill his lungs to capacity and exhale in a burst of turkey pillow talk. (The great Audubon called this phenomenon "pulmonic puff.")

As with males of most species (humans not excluded), wild turkey gobblers on the make are extremely hostile to rival suitors. Consequently, should two strutting toms meet, a battle generally ensues. The combatants lock beaks and use their leg spurs (which can be up to 24 millimeters in length and plenty sharp) to slash at each other's breasts. Such a tussle can last for hours, but rarely if ever ends in death—though head and neck injuries are common.

Once it's established which tom is the stronger, the defeated bird will flop down on the ground with his neck outstretched—a signal of submission that's always heeded by the victor, who backs off and allows the chicken turkey to retreat. In this manner a strong tom can assemble a harem of four to six hens and have their feathered affections all to himself.

Toward the end of mating season the harems break up, the hens wandering off to build nests consisting of shallow excavations scratched into the earth, then hastily lined with leaves and other forest-floor debris. But even though they're slovenly builders, wild turkey hens always conceal their nests carefully and cover their eggs with debris each time they leave the area to feed. A single hen often lays well over a dozen eggs, and several hens may share one nest. (Audubon reported finding 42 eggs in a single nest, with three hens in attendance.) The incubation period is 28 days, with a hatch success rate of 35% (which isn't so bad as such things go).

Newborn turkeys—called poults—are brooded on the ground until they're old enough to fly up to roost in trees at night. (Generally, poults can fly short distances at two weeks of age, and are accomplished aviators at six.) If a hen's poults are threatened by a predator, Mom sends them into hiding, then sounds a plaintive squawk intended to draw the predator's attention away from her young. She may even feign injury in order to fool a predator into thinking she's easy meat, and so lure the four-legged hunter into following her on a wild turkey chase leading far away from the hidden brood.

As table fare, wild turkey is tender, moist and delicious, and—since it contains very little fat, plenty of protein and no commercial poultry-feed additives or postmortem-injected butter—it's one of the most wholesome and nutritious of all meats. In fact, better gobbling can't be got.

In retrospect, perhaps old Ben Franklin's taste in birds wasn't so bad after all. At least at the dinner table.

Tree Squirrels

City-park beggar or sought-after wild game, the squirrel is a valuable resource.

Among both hunters and amateur naturalists, the squirrels (family Sciuridae) make up one of the most popular groups of wild creatures on this continent. These little animals are highly adaptable, and most species have proved able to survive, and even thrive, in areas where human destruction of habitat has long since eliminated less opportunistic mammals. They can be seen dancing limb to limb in city parks and on wilderness hillsides from coast to coast, and—being a very diverse bunch—include not only the *tree* squirrels, but also such seemingly dissimilar animals as chipmunks, woodchucks (or ground hogs), flying squirrels, prairie dogs, marmots and ground squirrels.

Still, to most of us, *squirrel* means one of the bushy-tailed tree dwellers. (In fact, the family name translates as "shadow tail.") These are the squirrels most commonly admired by students of nature and most often transformed into tasty meals by hunters.

Whether your chosen activity is observation or pursuit, your success and satisfaction will be increased if you take the time to learn about your quarry. So, to add to the fun you'll find in squirrel watching *or* hunting, we've prepared the following guide to the tree squirrels of North America.

DOUGLAS SQUIRREL
(*Tamiasciurus douglasii*)
Adult length and weight: under 16 inches, about ½ pound

Hunting: Some Tips for Tyros

There are a good many reasons why squirrels are among the most hunted animals in North America. For one thing, the bushy-tail season usually opens before that of any of the larger animals, and provides an excuse to enjoy the early-autumn woods. Then, too, squirrels are more numerous than any other huntable animal with the possible exception of rabbits. Because of this, productive woods are often accessible to youngsters who have to be able to reach their hunting areas by foot. The weapons used for squirrel hunting—and the skills required—also demand less of an investment on the part of beginners, be they young or old. And, finally, squirrel meat has been recognized as a delicious food since long before the first Europeans settled on our shores.

The best way to locate a good squirrel woods is simply to be in the country—hiking, camping or fishing—before the season begins. Listen for the barks and chatters of those often vocal animals, and keep your eyes peeled for nests and for the gnawed nutshells, pinecones, corncobs or fungi that indicate squirrels have been feeding.

Once you've located a spot and the season opens (in some parts of the country, squirrels are fair game year-round), your hunt can be as simple or as complicated as you'd like. The back-to-basics approach is simply to dress in comfortable clothes (with a blaze orange vest, in orange camouflage pattern if you prefer, for safety) and set yourself down in a likely-looking grove of trees. The early- to mid-morning and mid- to late-afternoon hours are often the most productive.

Most squirrel hunters use either a .22 rifle or a shotgun. If you choose the latter, which will make it possible to shoot running animals, it's best to use nothing smaller than No. 5 shot. Despite their size, squirrels are hard to kill; for that reason, hunters using a .22 should never shoot at a moving animal, and should always use hard-hitting hollow-point bullets. To do otherwise is to risk watching a wounded animal escape.

A variation of the sit-and-wait technique is still-hunting, which involves moving slowly and quietly through the woods, stopping in likely spots for up to half an hour at a time and keeping your eyes and ears peeled.

Or if you want to get complicated, you can use a call to locate your game, or even invest in a trained squirrel dog (called a feist dog in the South), which will tree squirrels and

EASTERN GRAY SQUIRREL
(*Sciurus carolinensis*)
Adult length and weight: 17 to 20 inches, 1 to 1¾ pounds

FOX SQUIRREL
(*Sciurus niger*)
Adult length and weight: to nearly 30 inches and 3 pounds

RED SQUIRREL
(*Tamiasciurus hudsonicus*)
Adult length and weight: under 16 inches, about ½ pound (average)

ABERT SQUIRREL
(*Sciurus aberti*)
Adult length and weight: 18 to 23 inches, 1½ to 2 pounds

Falling nut shucks often give away the positions of feeding squirrels.

circle the tree to force a hidden animal to give its position away.

Whatever method you use, keep in mind that a hunted squirrel can remain motionless, and all but invisible, for hours at a time. If you find yourself searching fruitlessly for a squirrel that suddenly disappears, you can follow several courses of action. First, if there's any breeze, look for the movement of blowing fur rather than trying to spot the whole animal. Or if you're with a friend, one of you can sit still while the other circles the tree noisily, perhaps causing the squirrel to move around the trunk to keep the tree between it and the more obvious hunter. If alone, you can try hanging your coat from a limb in view of the tree, then circling the trunk yourself. In fleeing you, the animal may think it's exposed itself to another hunter (the coat), and scoot into your view. Or, finally, you can just plunk yourself down and try to wait the squirrel out. It might take a long time, and you might even run out of day before that squirrel shows itself, but if you've never spent an afternoon sitting motionless in the woods, I can guarantee that you'll see and hear things that are every bit as rewarding as bringing a squirrel home for the pot!

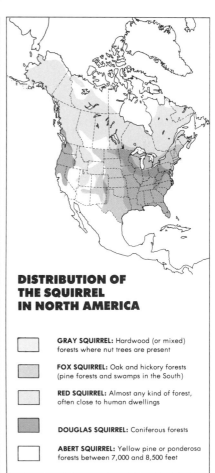

DISTRIBUTION OF THE SQUIRREL IN NORTH AMERICA

GRAY SQUIRREL: Hardwood (or mixed) forests where nut trees are present

FOX SQUIRREL: Oak and hickory forests (pine forests and swamps in the South)

RED SQUIRREL: Almost any kind of forest, often close to human dwellings

DOUGLAS SQUIRREL: Coniferous forests

ABERT SQUIRREL: Yellow pine or ponderosa forests between 7,000 and 8,500 feet

The Ground Hog Has Its Day

Woodchuck ways

How much wood would a woodchuck chuck if a woodchuck could chuck wood?

That old conundrum makes one wonder about the origins of the name *woodchuck*. And what of the big rodent's other titles—such as ground hog and whistle-pig and, in the western mountains, rockchuck and whistler?

No matter their local nicknames, both the woodchuck and its western cousins technically are marmots, members of the genus *Marmota* (from the Latin for "mountain rat"). And all marmots—there are three major species in North America, including the woodchuck—belong to the same family as the squirrels. That family is Sciuridae (from the Greek, meaning "shadow tail").

But back to the origin of the name *woodchuck*. Although there are other explanations, the currently popular theory traces back to the Choctaw Indian word *shukha*, meaning "hog." With the arrival of Europeans in North America, *shukha* soon enough was Anglicized to "chuck" and eventually merged with a word describing the place the little Indian hog was found—"woods." Woodchuck, then, can be taken to mean woods hog and, thus, has not a splinter of connection to chucking wood.

Then there's that other name, *ground hog*—and the day connected with the moniker.

Folk legend has it, you'll recall, that each February 2, this Rip Van Winkle of the mammal world rouses from his winter hibernation, emerges from his burrow and checks the weather, especially the presence or absence of sunshine. If the sun is shining and he sees his own plump shadow, that's bad, and means winter will last another six weeks;

if no shadow shows, that's good, indicating spring is at hand.

To understand the concept of ground-hog-as-meteorologist and how such an odd notion became elevated to the status of an annually observed folk tradition, it helps to know something of the nature of the beast.

The ground hog's species name is *Marmota monax*, the latter being a Lenape Indian word meaning "digger." Unlike so many other wild creatures of eastern North America, the ground hog did not suffer from the clearing of the forests as the pioneers and subsequent settlers made room for human enterprise, but indeed benefited from the creation of manmade pastures and fields.

Your basic ground hog is reddish brown in color with white-tipped guard hairs and dark brown or black feet. All-black (melanistic) individuals sometimes occur, as do albinos. True to its name, the animal is porcine in physique, weighing on the average around 10 pounds (the record, as reported by photographer-naturalist Leonard Lee Rue III, was a Pennsylvania behemoth of 30 pounds). Body length is a little over two feet, including a short tail.

Notwithstanding its unathletic build, the woodchuck can run at a respectable speed and, though rarely seen doing so, is capable of both climbing trees and swimming. One of the most distinctive identifying characteristics of the woodchuck is its high-pitched trilling call, or whistle, whence derives its nickname whistle-pig.

The ground hog eats about a tenth of its body weight in vegetation per day. Grasses and clover are favored, but the 'chuck will scarf down just about anything green, including, when available, garden, field and orchard crops.

Ground hogs and marmots, like all rodents, are toothed with outsize incisors that grow continuously except during hibernation. If the 'chuck doesn't use its incisors regularly to keep them worn down, or if the top and bottom teeth become misaligned so that they fail to contact when chewing, they can enlarge to the extent that the animal can no longer eat. Or the top teeth can curve back and up, eventually growing through the roof of the mouth and into the brain.

Each ground hog digs its own extensive tunnel system having at least two entrances, one made prominent by its mound of exca-

vated earth, the others hidden. The burrow can contain sleeping, nursery and even latrine chambers and is just large enough for the animal to squeeze into. Rarely will a ground hog tunnel exceed four feet in depth (though deeper excavations do occur), but it can be as much as 50 feet long. The animal digs with its forepaws, then heaves the loosened earth up and out of the burrow with paws, head and nose.

Ground hogs frequently vacate their previous winter's dens come spring and dig new homes. This provides an abundance of abandoned burrows as refuge for a variety of other wild creatures—including rabbits, several species of furbearers, various rodents and even game birds.

A top priority for a male ground hog just emerged from hibernation in early spring is the search for a mate. She's usually neither hard to find nor coy, and the male moves right in and makes himself at home in her home, if only for the nonce.

With mating normally taking place in March and gestation requiring a month, spring's new crop of whistle-pigs—usually four or five to the litter—is born during April. The young grow rapidly and are ready to move into their own digs by July or August, though they rarely relocate far from where they were born.

Woodchucks, especially the young, are playful by nature and have been observed enjoying their own version of sumo wrestling, wherein two opponents grapple atop a burrow mound until one throws the other into the tunnel opening. After a few moments of repose, the vanquished contestant pops up for another go-round.

Occasionally, the woodchuck's adeptness at reproduction combines with a dearth of natural predators, causing local populations to grow out of control. When that happens, the animals can become pests, causing damage to gardens, field crops, orchards and pastures. In time, a natural increase in predators (red foxes are among the most effective) would bring the 'chuck population back into balance with the environment. But no one wants to wait on nature these days, so excess woodchucks are generally shot, trapped or poisoned.

Although "yellow-belly" sounds like something the Duke might have called the villain in an old gun-and-gallop flick, the

A marmot "sits up and takes notice."

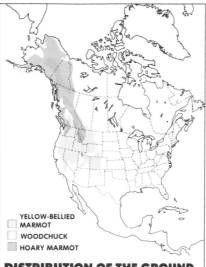

YELLOW-BELLIED
MARMOT

WOODCHUCK

HOARY MARMOT

DISTRIBUTION OF THE GROUND HOG IN NORTH AMERICA

name in fact is intended to describe the feature that most readily distinguishes *Marmota flaviventris* (literally, "yellow of the belly") from the other two primary species of the marmot family. Actually, this western animal's underbelly is burnt orange rather than yellow, but the name makers must have decided that "burnt-orange-belly" lacked sufficient melodic cadence.

Most often, yellow-bellies make their homes in boulder fields, preferring sizable rockslides located near green subalpine meadows at higher elevations. If there's a stream, lake or marsh nearby, all the better. Here a plenitude of food is at hand, and they can hie to the shelter of their burrows among the rocks when threatened by golden eagle, bobcat or fox.

Like woodchucks, marmots will eat almost anything vegetable, from wildflowers to wild berries. But since few gardens or commercial crops are grown on rockslides or in subalpine meadows, the marmot, unlike the ground hog, hasn't developed much of a reputation as a pest.

The hoary marmot is the northwestern-most representative of the genus, with a range extending no farther south than central Idaho, and north all the way to upper coastal Alaska. Its common name refers to the silver-gray color of its body hair, while its scientific name, *Marmota caligata* (literally, "booted marmot"), identifies a secondary coloration characteristic, its black feet.

Following Bergman's rule—a zoological tenet that says the farther north a species lives, the larger it will be in relation to its southern relatives—the hoary marmot, at around 20 pounds, weighs on the average a third more than the yellow-belly and twice

as much as the woodchuck. Like the yellow-belly, the hoary marmot prefers to make its home in montane boulder fields adjacent to subalpine meadows. Among its principal predators are the golden eagle and the grizzly bear.

Marmots and woodchucks are true hibernators, as opposed to bears, raccoons and other winter sleepers that snooze deeply but sometimes awaken and occasionally venture out. Yellow-bellied marmots enter their leaf-lined burrows among the rocks sometime from mid-August to early October, depending on the elevation and climate where they live, and sleep until late March or early April; hoary marmots retire as early as mid-September and usually emerge in April; woodchucks doze from late September or early October through late February or early March.

While in hibernation, woodchucks and marmots sleep curled up with their forepaws covering their eyes, and appear to be all but dead, which they are: They eliminate no body wastes, respiration slows to one breath every few minutes, the heart beats less than half a dozen times a minute, body temperature sinks to the upper 30s (from a waking temperature in the mid-90s); even their ever-growing incisor teeth take a vacation from elongation. Like miniature versions of winter-sleeping bears, hibernating marmots and woodchucks live by metabolizing the excess body fat they've stored during the summer months.

When spring finally arrives, woodchucks and marmots rouse slowly, taking several hours to come entirely awake. At that time they're hungry and, as previously mentioned, lonesome. Yellow-bellied and hoary marmots are free to get right about their search for food and love, but the ground hog

first must deal with his annual responsibilities as a folk hero.

The tradition of ground-hog day as we know it in the twentieth century evolved from an imaginative blend of medieval fact and fiction. Mostly the latter.

The tradition has its roots in Candlemas Day, an ancient Roman Catholic celebration honoring the Virgin Mary and held 40 days after Christmas—which just happens to be February 2. Candlemas Day was also the traditional time for forecasting the weather for the coming weeks and, thus, setting a date for spring planting. As the old saw says:

If Candlemas Day is fair and bright,
Winter will take another fight.
If Candlemas Day brings storm and rain,
Winter is gone and will not come again.

Since medieval French and German folklore credited ground hogs, along with badgers and bears, with the ability to predict the weather for the weeks following their emergence from hibernation (possibly because these winter sleepers seem to "know" when to awaken), it's not surprising that the weather-forecasting tradition associated with the celebration of Candlemas Day eventually merged with the idea of ground-hog-as-meteorologist, and the tradition of ground-hog day was born.

Does science support this charming tradition? In a word, no. But there's no need to disdain such a delightful folk belief simply because it lacks a scientifically established record of accuracy. One eminent wildlife authority who at least gave the notion of woodchuck weathermen the benefit of scientific possibility was naturalist Ernest Thompson Seton, who (in the 1920s) wrote:

"This superstition . . . has this much of truth for foundation: The woodchuck sometimes comes out as early as the first week in February. If at that time the sun shines brightly on the snow, it means frosty weather, and forecasts a late spring. On the other hand, *no snow* and low-hanging rain clouds are evidence of an open winter; and that fosters an early activity on the part of the woodchuck."

Seton concluded: "It must be obvious to the reader that I am trying hard to justify the picturesque popular notion; our lives and literature would be richer if we had more of such."

Just so.

Coyote: Survivor Supreme

A tale of the invincible "brush wolf"

For those who have heard it, the lonely, ethereal song of the coyote evokes either a primal fear of the wild and unknown, or the nostalgic, deeply felt pleasure of a music that has entertained and enthralled *Homo* since long before he became *sapiens*.

But for some western ranchers, especially sheepmen, the song of the coyote is a knell, a foreboding of disaster and doom. These ranchers charge the coyote with the crime of killing newborn calves and lambs. Especially lambs. In fact, so *much* stock is lost to coyotes, claim some sheepmen, that the little dogs are eating them right out of the ranching business.

This complaint is nothing new. The stockman's fear of, hatred for and war on predators extend back to frontier times, when cowboys battled not only coyotes, but bears, wolves, cougars, Indians and squatters for control of the vast western rangelands. The rancher long ago defeated those other, less adaptable, competitors, leaving the durable coyote as the last lonely rebel.

According to Defenders of Wildlife, a respected and effective conservation group with headquarters in Washington, D.C., the U.S. government for the past several years has spent some $20 million annually on predator control, with millions more being kicked in by states, counties and stockmen's associations. While the coyote is number one on the wanted list, other target species include bears, cougars and bobcats, as well as smaller "pest" species such as prairie dogs, ground squirrels, meadow mice, starlings and gulls.

And what have we gotten for all our trouble and expense?

Just more coyotes. *Lots* more coyotes.

Today, coyotes are more plentiful in the West and Midwest than ever before, and even the eastern states that traditionally have been coyoteless are beginning to look like home to the wayfaring canid. In fact, according to the U.S. Fish and Wildlife Service (FWS), 47 of the 48 contiguous states—Delaware being the sole holdout—currently host coyote populations.

How and why, when larger and more fierce predators such as wolves and grizzly bears have all but disappeared, have coyotes been able to survive and even prosper in the face of relentless attack by government and private trappers, aerial gunners, sport hunters, Compound 1080, sodium cyanide and denning (a particularly sporting endeavor wherein newborn coyote pups are dynamited, drowned, cremated, gassed or buried alive in their nursery dens—or snagged with wire hooks, dragged out and clubbed to death)? How and why, indeed?

Because, unlike wolves, bears and cougars, the coyote is highly prolific and not locked into any specific ecological niche. It can, like its human counterparts, change with the times and, when necessary, move on to greener pastures. Although *Canis latrans* (literally, "barking dog") prospers best in the mountains, deserts and prairies of the semi-arid West, the species can and readily will—as the FWS stats show—set up housekeeping virtually anyplace necessity demands.

In recent years, necessity has been most demanding indeed, frequently pushing the coyote to the very front yards of civilization. The resultant phenomenon of suburban predators has become particularly troublesome to pet owners living along the sprawling fringes of Los Angeles and other southern California burgs, where displaced coyotes stalk brazenly down residential streets at night, forced to subsist on a cosmopolitan diet of alley cats and Yorkshire terriers.

The coyote is at home in the snowy mountains and in the L.A. suburbs.

Of course, household pets aren't the coyote's food of first choice. In the northern Rockies, where he grows largest and his winter pelage becomes most beautiful, Wile E. Coyote's diet is both ample and varied, including—well, just about everything. Pocket gophers, voles, rabbits, hares, squirrels, chipmunks and other small mammals are among his favorite foods, though he also relishes carrion and regularly samples various vegetarian fare.

In winter, when times are hard, small game is scarce and hunting conditions are favorable (lots of deep, soft snow), a family of coyotes (not a "pack") will occasionally even make a go at bringing down a young, old, ill or otherwise less-than-prime deer, antelope or elk. This, of course, is entirely natural, being to the benefit of the prey species in keep-

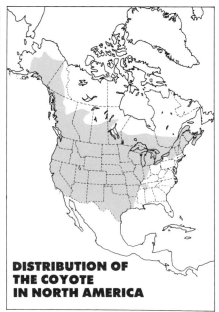

DISTRIBUTION OF THE COYOTE IN NORTH AMERICA

ing with the spirit of the old Eskimo maxim: "It is the wolf who keeps the caribou strong."

But it's his taste for the meat of ungulates that has gotten the coyote into so much hot water with sheepmen and, to some extent, with luckless hunters; you may have seen the bumper sticker that whines: "Did a coyote get your deer?" In answer to this redneck rationalization, the radical environmental group Earth First! counters with their own bumper sticker, which places the blame for any shortage of big game, actual or perceived, not on natural predators but on habitat destruction due to overgrazing of cattle and sheep. It reads: "Hunters, did a cow get your elk?"

Given the opportunity, a coyote will live to the age of 12 or so in the wild. These days, however, what with the predator wars and all, a coyote is lucky to enjoy even a couple of harassed and hungry years before being

shot, caught, poisoned or deprived of his livelihood through habitat destruction. To help offset these losses, nature has simply increased the modern coyote's range and rate of reproduction, with females becoming more fertile and litters growing ever larger.

While the grit of the western rancher must be admired and his need to protect his livestock acknowledged, recognition is also due the coyote for his cleverness, adaptability and stoic refusal to roll over and play dead. Both the western rancher and the coyote are tenacious fighters worthy of our respect.

But there is one significant difference: In contrast to the constant meddling and tireless efforts of human predators (who bag most of their meat these days at the supermarket) to dominate and control everything, even and especially each other, the song of the coyote remains in tune with nature and the species' assigned purpose on earth.

PART FOUR

Wilderness Workshop

A little time
with hammer and saw or
needle and scissors
can save some serious
money.

Consolidated Camper

A campground Conestoga that you can build

Though part of the fun of camping is shucking the amenities of society, it's obvious that the faster you set up camp, the sooner you can begin enjoying yourself. Since this compact camping trailer is already set up when it rolls into camp, "roughing it" is made smoother than you'd ever imagine.

The nearly 4′ cube is not a pop-out, sleep-in camper, but rather a combination storage locker and camp kitchen that'll hold everything necessary for a weekend (and maybe even a weeks-long) trip to anywhere you can

pull it. Five stowage compartments, three utensil and storage drawers, a cool box, a stove holder and a food preparation counter complete with overhead and sidewall weather protection make it one of the handiest conveyances to hit the trail since the days of the Conestoga wagon.

To keep the project within the capabilities of a person with average workshop skills, purchase, rather than fabricate, the 40″ X 48″ tubular steel trailer frame upon which the plywood camper rests. Believe it or not,

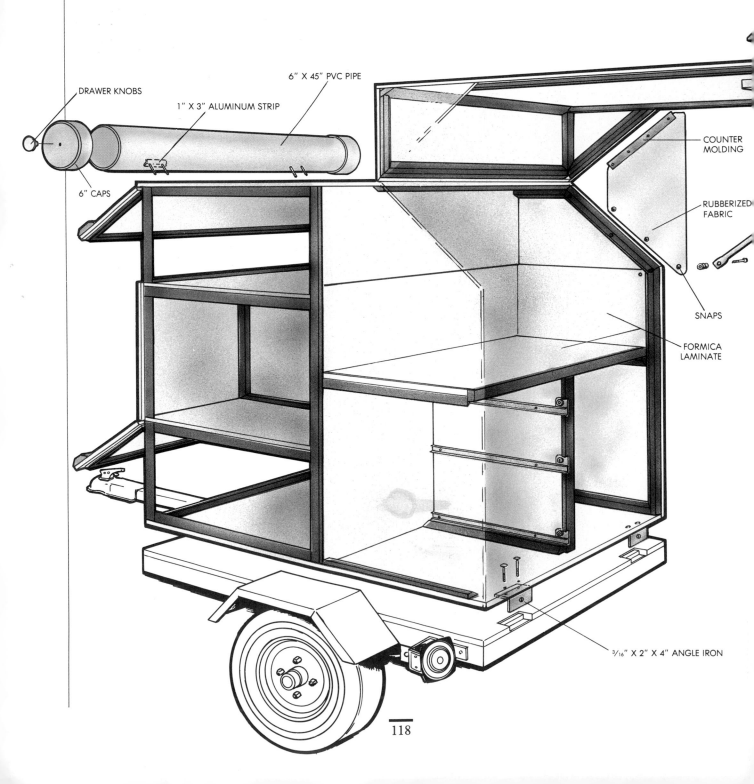

DRAWER KNOBS

1″ X 3″ ALUMINUM STRIP

6″ X 45″ PVC PIPE

6″ CAPS

COUNTER MOLDING

RUBBERIZED FABRIC

SNAPS

FORMICA LAMINATE

³/₁₆″ X 2″ X 4″ ANGLE IRON

the cost of buying just the parts to make a trailer can exceed the price of a new, manufactured one at a local hardware store.

The camper body is a self-contained unit built of ½" AC plywood on a ¾" plywood base. Internal rib members measuring ¾" X 1¾", and beveled to 45° on each side, strengthen the corners and provide bolsters for the horizontal and vertical inner partitions. Furthermore, angle-iron clips placed at each of the box's four lower corners bolt to the trailer frame and allow that chassis—

when the body is removed—to do double duty as a utility trailer. A ¾" plywood platform mounted to the trailer itself serves as a subfloor for either configuration.

Although the camper project demands only patience and a moderate selection of common workshop tools, the use of a table saw is almost mandatory to keep the panel edges straight and the rib bevels true. The other power tools you'll need are a drill with an assortment of bits, and a countersink, a router and perhaps a palm sander to prepare

the wooden surface for a coat of paint.

Start off by collecting one sheet of ¾" AC plywood, four sheets of the same material in ½" thickness, a section of ¼" plywood measuring 18" X 52" and a scrap of ¾" X 18" X 40" ply. The project requires about 20 linear feet of 1 X 4 fir or pine, one gross of 1" No. 8 flathead wood screws, several feet of ¾" X 3" hardwood (along with some larger hardwood scraps), a 40" X 42" piece of Formica or other plastic laminate and a 6" X 45" PVC pipe with two end caps. You'll

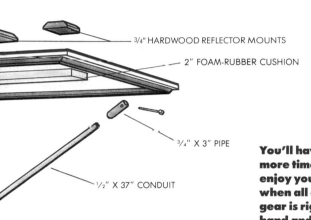

¾" HARDWOOD REFLECTOR MOUNTS

2" FOAM-RUBBER CUSHION

¾" X 3" PIPE

½" X 37" CONDUIT

You'll have more time to enjoy your trip when all of your gear is right at hand and ready to use as soon as you arrive.

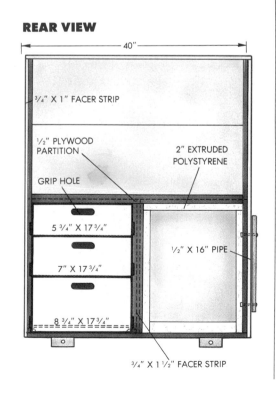

COOL BOX DETAIL

1½" X 3" BUTT HINGE

PANEL LOCK

2" EXTRUDED POLYSTYRENE
(BEVELED EDGES)

½" PLYWOOD

BEVELED RIBS

REAR VIEW

40"

¾" X 1" FACER STRIP

½" PLYWOOD PARTITION

GRIP HOLE

2" EXTRUDED POLYSTYRENE

5 ¾" X 17¾"

7" X 17¾"

8 ¾" X 17¾"

½" X 16" PIPE

¾" X 1½" FACER STRIP

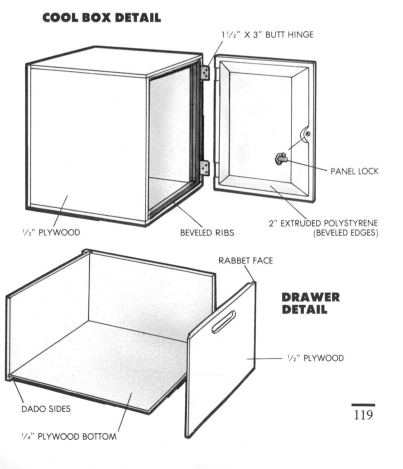

RABBET FACE

DRAWER DETAIL

½" PLYWOOD

DADO SIDES

¼" PLYWOOD BOTTOM

also need ten 3″ X 3″ butt hinges, two 2″ X 30″ continuous hinges, two 1½″ X 3″ butt hinges, two window-sash locks, a panel lock, six 3¾″ draw pull catches and three pairs of 18″ heavy-duty drawer slides.

The rest of the material consists of assorted fastener hardware and metal scrap, but in addition you'll have to find some extruded polystyrene board 2″ thick, 18″ wide and long enough to cover the equivalent of 11′, a 30″ X 60″ section of rubberized canvas or other waterproof material, a tube of silicone sealant, carpenter's glue and some contact upholstery adhesive.

To make your assembly chores easier, the camper is illustrated in an exploded view and in plan views of the rear, top and sides. Details of the drawer construction, cool box, stove holder and hinge layout are given.

Begin by cutting out the floor, front and sidewall panels. These will provide you with a reference from which to measure the placement of partitions, shelves and supporting ribs, as indicated in the illustrations. Note that not all the ribs are double-beveled: Some

have a single angle and a square side to meet stationary panels. Note, too, that the rib lengths aren't specified; it's simpler and more accurate to cut these to fit as you go along so they'll match *your* camper.

Use the left side–view illustration to guide you in determining the ribs' order of assembly, which is numbered—by group—from 1 through 4. Cut the plywood parts of the rear lift hatch, including the two 12″ X 12″ X 18″ corner gussets, so you can start construction on that component, and trim out the top and the vertical and horizontal partitions, as well. The ribs should be glued and clamped to the sheathing if possible, then the flathead screws fastened from the plywood side into the ribs at intervals of about 8″.

With the body roughed out, you can concentrate on the detail work as it suits you. The access holes to the side compartments at the front should be cut out to 12½″ X 24¼″ rough openings to meet the edges of the side and upper ribs. A fourth rib is cut and added to the lower edge of each opening to complete the perimeter. All but the upper

edges of both the door and the hole are beveled at 45° to match the ribs; once the doors are framed, you can add the full-length hinges and sash locks.

The upper and lower doors to the front stowage compartments also extend to their rib perimeters, but have square, rather than beveled, edges. (The frame ribs on the doors are beveled to meet the openings.) The exterior corners are strengthened with ¾″ X 3″ X 3½″ hardwood blocks, which hold the draw pull catches. Each door is fastened to the body with three butt hinges, and the joint is protected from the weather with a 6″ X 40″ strip of rubberized canvas, which is captured at each edge beneath ¾″ X 40″ strips of aluminum counter molding. A pole-storage tube made from a 45″ length of 6″ PVC pipe can be secured to the top edge of the upper door with ¼″ X 1¼″ carriage bolts backed with 1″ X 3″ aluminum strips in lieu of washers.

In the rear, the lower left compartment is equipped with three drawers, 5¾″, 7″ and 8¾″ deep. All share the same construction,

LEFT SIDE VIEW (SECTIONED)

RIBS INSTALLED IN NUMBER ORDER

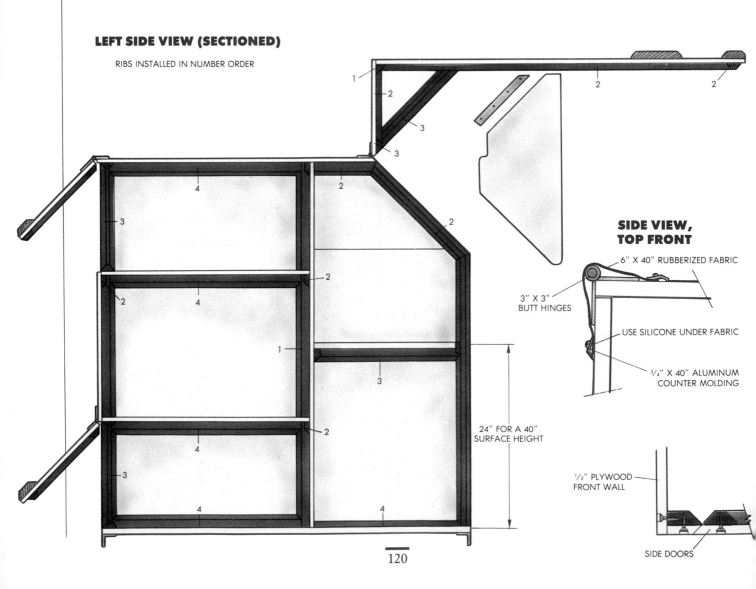

SIDE VIEW, TOP FRONT

6″ X 40″ RUBBERIZED FABRIC

3″ X 3″ BUTT HINGES

USE SILICONE UNDER FABRIC

¾″ X 40″ ALUMINUM COUNTER MOLDING

24″ FOR A 40″ SURFACE HEIGHT

½″ PLYWOOD FRONT WALL

SIDE DOORS

the bottoms being set in ¼" dadoes cut into the sides and ends, and the rear panels secured in ½" grooves made in the sides alone. The drawer fronts are rabbeted on all edges but the top, save for the lower one, which uses a dado groove 1¼" up from its bottom edge to allow that drawer to clear the ribs directly beneath it. Once the drawers are built and trial-fit, fasten the slides and install facer strips (relieved at the three slide locations) on either side.

The cool box, an optional feature, is simply a ½" plywood case sized to fit in the lower right opening once the 2"-thick polystyrene jacket is installed. Remember to trim the outer corners of the foam board to allow for the ribs, so the insulative panels will be square. The box opening is faced with beveled ribs, and the door is insulated with a block of foam trimmed at the edges to make a perfect seal. After the hinges and panel lock are installed, the foam board is glued to the door with upholstery adhesive; the door lock will hold the foam in place until the glue cures. (As an alternative to this time-consuming procedure, you might consider making the drawer compartment narrower and using the increased space to accommodate your own portable cooler.)

Directly above both lower compartments, the food preparation counter is covered with an easily cleaned surface that can be extended around the sides as a surround. Formica laminate can be glued to the plywood with contact cement, and the counter's exposed edge given a 1½" facer strip to be covered, as well. If you'd rather not clutter the counter with a cooking surface, the details of an external, removable angle-iron stove holder are shown in the illustrations.

The last major component needed to make your camper complete is the rear lift hatch, which is fastened to the upper rear edge with the four remaining butt hinges and equipped with the fabric hinge seal and two draw pull catches. The door is held up with a 37" length of ½" conduit fastened to the corner of the sidewall; a short section of ¾" pipe screwed into the side of the hatch provides a socket for that pole.

The remaining section of rubberized canvas is cut to form two trianglelike side curtains. Fasten their top edges to the hatch's corner gussets with strips of aluminum counter molding, and use snap fasteners at the bottom to secure the flaps to the body. Finish up by gluing some foam rubber padding to the inner surface of the door where it meets the drawer faces; it'll prevent the bins from sliding back and forth in transit.

Before dressing up your camping trailer with a coat of paint, you might want to carefully look over the outside surfaces, and especially the edges, for gaps, knotholes and cracks that would eventually allow water to enter the plywood's inner layers. Auto body putty, such as Bondo, makes an excellent filler for such imperfections because it's easily applied, seals well and sands to a smooth, paint-ready finish. Once you've painted your camper trailer, you'll be ready to pack up and hit the trail. But don't forget to check your state's licensing and insurance requirements before you roll; even the road to the wilderness has its rules.

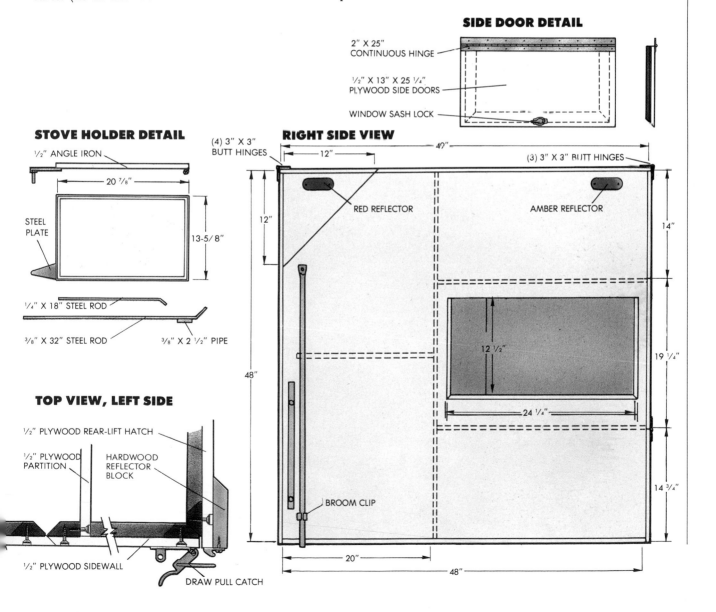

SIDE DOOR DETAIL

2" X 25" CONTINUOUS HINGE

½" X 13" X 25 ¼" PLYWOOD SIDE DOORS

WINDOW SASH LOCK

STOVE HOLDER DETAIL

½" ANGLE IRON

20 ⅞"

STEEL PLATE

13-5/8"

¼" X 18" STEEL ROD

⅜" X 32" STEEL ROD

⅜" X 2 ½" PIPE

RIGHT SIDE VIEW

(4) 3" X 3" BUTT HINGES

12"

48"

(3) 3" X 3" BUTT HINGES

RED REFLECTOR

AMBER REFLECTOR

12"

14"

12 ½"

19 ¼"

24 ¼"

14 ¾"

BROOM CLIP

20"

48"

TOP VIEW, LEFT SIDE

½" PLYWOOD REAR-LIFT HATCH

½" PLYWOOD PARTITION

HARDWOOD REFLECTOR BLOCK

½" PLYWOOD SIDEWALL

DRAW PULL CATCH

An Ice-Fishing Shack

When the frozen lakes call you to fish, this handy heated shelter will rise to the occasion.

Northern anglers can enjoy a special brand of sport fishing that those in warmer climates can't experience close to home. The lure of a frozen lake's wintry solitude draws untold people away from their hearths and onto the solid surfaces of countless bodies of water across the land to participate in the popular pastime of ice fishing.

Now, the old regulars know that being comfortable while hunkering over a hole in the ice is tantamount to being successful, simply because an alert angler is less likely to miss a strike. It follows, then, that a completely enclosed, weathertight structure equipped with a convenient and safe form of heat would make for more-successful outings than would the open-faced windbreaks that many fisherfolk pit against winter's cruelty.

Let's look at some of the benefits of the utilitarian design shown here. To begin, at 4' wide, 6' long and nearly 6½' tall, the structure is spacious enough to comfortably accommodate even two large adults for the eight- or 10-hour stints expected of it. Yet in three minutes' time it can be folded up into a 9"-high, 4' X 8' self-contained package that can be pulled along the ice on built-in runners or lifted into the back of a pickup truck with little trouble.

Inside, the shelter sports two sizable fold-down seats, removable floor-hatch covers, armrests, coat hooks and a window with a sliding shade. Furthermore, it's designed to externally vent a kerosene or propane heater. Finally, the hut's polyethylene tarp skin (which allows the shack to fold and reduces its weight and expense) is lined with a reflective plastic which helps insulate the shelter and retain interior warmth.

Tackling the Shack

A look at the accompanying illustrations will reveal that the structure is, in the main, made of ¼" and ⅝" plywood sheathing (AB or AC grade), 1 X 3 and 1 X 4 furring strips, a couple of 4'-long 1 X 5s, ⅛" metal stock, and hinges and other assorted hardware.

To aid in your understanding of how the project goes together, there are separate detail drawings of the two end walls and the roof components. Essentially, the shelter is just a tray on runners; the stove wall is designed to hinge down on top of the tray, with the window-and-door wall folding to cover it. The structural members that hold the walls steady and give the roof shape fit easily into the tray once the framework is dismantled, and the flexible sidewalls and roof fold neatly between the two end walls.

This explanation won't cover *every* facet of construction, since the illustrations are quite thorough in that regard. But there are a few areas in which you might appreciate additional help, and these follow in appropriate sequence.

To start, it's simplest to build the base first, complete with angle-iron runners (miter their ends), hatch covers and stops, and end boards with handles. Be true to the dimensions on the end boards, since the geometry

Lift the door wall and hold in place while raising the rear wall.

Next, slip the arm rails into their support sockets to hold the wall in position.

of the folding walls depends upon them. Don't install the two sideboards yet, because they have to cover the tarp layers, which are added later.

Next, assemble the window-and-door wall according to the plan. Again, pay attention to the dimensions given, and be especially careful around the door opening, since there must be a good seal at that point. For a really topnotch job, use carpenter's glue as well as ³/₄″ brick-siding nails to secure the furring strips to the ¹/₄″ plywood sheathing. The acrylic window is merely joined to the edges of its opening with silicone sealant, and the sliding plywood shade fits behind two narrow plywood tracks mounted to the cross braces. Finally, be sure to allow a ³/₄″ clearance above the roof rail hangers and the stops attached to them. And don't forget the stops, because they'll help keep the wall off the poly in transport.

The stove wall is assembled in much the same manner as its opposite, but its construction is even more critical because it must fit snugly beneath its mate. Pay close attention to the position and length of the dowel stops, which bear the weight of the wall when the shelter is folded. To ensure a safe and proper installation, don't cut the openings in the sheathing for the stove inlet and flue until you've acquired a heater and can set it in place. Note that the openings in the pie plates are just slightly larger than the rectangular downspout elbows used for venting and that the bottom of the inside plate faces inward, while the inside of the outside, or in-

let, plate faces outward. For safety's sake, mount the two-layer reflective aluminum shield behind the stove housing, and fabricate the folding heat shield as shown. Even though you'll be in the shelter when the heater's running, and thus able to keep an eye on it, these extra precautions provide a necessary margin of safety.

With both walls completed, you can concentrate on mounting them to their respective end boards using the larger surface hinges. Once that's done, assemble the arm rails and roof rails as illustrated, paying particular attention to the placement of the joist stops and the angle-iron brackets. Don't fasten the arm-rail supports or the wall brackets until you've trial-fitted the rail sets to see where the steel struts and the arm-rail shoulders will fall. Then drill the holes, and install the bolts that hold the metal parts together. (The wall-bracket bolts are fixed in place with locking nuts tightened against their shoulders.) The two roof joists should have a symmetrical pitch cut into their upper surfaces, and 1″ X 2″ notches included in their lower corners.

At this point, the structural portion of the shelter is complete. To finish the project, you'll need to install the three layers of plastic sheeting as follows: First, drape the clear poly inner liner over the erected structure so the material is slightly loose and all the wall edges are covered. Staple the plastic at appropriate locations to hold it in place, then trim it if necessary, leaving a bit of border for fold-over. Next, cut your roll of reflective

film into three 30″ X 208″ sections, and lay them over the poly so they overlap at the inside edges and meet the walls. Finally, place the outer layer of reinforced tarpaulin over the film, and fold over the edges and bottom to create a hem. Again, use some staples to hold it temporarily in place.

The last step is to secure the layers of plastic to the edges of the walls with carefully trimmed counter edging held in place with ³/₄″ oval-head screws. These molding strips should be fastened at the top and sides, terminating about 3″ from the lower ends of the walls. When this is done, the two sideboards can be installed, and your shelter is complete.

Flagship of the Frozen Fleet

Without a doubt, you'll be the envy of the lake the minute you unfold your shelter and start your heater cooking. Though the hut has not been tested in subzero weather, it's certainly capable of maintaining at least a subsistence-level interior temperature even in severe cold, and probably will be more than adequate under more moderate conditions.

Finally, one word of caution: Before you set up your shelter on the ice, make absolutely certain that the frozen surface is thick and *solid* enough to support the 245-pound shed—plus you and a friend. And be sure to check your state's licensing requirements before boring your hole. That could save you from a fine—and from a *very* bad day. Happy angling!

Place the two roof joists between the rails, and slide them between their stops.

Now step inside and position the roof rails between their supports at the upper corners.

Finally, secure the walls to the roof rails with the four steel struts.

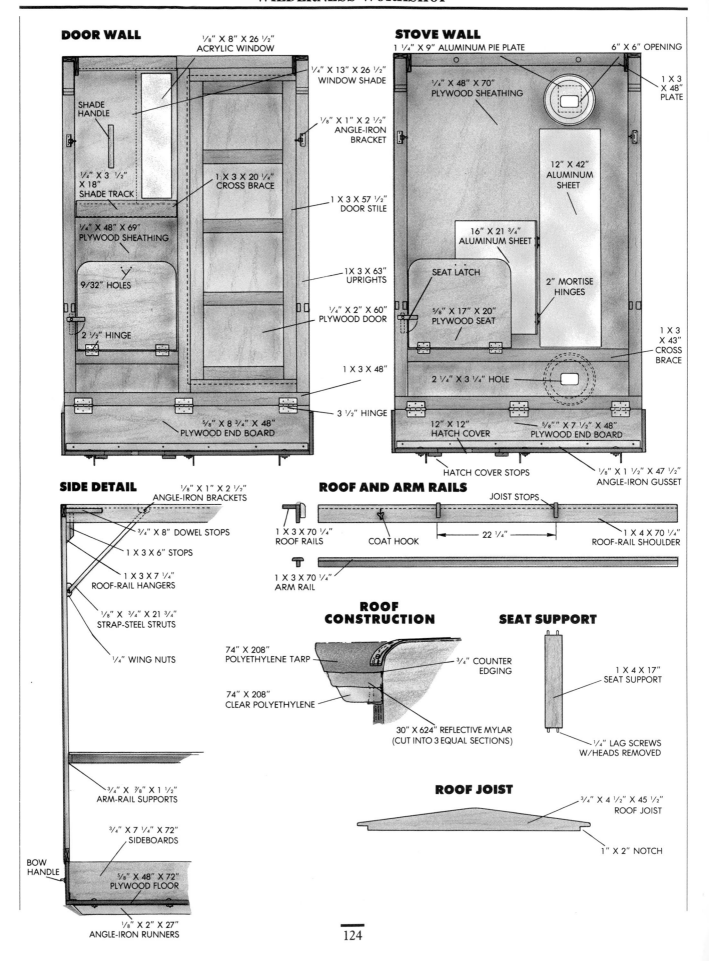

DOOR WALL

⅛" X 8" X 26 ½" ACRYLIC WINDOW

¼" X 13" X 26 ½" WINDOW SHADE

SHADE HANDLE

⅛" X 1" X 2 ½" ANGLE-IRON BRACKET

¼" X 3 ½" X 18" SHADE TRACK

1 X 3 X 20 ¼" CROSS BRACE

1 X 3 X 57 ½" DOOR STILE

¼" X 48" X 69" PLYWOOD SHEATHING

9/32" HOLES

1 X 3 X 63" UPRIGHTS

¼" X 2" X 60" PLYWOOD DOOR

2 ½" HINGE

1 X 3 X 48"

3 ½" HINGE

⅝" X 8 ¾" X 48" PLYWOOD END BOARD

STOVE WALL

1 ¼" X 9" ALUMINUM PIE PLATE

6" X 6" OPENING

¼" X 48" X 70" PLYWOOD SHEATHING

1 X 3 X 48" PLATE

12" X 42" ALUMINUM SHEET

16" X 21 ¾" ALUMINUM SHEET

SEAT LATCH

2" MORTISE HINGES

⅝" X 17" X 20" PLYWOOD SEAT

1 X 3 X 43" CROSS BRACE

2 ¼" X 3 ¼" HOLE

3 ½" HINGE

12" X 12" HATCH COVER

⅝" X 7 ½" X 48" PLYWOOD END BOARD

HATCH COVER STOPS

⅛" X 1 ½" X 47 ½" ANGLE-IRON GUSSET

SIDE DETAIL

⅛" X 1" X 2 ½" ANGLE-IRON BRACKETS

¾" X 8" DOWEL STOPS

1 X 3 X 6" STOPS

1 X 3 X 7 ¼" ROOF-RAIL HANGERS

⅛" X ¾" X 21 ¾" STRAP-STEEL STRUTS

¼" WING NUTS

¾" X ⅞" X 1 ½" ARM-RAIL SUPPORTS

¾" X 7 ¼" X 72" SIDEBOARDS

BOW HANDLE

⅝" X 48" X 72" PLYWOOD FLOOR

⅛" X 2" X 27" ANGLE-IRON RUNNERS

ROOF AND ARM RAILS

JOIST STOPS

1 X 3 X 70 ¼" ROOF RAILS

COAT HOOK

22 ¼"

1 X 4 X 70 ¼" ROOF-RAIL SHOULDER

1 X 3 X 70 ¼" ARM RAIL

ROOF CONSTRUCTION

74" X 208" POLYETHYLENE TARP

¾" COUNTER EDGING

74" X 208" CLEAR POLYETHYLENE

30" X 624" REFLECTIVE MYLAR (CUT INTO 3 EQUAL SECTIONS)

SEAT SUPPORT

1 X 4 X 17" SEAT SUPPORT

¼" LAG SCREWS W/HEADS REMOVED

ROOF JOIST

¾" X 4 ½" X 45 ½" ROOF JOIST

1" X 2" NOTCH

The Incredible Beanbag Tripod

Give your camera a rest.

The lowly beanbag hasn't a leg to stand on, but that doesn't keep it from being a superb photographic "tripod." It's sturdier, lighter, simpler to use and more versatile than most three-legged support systems, and if you make it yourself, it costs next to nothing.

Professional photographers have long known that one of the reasons their photos are consistently superior to the snapshots taken by amateurs is the pros' use of solid camera-mounting systems; too many novice shutterbugs are willing to risk the clarity of their images to shaky hands and wobbly knees.

But by simply filling a home-sewn cloth sack with dried grain, even the lowest-budgeted photographer can "support" his or her camera habit in style. A beanbag can be poked, pounded and fluffed to form a comfortable rest for just about any camera-and-lens combination you can come up with, and will anchor that equipment to odd shapes and inclines seemingly steep enough to defy gravity.

A beanbag placed on the ground gives an ant's-eye view of wildflowers, mice, mushrooms, insects and other terrain-hugging forms of life. This down-to-earth perspective adds an interesting new dimension to any slide show or photograph album—and dollars to your income if you're a pro.

For shooting landscapes—when it's necessary to sacrifice shutter speed in favor of in-

creased depth of field—haul out a beanbag, plop it firmly down on top of a fence post, stump or rock, seat your camera securely in the bag, and squeeze off dead-sharp shots with shutter speeds as slow as two or three seconds.

Because this homemade photo accessory supports so much of the bottom surface of a camera and lens (rather than balancing all the weight at a single point as a tripod screw does), it's often actually sturdier than a traditional three-legged stand. Wind, a slight tremor of the shutter release finger and even the movement of the camera's own mirror can blur a slow shot taken atop a tripod. That seldom happens on a beanbag.

The trick is to snuggle your camera securely into the lump of beans (or whatever you're using in their place), then press down firmly so that the instrument is comfortably seated in its rest. Once you master the system (which takes the average photographer all of two minutes), you'll discover that it's possible to make successful slow-shutter shots without employing a cable release.

Occasionally you'll need to anchor your camera someplace where there are no horizontal (or even semihorizontal) supports. With a beanbag, you can create a support by holding the pouch against a wall, tree or whatever surface is handy, then resting your camera on the bag. That leaves one hand free to manipulate the instrument. Of course, this particular variation of the beanbag system can't be called steady as a rock, but if you take a deep breath, exhale half of it, relax and squeeze the shutter, you should be able to make top-quality exposures at shutter speeds down to one-fifteenth of a second or so.

Beanbags, in addition to substituting for tripods, can also be used in conjunction with them. Beanbag-wise professionals sometimes lay bean sacks on *top* of cameras mounted on sturdy tripods. That extra mass of weight atop the camera absorbs the minuscule flicker of shutter-induced movement, allowing for absolute steadiness when professional-quality results are a must.

Anyone with the coordination necessary to use a camera can make a beanbag tripod,

either by hand or with a sewing machine.

The fabric you use for the sack should be nonabrasive, tightly woven and tough enough to withstand hard knocks and rugged use without ripping. Denim is perfect; a section of old jeans leg is ideal, and is half-finished before you even touch it. Just cut a piece of leg to the length you want your beanbag to be, sew one end shut, fill the resulting pouch loosely with the "beans" of your choice, and sew the top shut. (For added strength, the seams should be double- or even triple-stitched.)

Naturally, the dimensions—and to some extent, shape—of your beanbag will be determined by the photo equipment you'll use with it: A tiny rangefinder camera will rest comfortably on a 3″ X 6″ pant's pocket filled to a thickness of less than an inch; a massive 500-mm lens attached to a motorized 35-mm SLR (single lens reflex) camera body might require a large bag as much as six inches thick. If you'll be resting your makeshift tripod over the windowsill of your car or truck, give it some floppy "legs" to hang down either side of the door. And when maximum stability is your goal, think *big*.

For added versatility, you can make an "inflatable" beanbag by sewing a zipper into one end of the sack. (Plastic zippers are less durable than metal, but they're also less likely to mar expensive and delicate photo equipment.) To assure that you don't lose your beans at an inopportune moment, make several extra passes over the ends and corners of the zipper with strong thread.

This closable opening will let you pack a virtually weightless and bulkless wad of cloth deep into the woods or to the top of a mountain. There, you can fatten the slack sack with wild nuts, stream gravel, sand, dirt or whatever natural materials are at hand, and have an instant tripod for that "I've been there and I can prove it with pictures" photo session.

If you carry your zippered sack into the woods prestuffed with nuts, seeds, popcorn, gorp, jelly beans or anything else edible, you can lunch on your beanbag to help fuel the return hike.

Once the sack is sewn and ready . . .

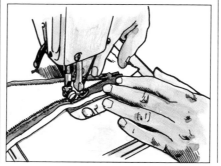

. . . fill it up and start shooting.

There aren't too many homesites in North America that aren't within easy driving distance of a good-sized body of water. So it's a safe bet that those of you who *don't* own a boat have had, over past summers, occasions to wish you did. The little beauty shown here is fairly easy to construct; this brightly painted model was finished in four days by its two designers, and most of that time was spent waiting for glue to dry!

Your first task will be to collect two 4' X 8' sheets of ¼" marine plywood, about 160 feet of ¾" X 1⅛" flexible, clear-grained hardwood, a foot or so of ¾" X 8" hardwood for the motor-mount brace (you'll measure it for exact fit later), about 500 No. 6 X ¾" brass wood screws, two dozen No. 8 X 1½" brass wood screws (nickle-plated fasteners can also be used) and a supply of plastic resin glue.

To begin, scribe a center line down each sheet of plywood (it'll serve as a reference point for several of the measurements to come). Then go on to mark the cutting lines for one of the boat's sides. To do so, select a long, straight-grained strip of 1⅛" X ¾" hardwood to use as a straightedge. (Keep this strip separate, because the same one should be used later to draw the curves for the boat's bottom.) Clamp its center to one of your plywood sheets, placing the clamp about ⅛" in from the edge at a point 3'6½" from one end (that end will be the boat's stern). Then, with a friend's help, bend the hardwood into a bow, clamping it so that its outer edges intersect the edges of the plywood 3" from the corner in the stern and 5⅛" from the corner in the bow. With that done, scribe a line along the outer surface of the hardwood strip.

Next, you'll want to draw the upper edge of the boat's side. To do so, mark the clamp positions as in the accompanying illustration, then—using a bar clamp positioned 3'6½" from the stern end—secure the hardwood strip with its outer edge 1'3¼" from the edge of the plywood, clamp the ends of the strip as marked, and trace the line. Now mark the angles of the bow and stern as shown, cut out the side, and flop it over to use as a pattern for the boat's other side. (It's best to draw in the patterns for the bow and stern transoms, allowing room for the four corner pieces, before doing any more cutting, to make sure all of the components will fit on the one plywood sheet.)

Now, going to the other plywood sheet, use your hardwood strip "ruler" to draw the boat's bottom, employing the same bend-and-trace technique used when drawing the sides. Then cut out the bottom, leaving a surplus of 1½" to 2" around the pattern on the sides and at the bow (it'll be trimmed away later).

With that done, you can cut out the second side and the transoms and also draw and cut out the central support frame. Then glue and screw the hardwood support strips, and the cut-to-fit motor-mount brace, to the front and rear transoms and the central support, using No. 6 X ¾" wood screws set at 3" intervals. (The upper support strips for the front and rear transoms will have to be trimmed to match the angles of the bow and stern. To do so, simply use a sliding bevel to measure the appropriate angle on the bottom panel—use the pattern lines, not the "hem"—then set your saw's miter gauge to that angle, and trim away.)

In the next step, use glue and 3"-spaced No. 6 X ¾" wood screws to secure the two sides to the central support frame, which should be positioned 3'6½" from the boat's stern. Then swing in the sides and, starting with the stern transom (you might want to loop a rope around the two sides at a point near the front to keep them from spreading too much while you do this), glue and screw the sides to the stern transom support frame—again setting the screws at 3" intervals. Now go on to secure the sides to the bow transom in the same manner, and let the glue dry for its full recommended period of time.

At this point, we come to the only really awkward part of the construction process. After the glue has dried, you'll have to beg, borrow or buy at least *20* clamps to secure the hardwood support strips to the bottom edges of the two sides. Cut the strips to length, leaving a 6" overhang on each end, and then start each one—at the stern—by running a No. 8 X 1½" wood screw through it and into the transom support frame. Then—working with a helper and using glue and ¾" wood screws set at 3" intervals—bend, fasten and clamp both strips in place a bit at a time. (A brace and bit, and predrilled pilot holes, will make this task go quickly.) Secure the far ends of each strip with 1½" screws, and when the adhesive has thoroughly dried, trim the ends of the strips, and plane them flush with the bottom of the plywood.

When the next step's completed, your boat will begin to *look* like a water-worthy craft. Now's the time to invert the sides-and-transoms assembly and to glue and screw the bottom in place. Once that's done, you can go on to install the bottom support strips, using the overlapping bottom "hem" to clamp them in place as you glue and screw them down (these ¾" screws are inserted from the *inside* of the boat).

Later, after waiting for the previously added pieces to dry in place, you can trim off the excess plywood on the bottom. At this point, flip the boat over and attach the gun-

A simple boat will greatly increase your opportunities for outdoor fun. And you can build this one with inexpensive materials.

It'll take a little time and care to finish this boat, but after that you'll enjoy "smooth sailing."

nels (top support strips) to the upper edge of each side, employing the multiple clamps to attach the two gunnels simultaneously as you did when installing the lower side support strips.

And, finally, it's time for the finishing touches. Take your scrap of plywood, and using the sliding bevel to get the angles right, draw and cut out the four corner braces. Secure strips of hardwood brace to these at the points at which they'll be fastened to the boat. Bring the sliding bevel into play again, this time to measure the slope of the boat's sides and transoms at the appropriate points;

A Basic (and Beautiful) Boat

then set your miter gauge to the indicated angle, and rip the support strips before gluing and screwing them into place.

You'll have to use the sliding bevel once more to fit the bow seat support in place; then run a strip of hardwood from it, allowing the strip to rest on the central support

brace, to mark the correct height for the stern seat support. With that done, go on to assemble the hardwood-strip seat as shown in the detail drawing, leaving off one of the side braces so you'll be able to paint the interior of the boat and slip some polystyrene flotation blocks beneath the seat. (Simply attach

the remaining side brace to hold the foam in position.)

The skiff should be painted with at least three coats of urethane floor enamel (about one gallon total), and a primer coat of Thompson's Water Seal (or a similar product) would certainly be a worthwhile investment.

Once the paint has dried and you've positioned your oarlocks (they work best when the holes are centered 7¹/₄" behind the center support brace), grab a pair of oars and a life preserver, head for the nearest lake, pond, bay or slow-moving river, and discover, as Water Rat noted in *The Wind in the Willows*, that "there is *nothing*—absolutely nothing—half so much worth doing as simply messing about in boats."

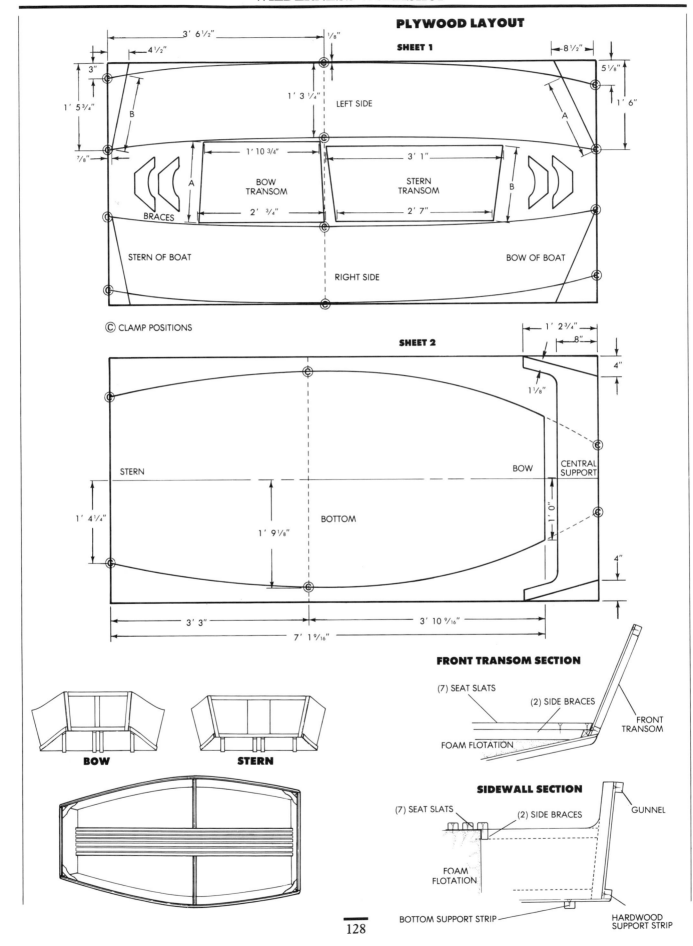

PLYWOOD LAYOUT

SHEET 1

3' 6½"

4½"

1/8"

8½"

5⅛"

3"

LEFT SIDE

1' 5¾"

B

1' 3¼"

A

1' 6"

7/8"

A

1' 10¾"

3' 1"

BOW TRANSOM

STERN TRANSOM

BRACES

2' ¾"

2' 7"

B

STERN OF BOAT

BOW OF BOAT

RIGHT SIDE

Ⓒ CLAMP POSITIONS

SHEET 2

1' 3¾"

8"

4"

1⅛"

STERN

BOW

CENTRAL SUPPORT

1' 4¼"

BOTTOM

1' 9⅛"

1' 0"

4"

3' 3"

3' 10 9/16"

7' 1 9/16"

BOW

STERN

FRONT TRANSOM SECTION

(7) SEAT SLATS

(2) SIDE BRACES

FRONT TRANSOM

FOAM FLOTATION

SIDEWALL SECTION

(7) SEAT SLATS

(2) SIDE BRACES

GUNNEL

FOAM FLOTATION

BOTTOM SUPPORT STRIP

HARDWOOD SUPPORT STRIP

An Instant Sailboat

Just add a spritsail.

Clamp this simple spritsail onto any small, square-sterned rowboat or dinghy (such as the build-your-own "basic boat" featured on page 126), and you'll have a fine little wind cruiser! The rig, though admittedly not quite as efficient (*or* complicated) as those on "real" sailboats, performs nicely on a broad reach, and with a good breeze can even bring a boat around to head up at about 30° off the wind. Moreover, since the mast, boom and rudder work as a single unit, even a novice can readily master the sail's operation.

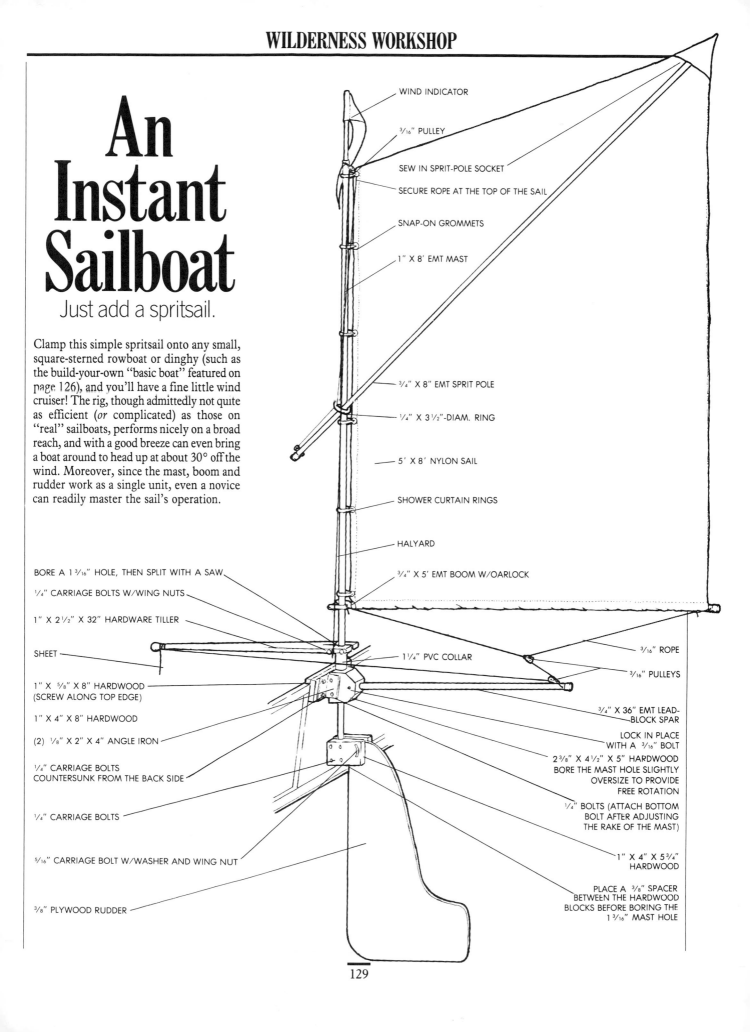

WIND INDICATOR

³/₁₆" PULLEY

SEW IN SPRIT-POLE SOCKET

SECURE ROPE AT THE TOP OF THE SAIL

SNAP-ON GROMMETS

1" X 8' EMT MAST

³/₄" X 8" EMT SPRIT POLE

¹/₄" X 3¹/₂"-DIAM. RING

5' X 8' NYLON SAIL

SHOWER CURTAIN RINGS

HALYARD

³/₄" X 5' EMT BOOM W/OARLOCK

BORE A 1 ³/₁₆" HOLE, THEN SPLIT WITH A SAW

¹/₄" CARRIAGE BOLTS W/WING NUTS

1" X 2¹/₂" X 32" HARDWARE TILLER

SHEET

1" X ⁵/₈" X 8" HARDWOOD (SCREW ALONG TOP EDGE)

1" X 4" X 8" HARDWOOD

(2) ¹/₈" X 2" X 4" ANGLE IRON

¹/₄" CARRIAGE BOLTS COUNTERSUNK FROM THE BACK SIDE

¹/₄" CARRIAGE BOLTS

⁵/₁₆" CARRIAGE BOLT W/WASHER AND WING NUT

³/₈" PLYWOOD RUDDER

1¹/₄" PVC COLLAR

³/₁₆" ROPE

³/₁₆" PULLEYS

³/₄" X 36" EMT LEAD-BLOCK SPAR

LOCK IN PLACE WITH A ³/₁₆" BOLT

2 ³/₈" X 4¹/₂" X 5" HARDWOOD BORE THE MAST HOLE SLIGHTLY OVERSIZE TO PROVIDE FREE ROTATION

¹/₄" BOLTS (ATTACH BOTTOM BOLT AFTER ADJUSTING THE RAKE OF THE MAST)

1" X 4" X 5³/₄" HARDWOOD

PLACE A ³/₈" SPACER BETWEEN THE HARDWOOD BLOCKS BEFORE BORING THE 1 ³/₁₆" MAST HOLE

A Pair of Tree Stands

For better hunting or wildlife photography, just climb a tree.

People who appreciate the outdoors realize that it's necessary to be *unobtrusive* in order to best enjoy its appeal; those who are least conspicuous are the ones most likely to view nature's surprisingly busy agenda. To a hunter or wildlife photographer, this frequently means picking an advantageous spot in the woods and simply staying put until something of interest comes along. And, for a number of reasons, the best spot is often one that's a dozen or more feet off the ground, where the lanes of sight are less obstructed, the view is nearly panoramic and the possibility that wildlife will notice human scent is reduced considerably.

The two tree stands detailed here can both provide efficient observation or shooting platforms. One is a stationary stand that folds flat, weighs 20 pounds and can be hauled up a tree with a line or positioned with the help of a ladder. Once raised, it's chained, top and bottom, around the trunk of the tree and secured with lever binders that draw the coils tight. The foot platform measures a comfortable 23″ X 31″, and the seat is contoured to accommodate the thighs. The metal parts are lightweight extruded aluminum, available from a fabricator's supply house, but steel angle and channel can be used as an alternative if weight is not a factor.

Since installing the stationary model is enough of a chore to convince most people to leave the stand in place for an extended period once it's secured to a tree, it's best suited for use on private property rather than public lands (where, in most cases, tree stands must be removed daily). Therefore, we've also illustrated a two-piece climbing version that has staggered girths that grip the tree trunk when the platforms are in a hor-

To use our climbing tree stand, lift the seat as high as you can, hook your feet into the straps, and pull the platform up.

Continue to raise the seat, and then pull the base up after you until you've reached the desired height.

Always use a safety belt when on a tree stand. And use care not to damage the tree that hosts your perch.

STATIONARY STAND

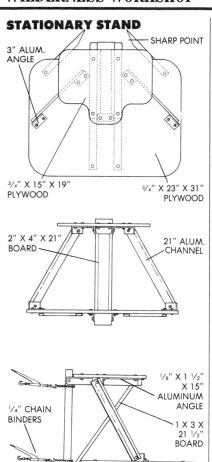

SHARP POINT

3" ALUM. ANGLE

¾" X 15" X 19" PLYWOOD

¾" X 23" X 31" PLYWOOD

2" X 4" X 21" BOARD

21" ALUM. CHANNEL

⅛" X 1 ½" X 15" ALUMINUM ANGLE

1 X 3 X 21 ½" BOARD

¼" CHAIN BINDERS

¼" X 60" PROOF COIL CHAIN

24" ALUM. ANGLE

izontal position. To use it, a climber merely has to stand on the installed foot platform with the seat section dug in overhead, then pull him- or herself up—using the built-in handles—while lifting the lower platform with the foot loops provided. Once the bottom section is locked in its new position, the process is repeated until the desired height is achieved.

The framework on this model is ⅛" X 1" angle iron, which should easily support an average-sized individual. If necessary, however, feel free to upgrade the stand by using larger sections of angle. And, of course, check all of the components for signs of wear before taking to the trees. Eight pairs of mounting holes allow the girths to be adjusted to suit the diameter of the trunk you choose to climb, and nylon utility straps help secure the grip once you've attained the height you want.

Before you start your trek into the wilderness, keep these points in mind: Never climb a tree while carrying a firearm or any sharp or pointed equipment that could injure you in a fall; instead, pull your gear up once you're perched. Always wear a safety belt and extension strap when using a tree stand, no matter how comfortable you feel with heights. And please be considerate of the forest that's hosting your visit; choose a tree that'll require little or no trimming, so your impact on it will be minimal.

CLIMBING STAND

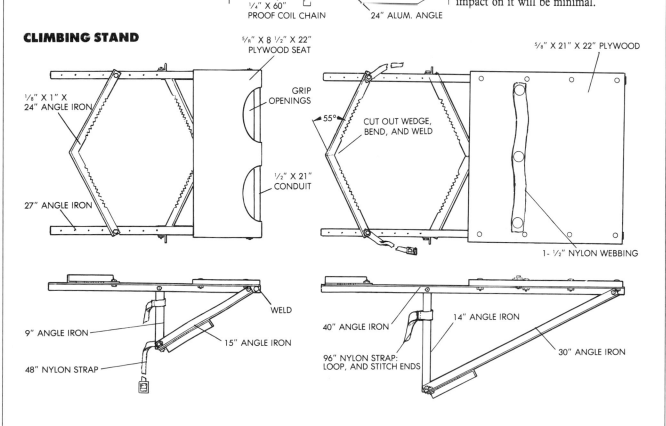

⅝" X 8 ½" X 22" PLYWOOD SEAT

⅝" X 21" X 22" PLYWOOD

⅛" X 1" X 24" ANGLE IRON

GRIP OPENINGS

55°

CUT OUT WEDGE, BEND, AND WELD

27" ANGLE IRON

½" X 21" CONDUIT

1- ½" NYLON WEBBING

9" ANGLE IRON

WELD

15" ANGLE IRON

48" NYLON STRAP

40" ANGLE IRON

14" ANGLE IRON

96" NYLON STRAP: LOOP, AND STITCH ENDS

30" ANGLE IRON

PART FIVE

Backcountry Lore

The great outdoors
is seen as threatening
only by those who
dare it unprepared.

Survival Kits

To augment, not replace, your wilderness skills

Anyone who frequently, or even occasionally, hikes, camps or cross-country skis any distance from civilization should know how to live through a wilderness emergency. Many of the survival skills involved are presented throughout this book, but a small kit containing survival necessities—to be carried on *every* outing—is a vital accessory. To that end, here are five survival kits that are compact and light enough to be carried easily. Four kits were supplied by America's leading authorities on wilderness living, and the fifth was assembled by several outdoor experts at *Mother Earth News*.

When assembling your own survival kit, you'll want to include those items that are in *all* the experts' lists. As for the rest, choose to suit the conditions prevalent in the backwoods areas you most often frequent.

Outward Bound USA

Ian R. Wade, of Outward Bound USA (384 Field Point Rd., Greenwich, CT 06830), reports that his goal in designing a survival kit was to "keep it small and light so it would actually be carried." Ian spent $46 assembling a 1 pound 9 ounce kit that's wrapped in a large, black-plastic garbage bag. The bundle is compact enough (2″ X 6″ X 9″) to fit into a large pocket in a jacket or pants, and includes the following:

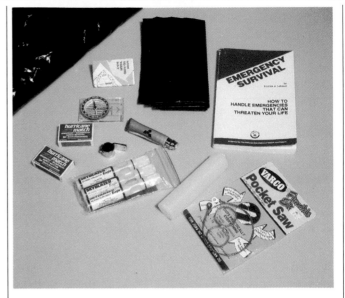

● 1 copy of *Emergency Survival: How to Handle Emergencies That Can Threaten Your Life* by Charles A. Lehman (Technical Book Co., 2056 Westwood Blvd., Los Angeles, CA 90025)—for information to help a person make sensible decisions in a survival situation
● 1 large black-plastic garbage bag (in addition to the one the kit is in)—for shelter from wind and rain
● 2 boxes of wind- and waterproof matches
● 1 flexible steel (wire) pocket saw—for cutting firewood and constructing shelter
● 1 large candle
● 1 folding knife
● 1 Silva compass (with instructions for use)
● 1 metal whistle
● 3 small, red aerial signal flares (with launchers)

Boulder Outdoor Survival School

Doug Nelson, former director of the Boulder Outdoor Survival School (P.O. Box 905, Rexburg, ID 83440), puts "the will to live" at the top of his survival necessities list.

"So often," Doug explains, "our self-confidence is derived from external objects. But objects can be taken away from us. Consequently, the will to survive a life-threatening situation must come from inside."

Therefore, Doug stresses that experience in survival skills is probably the most valuable "kit" that an outdoorsperson could hope for. Practice can produce the needed self-confidence.

But there's no denying that a few essentials can go a long way in assisting that will to survive, so Doug put together the following quite comprehensive kit:

● 2 packets of Pripps Plus powdered drink mix—for energy and to replace body salts
● 6 bouillon cubes—for improving the taste of water and to replace salts
● 1 6-foot length of twisted wire fishing leader—for fishing and for making snares
● 6 size-12 snelled fishhooks with leaders
● 1 small, clear-plastic fishing float
● 1 dry fly—for fishing and for catching frogs
● 30 small split-shot sinkers
● 1 sliding sinker
● 1 inexpensive aluminum canteen
● 50 iodine water-purification tablets
● 2 small candles—for illumination, starting fires and signaling for help
● 1 Cyalume Light-stick—for illumination and signaling
● 1 vinyl poncho—for a raincoat, shelter, rainwater collection, extra warmth and signaling
● 1 Space Blanket–type foil blanket—for signaling and warmth
● 2 boxes of wind- and waterproof matches—for lighting fires and signaling
● 1 army surplus chemical-heat bar—for starting fires
● 1 fuel-tablet stove—for heating food and boiling water for purification
● 6 compressed chemi-

cal-fuel tablets—for stove fuel and starting fires
● 1 carbon steel multi-bladed (including fork and spoon) knife—for cutting and as a striker for starting fires with flint and steel
● 1 Sierra-type camper's cup—for drinking, eating, cooking and sending signals
● 1 multiuse plastic canister—for water-proof storage of matches (includes built-in whistle, mirror, flint striker and compass)
● 1 packet of toilet paper in a damp-proof pouch
● 1 50-foot length of nylon parachute cord—for fastening and building
● 1 small waterproof plastic container—for any important personal medications
● 1 packet of plasticized survival cards—printed with information on wilderness survival and first aid
● 1 small first-aid kit

Doug's kit cost $47.13 to assemble (the price includes a durable nylon belt pack that houses the works), weighs 3 pounds 7 ounces and measures 5″ X 5″ X 11″.

National Outdoor Leadership School

Web Webster, of the National Outdoor Leadership School (P.O. Box AA, Lander, WY 82520), says, "My intent was to build a kit using, as much as possible, items that can be found around the house." Consequently, he was able to assemble his kit for only $24. Web believes in the usefulness of these items but cautions that "remaining calm and rational are the main ingredients for staying alive and healthy in a wilderness survival situation."

The National Outdoor Leadership School kit is housed in a three-pound coffee can (total weight, including the can, is 3 pounds 11 ounces) and contains (in order of importance as ranked by Webster):

- 1 Space Blanket–type foil blanket
- 1 box of waterproof matches
- 1 multibladed knife
- 1 3-pound coffee can—for housing survival kit items, collecting and carrying water and food (berries, nuts, etc.), and use as a hobo stove (the can would, of course, require that the kit be carried in a backpack, but its items *could* be stored in a more convenient belt pouch)
- 1 small roll of strapping tape—for first aid, repairs and shelter building
- 3 large plastic garbage bags
- 2 smaller plastic bags—for water storage and use as vapor-barrier socks
- 1 large candle
- 1 10-inch-long, coarse-toothed hacksaw blade
- 1 50-foot length of nylon parachute cord
- 1 small (partial) roll of toilet paper
- 4 granola bars—for energy
- 2 packets of instant soup powder—for salt and to make water more palatable
- 4 packets of powdered spiced cider mix—to make water more palatable
- 15 tea bags—to make water more palatable
- 1 waterproof plastic container with several dozen matches

- 1 pencil—for taking or leaving notes
- 6 3X5 cards—for taking or leaving notes
- 1 small stainless-steel camper's mirror—for signaling
- 1 7-ounce can of

Sterno-brand canned heat—for heating water, cooking and starting fires

The Tracker

"The trouble with survival kits," cautions Tom Brown, Jr. (The Tracker, P.O. Box 173, Asbury, NJ 08802), "is that people too often rely on them to replace essential survival skills, rather than merely to augment them. Before carrying any survival kit into the woods, first be sure you know how to use the items it contains."

The Tracker's low-priced ($10) kit is stored in a waterproof 4" X 5" X 6" belt bag and weighs a mere 1 pound 2 ounces.

- 1 large plastic garbage bag—for rain protection and to serve as a ground cloth. Tom says that while a Space Blanket would do both jobs better, the plastic bag is sufficient if the survivor knows how to build a debris hut.
- 1 solar still (consisting of 6 feet of plastic tubing, a 3' X 3' sheet of heavy plastic and a metal cup for collecting the condensed water)
- 1 Bic disposable lighter
- 1 small candle
- 1 50-foot length of nylon cord—for making a bow-drill fire-starting apparatus, attaching spearheads to saplings and repairing equipment
- 1 multibladed knife
- 1 60-foot length of 80-pound-test nylon fishing line—for fishing and making snares
- 12 assorted fishhooks
- 1 compass
- 1 plastic whistle
- 1 bottle of chlorine water-purification tablets

Mother Earth News

The staff of *Mother Earth News* pooled their collective wilderness experience, purloined a few choice ideas from the authorities who put together the other packs shown here and came up with Mother's Wilderness Survival Kit. While the components cost more—$50—than those in the other kits, the whole shebang fits into a compact (3" X 6" X 8") belt pouch and weighs only 1 pound 7 ounces.

- 1 heavy-duty Velcro-sealed waterproof plastic pouch—for waterproof storage of small kit items and for dipping up and storing water
- 2 boxes of waterproof matches
- 5 fishhooks in assorted sizes
- 5 "matchstick" lead sinker strips
- 1 small rabbit-fur fishing jig—alluring to most species of fish
- 1 candle, wrapped with 30 feet of strapping tape for equipment repairs
- 1 pencil stub, wrapped with 20 feet of strapping tape for equipment repairs
- 1 small, lock-blade folding knife (we assume that any outdoorsperson will carry a better knife *outside* the kit)
- 1 ceramic insulator—for knife-sharpening—wrapped with 30 feet of 50-pound-test Dacron fishing line (ceramic insulators can often be purchased for pennies at hardware and electrical supply outlets)
- 1 plastic signal whistle
- 2 packets of instant coffee
- 12 aspirin (in a small, sealed plastic bag)
- 1 waterproof container of personal prescriptions
- 1 straw-type water purifier
- 1 solar still kit—consisting of 6 feet of plastic tubing, a 3' X 3' sheet of heavy clear plastic and a Sierra-type camper's cup
- 2 Space Blanket–type foil blankets—strapping-taped along three edges to form a make-

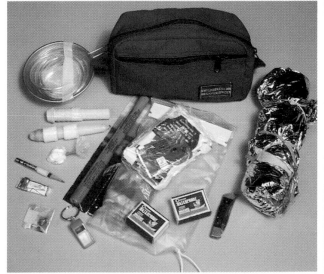

do sleeping bag or shelter, with a collection of Tom Brown, Jr.'s survival articles, photocopied from back issues of *Mother Earth News*, folded up inside the waterproof bundle of blankets.

Giardiasis in Paradise

The microorganism with the smiling face might be an unwelcome souvenir of your next excursion.

Giardiasis is sometimes called backpacker's fever (because backwoods hikers catch it from drinking untreated water) or beaver fever (because these large rodents often carry and spread the disease as they travel between aquatic environments). But giardiasis is not limited to remote waters. It's now the most common parasitic disease of humans in the U.S., and it's fast becoming a national concern. It is, in fact, worldwide—present in all climates from the equator to the poles—and a major cause of traveler's diarrhea. (So many tourists have returned from the Soviet Union—to cite one example—with giardiasis that another name for the disease is the trotskys.)

So what do you do about it? How can you keep from getting giardiasis or get rid of a case you do contract? To answer these questions, you first need to understand what both the organism and the ailment are.

Smiling Faces

Giardia lamblia is a microscopic, one-celled protozoan that can exist in two different forms: one, a dormant, tough-walled cyst; the other, a mobile, vegetative trophozoite that can swim around with four pairs of flagella and adhere to your intestinal lining with a sucking disk. The trophozoite is very distinctive (see illustration). Its two nuclei and organelles make it look like a happy face—a very tiny happy face: It's only 10 to 12 microns long by seven to 10 microns wide. About 8,000 trophozoites can fit on the head of a pin.

The ovoid cyst is less jovial-looking, but it has a sterner function: This form helps the parasite survive hard times. The cyst can live for four days in 98.6°F (body temperature)

water and more than two months at 39°F (for example, in the bottom of a winter pond). And taken into a host with food or drink, the hard-walled, dormant invader can survive the acid digestive juices of its host's stomach.

Once the cyst gets to the safety of the intestines, its tough wall breaks down and it "hatches" into a trophozoite, which attaches itself to the intestinal mucosa. There the little giardia feeds and multiplies (by simple fission), producing enormous numbers of progeny, which are passed as cysts in the feces, enhancing the organism's chances of getting to another host. (One estimate places the number at 14 billion protozoa per defecation!)

Giardiasis

The most surprising thing about giardiasis is the variation in host response to infection, which covers the spectrum from no symptoms at all to serious disease. Many people who carry giardiasis appear to be completely asymptomatic. That probably explains why the pathogenic nature of the organism has been recognized only in the last 40 years, even though the giardia itself has been known for 300 years—since the inventor of the microscope, Anton van Leeuwenhoek, spied the smiling trophozoite in 1681. (*Giardia lamblia* was previously thought to be a harmless commensal resident of the gut, merely "eating at the same table" as its host.)

Those who do become ill don't experience symptoms until the trophozoites have multiplied enough to have effects; this incubation period is usually around six to 20 days. The malady then experienced varies from mild—but often recurring—diarrhea to severely debilitating malabsorption and weight loss. The results can include painful illness and weakness, dehydration, lactase and vitamin deficiencies and electrolyte imbalance. The Pandora's box of complaints goes on: abdominal pain, cramps, nausea, flatulence, belching, anorexia, fever, diarrhea alternating with constipation, and stools that often contain unusual amounts of mucus.

Giardiasis is not considered to be a killing disease (although it may make you wish you were dead), and some people experience self-limiting infections that disappear after one to several weeks. Then again, many afflicted individuals struggle through prolonged illnesses that continue for months or even years with symptoms waxing and waning. (For example, if you have an unexplained periodic recurrence of diarrhea, you could be the victim of a persistent case of giardiasis.) Even if you've been cleansed of the parasite, you can still recontract the disease over and over.

Transmission

The giardia spreads by waterborne infection and by direct person-to-person (and animal-to-human) contact.

The most common source of infection is drinking water that contains cysts. (Swimming in infected water will also expose you to the parasite.) The organism enters the watershed with the feces from an infected human or animal or by sewage contamination. The cyst is apparently not host-specific and has been found in beavers, muskrats, cattle, sheep, deer, moose, rats, mice, cats, dogs, rabbits, gerbils and guinea pigs. (Beavers earned their top billing because they were the first identified animal carriers and because their sometimes migratory, aquatic lifestyle made them the Johnny Appleseeds of this disease.) Any infected animal becomes a parasite factory, releasing millions of the cysts into the environment.

It's easy, then, to see why pure tap water can no longer be taken for granted. Indeed, outbreaks of the disease caused by organisms in the municipal water supplies have occurred in Rome, New York; Banff, Alberta, Canada; Camas, Washington; Scranton, Pennsylvania; Leningrad, Russia; Reno, Nevada; and at least half a dozen cities in Colorado.

Such outbreaks are difficult to combat. The cyst is not necessarily killed by the concentrations of chlorine used in municipal water supplies. While proper filtration at the treatment plant is effective, the equipment must be carefully installed, operated and maintained. (Since present identification procedures are intricate and fallible, it's not always possible to confirm when a water supply has been infected.)

Colorado's solution to the problem has been to require filtration—as well as disinfection—of all public water supplies that rely on surface water. And don't feel smug if you have your own private well. Although the giardia is much less common in under-

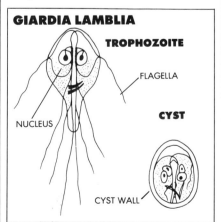

GIARDIA LAMBLIA

TROPHOZOITE

FLAGELLA

NUCLEUS

CYST

CYST WALL

No matter how pristine the water appears to be, a wilderness stream may not be free of *Giardia lamblia*.

ground water supplies, it has been found in wells, cisterns and springs.

The persistent protozoan is also transmitted directly by what is known in medical circles as the fecal-oral route, being passed from person to person or from pet to person and by food handlers. (Giardiasis can also be transmitted sexually.)

Outbreaks have occurred in orphanages and institutions for the mentally retarded. Recently, many epidemics have been traced to day-care centers, where the infection has been passed from one (often asymptomatic) child to another and then brought home to the diaper-changing parents. Pets, too, play an important role as reservoir hosts, making every gutter and drainage ditch a potential source of infection.

Of course, the best way to break the fecal-oral cycle of infection is to practice good personal hygiene habits. Make sure all the members of your family wash their hands carefully with soap after toileting and handling diapers or other fecally soiled materials. And don't overlook pets or even yourself (you could be asymptomatic) as carriers.

Treatment

Giardiasis is commonly treated with one of three drugs (prescribed by a doctor after diagnosis):

Quinacrine hydrochloride (brand name Atabrine): This quinine-based drug is now considered the most effective treatment.

Metronidazole (brand name Flagyl): The FDA regards this as an "investigational" drug for giardiasis.

Furazolidone (brand name Furoxone): As the only antigiardiasis drug available in sus-

pension, this one is useful for infants.

One course of treatment usually eradicates the organisms, although resolution may be slow.

Backcountry Protection

How can people camping in the wilderness, traveling abroad or even just living at home make sure the water they're drinking is safe?

Treatment with chemicals is not reliable. There are too many resistant organisms and critical variables (such as temperature, dosage, exposure time and percentage of organic matter in the water). Consequently, neither chlorine nor iodine—two of the most common backcountry water purifiers—is 100% effective against giardia cysts. In addition, iodine is itself tricky to use and, indeed, potentially toxic. Accidentally swallowing a crystal or inhaling its gaseous fumes in a closed tent could cause serious illness. Chlorine, too, has drawbacks other than its partial effectiveness. It can form dangerous by-products, and it definitely makes water taste bad.

Boiling *will* kill giardia cysts. A rolling boil will knock out giardias, other protozoa and bacteria (not viruses, however). But boiling is inconvenient and time-consuming.

For many the answer is a pocket filter. Be sure to select a model with a maximum pore size of .2 microns. All particles and pathogens larger than this (including all protozoa and bacteria and some viruses) must be physically prevented from passing through the filter.

Lucky Us

We're really quite lucky. Compared with the crippling, blinding and terminal diseases of the tropics that affect millions of people each year, giardiasis seems quite benign. And we have effective treatment for it, whereas some tropical diseases are resistant to all known drugs.

Then again, giardiasis is not the only waterborne infectious disease in the U.S. There are hosts of bacteria, viruses and other parasites. Still, *Giardia lamblia* is the American backcountry's most prevalent waterborne parasite, and one we're stuck with. We'll never be able to eradicate it from every stream and carrier (especially since most of the latter are asymptomatic).

This protozoan is here to stay—a fact of life, like pesty insects. Indeed, it's probably been around a heck of a lot longer than humans (the word *protozoa* actually means "first animal"). We just have to learn to live with *Giardia lamblia*.

By trying to live *without* it.

BACKCOUNTRY LORE

It's a statistical fact that far too many backcountry wanderers give far too little thought to where they've come from, where they're going and where they are. Until they find themselves lost, that is. Then it's too late.

Why do so many adventuresome outdoors folk seem to be so resistant to learning the essentials of land navigation—an aspect of woodcraft that's critical to their own well-being? It may well be a problem of attitude:

A lot of people hold the belief that using map and compass to steer their way through the boonies is a dryly technical chore that will detract from the carefree pleasures of their wilderness experience.

To the contrary, gaining a working knowledge of the basics of land navigation will enable you to escape the heavily trafficked hiking trails, the crowded campgrounds and the hunted-out and fished-out roadside acreage to which the overwhelming majority of

today's outdoors enthusiasts are shackled by chains of navigational insecurity.

The good news is that learning to find your way in the woods isn't all that difficult, especially if your education comes one step at a time—the approach that follows.

Topographic Maps

Topography, according to dictionary definition, is "the art or practice of graphic

Learn to use a map and compass, and the wilds will be as easy to navigate as the streets of your hometown.

Finding Your Way

Avoiding the risk of getting lost in the wilds is simply a matter of knowing where you are.

delineation in detail, usually on maps or charts, of natural and manmade features of a place or region, especially in a way to show their relative positions and elevations." In other (and fewer) words, a topographic map employs symbols to provide a three-dimensional likeness of a chunk of the earth's surface on a flat sheet of paper.

Contour lines: The most elusive landform dimension to envision—elevation—is represented on topographic maps (topos) by a sea

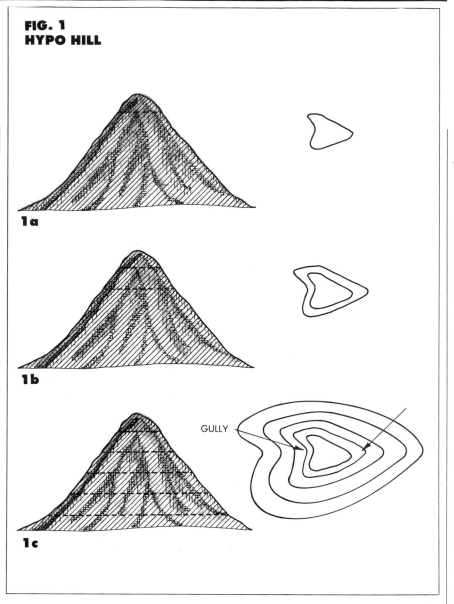

FIG. 1
HYPO HILL

1a

1b

1c

GULLY

of wavy brown lines. These lines are called *contours*, and they symbolically connect points of equal elevation on the ground. The best way to visualize this is to imagine a hill—let's call it Hypothetical Hill—with its top sliced off in a perfectly horizontal plane. If a line were traced around the edge of the now-flat top of Hypo Hill, that line would form a ring that waves in and out and generally swims around to conform to the gullies, ridges and other convolutions of the hill's rim at the point where the cut was made. This ragged circle would represent a plane of equal elevation above sea level (ASL) all the way around Hypo Hill (Fig. 1a).

If we went a step further and lopped off a second slice some distance below the first cut, then traced a line around the new top's perimeter, the second contour line would fit like a loose ring around the original circle (Fig. 1b).

Likewise, if we went on to slice our imaginary hill at equal elevation intervals—let's say every 40 feet—from peak to base and traced a contour line around the perimeter of each cut, we'd wind up with a three-dimensional (topographic) representation of Hypo Hill (Fig. 1c)—a representation that demonstrates a basic principle of topographic maps: *Contours that form concentric Vs pointing downhill portray ridges, while valleys and other depressions are represented by contours that V in an uphill direction.*

Since Hypo Hill is essentially a ragged cone with sides that slope off more or less equally all around, the concentric rings formed by the contour lines are fairly evenly spaced one from another. But what if, rather than a cone, we have a hill that rises gradually on its east side and falls off abruptly to the west; what will our contours look like then? Well, because we're saying that the distance between each contour line represents 40 feet of elevation, the contours of such a lopsided hill would be widespread on the gentle east slope and closely spaced on the much steeper west flank (Fig. 2). This example represents a second basic principle of map contours: *The closer together the contour lines, the steeper the terrain they represent.*

What's more, if we know the elevation gain represented by the space between each contour line—which is called the *contour interval*—we can determine the approximate height of any mapped terrain feature by counting the number of contour intervals from the feature's base to its peak and multiplying that number by the contour interval listed at the bottom of the map. In Fig. 2 there are seven contours (and six contour intervals between them), with the outer (base) line representing ground level. By multiplying six by the contour interval of 40 feet, we find that the height of the hill above ground level (AGL) at the top contour line is 240 feet. From there we can extrapolate that the very peak of the hill is higher than 240 feet but lower than 280 feet (else there would be an eighth contour line).

Index contours: A typical topo map, known officially as a *quadrangle*, is a 23″ X 19″ rectangle representing from 49 to 70 square miles. That's a lot of ground. And if the terrain represented on a particular map is mountainous, with numerous steep slopes and abrupt changes in elevation, the contour lines can be spaced so closely that counting them without the aid of a magnifying glass can be a real headache.

In order to overcome this problem, the clever cartographers at the U.S. Geological Survey (USGS) draw every fifth contour line darker than the intervening four and write in its elevation above sea level (ASL). These bold contour lines are called *index contours*. This indexing system allows a navigator to find the ASL height of any point on any topo map simply by noting the elevation written on the nearest index contour, then counting the intermediate contour lines up or down from the index to the point in question. If, for example, a map's contour interval is 40 feet, the index contour nearest to a spot called Mystery Point is marked 3,500 feet, and Mystery Point falls halfway between the first and second contour lines above the 3,500-foot index, we can extrapolate that its eleva-

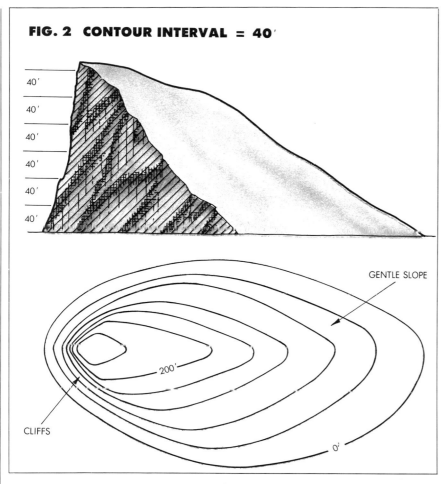

FIG. 2 CONTOUR INTERVAL = 40'

40'
40'
40'
40'
40'
40'

GENTLE SLOPE

200'

CLIFFS

0'

tion is very near to 3,560 feet ASL (higher than the 3,540-foot contour, but lower than 3,580 feet).

Scale: A topo's *scale* indicates the physical size of the map sheet in relation to the area it represents on the ground. For example, a scale of 1:24,000 means that 24,000 units of measure on the ground are represented by one unit of measure on the map. Thus, the smaller the denominator of a map's scale, the larger the map's detail: A 1:24,000 map is slightly more than twice as large in scale (and detail) as a 1:50,000.

Color: The general classifications of significant features noted on topo maps are indicated by color. We've already seen that elevation contours come in different shades of brown. Other coloration symbols include the following:

Black = manmade features such as buildings and roads.

Blue = water (lakes, rivers, creeks, marshes, oceans, etc.).

Green = vegetation.

Purple = relatively new terrain features, almost always manmade, identified from recent aerial photos and used to update a map. Purple features haven't been field-checked for accuracy but are generally dependable.

Red = major roads, as well as lines and numbers indicating various boundaries.

White = unforested terrain (although it may contain low vegetation).

Symbolic logic: Unlike some government agencies, the USGS seems to make an honest effort to turn out a product that's at least somewhat comprehensible to the general public. Consequently, few topo symbols are cryptic, and the meanings of most can be grasped at a glance.

For instance, small buildings are represented by solid black rectangles, while larger buildings are represented by larger, cross-hatched rectangles. If a building is a church, the rectangle that represents it will be topped with a cross; if a school, with a flag. Campgrounds are denoted by black tipis, mines by crossed pickaxes, and cemeteries by dashed-line rectangles enclosing the abbreviation "Cem," or a cross. Highways and byways are depicted the same as on standard road maps, with foot trails being represented by single dashed black lines; unimproved dirt roads (jeep trails) by parallel dashed black lines; improved dirt roads by parallel solid black lines; medium-duty hard-surface highways by parallel black lines filled with alternating red and white blocks; and primary highways by thick solid red lines. (For information on ordering a free USGS pamphlet that details all there is to know about map symbols, scale and other topographic trivia, see "Sources for Topographic Maps of North America" on page 146.)

Which north is north? The term *true north* refers to the geographic North Pole—the top of the world, the northern axis about which the earth rotates. Topographic maps are drawn in reference to true north. Unfortunately for the navigators of the world, magnetic compasses point to a slightly different place, called *magnetic north*, located more than a thousand miles south of the North Pole.

It follows, then, that from any given point in the Northern Hemisphere, the direction a compass tells you is north will be a few degrees either east or west of true north, with the direction and severity of error dictated by your location. This difference in degrees between the two norths is known as *magnetic declination*. If you're east of a line extending roughly from the Great Lakes down through the center of Florida, the declination is west; if you're west of that line—as most of the U.S. is—the declination is east.

The navigator's problem, therefore, is to reconcile the magnetic north bearing provided by a compass with the true north orientation of topo maps—which is why the USGS provides a *declination diagram* in the marginalia of every map (Figs. 3 and 4). For most land-nav purposes, if a map's declination diagram contains a third line (not all do) labeled GN (for grid north), it can be ignored.

The declination diagram shows whether

FIG. 3
USING A TOPOGRAPHIC MAP

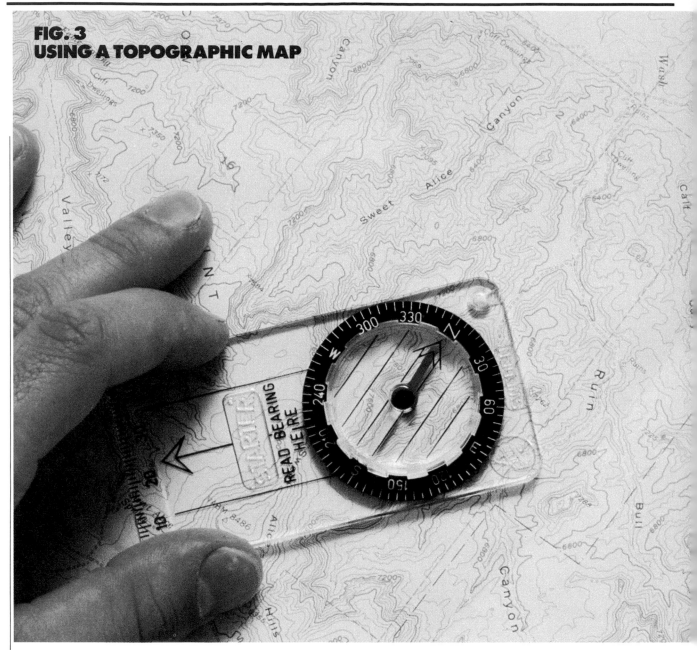

FIG. 4
DECLINATION DIAGRAM

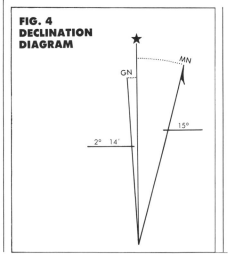

FIG. 5
ORIENTEERING COMPASS

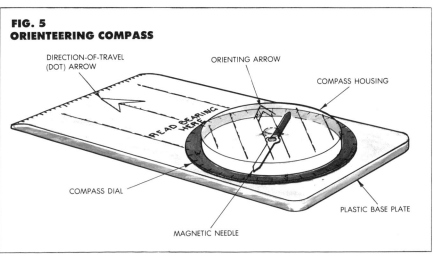

the magnetic declination for the area covered by a particular map is east or west of true north and by how many degrees. To reconcile magnetic north with true north (that is, to make compass and map bearings agree), the rule is to *subtract if the declination is east, and add if the declination is west.* As an aid in remembering this rule, some clever navigator long ago came up with the rhyme "east is least and west is best." If you can remember that one rule—subtract eastern declination and add western—you've got the single most confusing aspect of map-and-compass work licked.

But before we talk any more about topos, magnetic declination, declination diagrams, et cetera, let's familiarize ourselves with the second half of the map-and-compass team.

Compasses

The heart of any magnetic compass is an ionized, slightly magnetized iron needle that swings freely (often on a sapphire bearing) to align itself in parallel with the earth's magnetic force fields. Since these force fields run in north-south planes, one end of a compass needle (usually painted red) points toward magnetic north.

To provide for precise directional measurement, the compass needle is surrounded by a *compass dial*—a ring marked off, clockwise, into the 360° of a full circle: North is 0°, east 90°, south 180° and west 270°, with 360° coinciding with 0° as north. **The orienteering compass:** The *orienteering* compass is preferable to other designs (such as the watchlike *lensatic*) for most map-and-compass work because it's designed specifically to minimize the confusion caused by magnetic declination.

The needle of an orienteering compass (Fig. 5) is enclosed in a circular capsule called the *compass housing.* The compass housing can be rotated with the fingers and often is filled with a freeze-resistant liquid to damp excess needle gyrations, making the compass easier to read while on the move. Typically, the compass housing is mounted on a rectangular plastic base.

A further distinguishing feature of the orienteering compass is that it has two reference pointers: The *direction-of-travel* (DOT) arrow runs down the longitudinal center of the rectangular plastic base and is stationary;

that is, painted on or etched in. The *orienting arrow* is painted or etched onto the rotating compass housing and—though it turns with the housing—always points to north (N) on the compass dial.

Now let's jump back to where we paused in our discussion of topo maps to see how we can take advantage of the special design features of the orienteering compass to minimize, but not eliminate, the hassles caused by the need to compensate for magnetic declination.

Marrying Map and Compass

First, take a minute to connect, with pencil lines, the light blue tick marks (representing meridians) located along the top and bottom of the map sheet. These north-south lines will provide convenient references for aligning your compass. Now, let's get on with it.

Anytime a map and compass are to be used together, the first order of business is to orient the map to true north so that it will correspond to the terrain features it represents. Spread your map out on a flat, level spot well away from any metallic object that could magnetically deflect the needle of your compass (a phenomenon known as *deviation*). Place your compass over the map's declination diagram so that the needle's pivot pin is sitting directly over the base of the diagram, where the true north (designated by a star at its tip) and magnetic north (MN) lines originate (Fig. 6). Now hold the compass steady, and rotate the map until the declination diagram's MN line is directly under the compass needle. Your map is now oriented to true north.

Plotting a course—the traditional method: The most common use for map and compass arises when you can pinpoint on a map both where you are and where you wish to go, and you need to figure out a compass heading (azimuth) to follow in order to get there. Here's how it's done:

With the map oriented to true north, position your compass so that one long side of its rectangular base is lying along a line (either drawn or imagined) extending from your present position, Point A, to your goal, Point B. Caution: The DOT arrow should be pointing *toward* Point B (Fig. 7); if it's not, turn the compass around 180°.

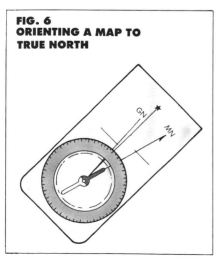

**FIG. 6
ORIENTING A MAP TO
TRUE NORTH**

While holding the compass base in place on the map, rotate the compass housing until the orienting arrow (or one of the parallel lines on either side of the arrow) aligns perfectly with one of the north-south lines you drew on your map (or with either edge of the map sheet); disregard the compass needle for now. The rough heading to Point B can now be read on the compass dial at the base of the DOT arrow (see "Read Bearing Here" notation on Fig. 5)—for example's sake we'll say that this rough heading is 250°.

The final step in obtaining an exact heading is to adjust for magnetic declination. Consult your map's declination diagram to find the amount and direction of declination, and add or subtract as necessary. Let's say the declination given on your map is 15° east. By mentally reciting the old navigator's saw "east is least and west is best," you're reminded to *subtract* easterly declination. Thus, 250 less 15 gives you a final heading of 235°. To guard against forgetting this figure somewhere down the trail, jot it down in a pocket-sized notebook.

Plotting a course—an easier way: We've just seen the traditional method of computing a heading—a bit clumsy at first, like learning to drive a stick-shift car, but it gets easier with practice. Fortunately, there's a better way, thanks to the two built-in "automatic transmission" features of orienteering compasses—the DOT and orienting arrows. By offsetting the orienting arrow from the DOT arrow by the amount and in the direction of magnetic declination, an orienteering compass will automatically compensate for declination, freeing you from the need to add or subtract each time you figure a map heading. Here's how it works:

With your map oriented to true north, place your compass along the line of intended travel (A to B). Now—here's where we shift into automatic—instead of aligning the orienting arrow with *true* north as in the standard method, align it with the compass needle (magnetic north). *If* you're careful in orienting your map, *if* you make sure there's no metal near your compass to induce variation and *if* you align needle and arrow *perfectly*—the degree heading shown at the base of the DOT arrow will be route-ready. (To crosscheck the accuracy of this method, go back and do it stick-shift style: The two headings should be the same.)

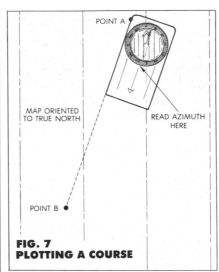

**FIG. 7
PLOTTING A COURSE**

Determining route mileage and difficulty: With your heading from Point A to Point B calculated, the next step is to determine distance. Using a strip of paper from your pocket notebook laid alongside the route line on the map (and bent to follow curves where necessary), mark off the distance from Point A to Point B by making a tick on the paper at each of these two points. Now position the marked section of the paper alongside the mileage conversion scale in your map's marginalia to determine the approximate length of your route. Jot this number down in your notebook next to the route heading. (If the route includes a lot of ups and downs and twist-arounds, compensate by adding 25% to the measured distance.)

Since it's nice to know the lay of the land up ahead—elevation gain and loss, availability of water, obstacles that must be crossed, vegetation type and so forth—your final pre-hike task is to make a map inspection of the territory between Points A and B. If the terrain is vegetated, it will be tinted green on the map. If there are streams or lakes along the route, they'll be shown in blue. Extremely steep terrain can be recognized by contour lines jammed close together, and you can calculate elevation gain and loss by inspecting the numbers written on the dark brown index contours falling between A and B.

Bushwhacking: With map and route notebook tucked away in pocket or pack, and your compass in your fist, you're ready to strike out across that mysterious, untrailed

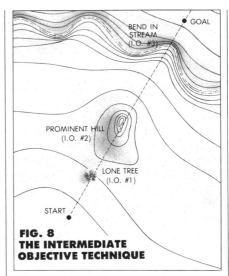

**FIG. 8
THE INTERMEDIATE
OBJECTIVE TECHNIQUE**

wilderness. With the compass dial set to the proper heading, hold the instrument in your hands, as level as possible, and turn slowly around until the red end of the magnetic needle aligns with N on the compass card. The DOT arrow is now pointing toward your goal (235° in our example).

You *could* just strike out with compass in hand, doing your best as you jostle along to keep the needle's red tip aligned with N on the compass card. In fact, that's about the *only* way to follow a course through densely vegetated country where you can see only a few feet ahead, or when you're out on a fogged-in day or at night. But most of the time there's an easier and far more accurate way to follow a compass—the *intermediate objective* method (Fig. 8).

Holding your compass up to your eye (being careful not to tilt or rotate it) and sighting down the DOT arrow, choose a prominent and unique landmark somewhere in the middle distance along your course—an object you can identify at a glance and one that's not likely to drop below your level of sight before you reach it. Prominent rock outcroppings, isolated trees, odd-shaped mountain peaks, manmade structures and bends in streams are examples.

By keeping this intermediate objective in sight as you walk, you're free to look around and enjoy the scenery—you can even stray off course to explore—just so long as you don't lose sight of the marker. This method also eliminates any worry about whether or not you're walking a straight line—which

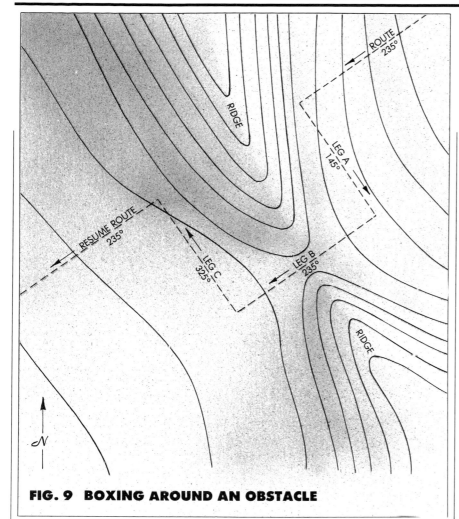

FIG. 9 BOXING AROUND AN OBSTACLE

hardly anyone can do freestyle, even with compass in hand.

When you reach your first intermediate objective, again sight down your compass to choose a second marker, and so on until you attain your final goal.

Two can walk straighter than one: If you're traveling with a partner, and if visibility or terrain won't allow for the use of *natural* intermediate objectives, you can create your own route markers by having your companion walk on ahead while you sight along the DOT arrow of your compass. When your friend reaches the limit of vision or voice—whichever comes first—guide him or her left or right, with spoken or visual commands, to a point directly in line with the DOT arrow. Now your partner can sit and rest for a spell while you stroll up to that spot. Continue this leapfrogging until you've reached your goal.

Obstacles: In theory, that's all there is to compass following. But theory and practice rarely hold hands. That nice straight route line on your map might prove to hold a few surprises out there on the ground—like a river that can't be forded where your course

intersects it, a lake that's too wide (or too cold or just too *wet*) to swim or a ridge that's too steep to climb. How do you get around such obstacles without straying off course?

The question answers itself: You get around obstacles by getting around them.

If the barrier is a stream, a lake or any other feature that's small enough and low enough to see across, simply sight along the DOT arrow, and choose a prominent terrain feature on the far side to mark your course. (For insurance, you might also build a brush cairn at your present location—something large enough that you can pick it out visually to check your position when you reach the other side.) Now simply walk along the obstacle until you find a safe place to cross, then mosey back along the far side until you strike your landmark. Finally, use your compass to realign yourself with your original course bearing, choose another intermediate objective up ahead, and resume your march.

But what about obstacles you *can't* see across or over, like steep ridges? In that case, use your compass to *box around* the hurdle (Fig. 9).

Let's assume you're still following a head-

ing of 235° southwest when you strike the foot of an impassable ridge. Break out your map, and locate your present position by noting where your route intersects the ridge. A quick study of the topography of the ridge (via contour lines) will tell you which way—left or right—you should walk to find the shortest or easiest route over or around. Let's say this ridge rises gently on the north but drops off in steep cliffs a quarter mile south of your position. The choice is obvious: The shortest, easiest and fastest course will be to circumnavigate the ridge below its south rim.

You *could* just stroll around to the far side. But how, then, would you realign yourself with your original course? The solution is to box around the obstacle, using your compass in conjunction with time traveled. Or, if the distance isn't too great, you can count paces to keep yourself on track.

The trick in compass boxing is to walk each of the three legs of the box (A, B and C) at right angles to one another. In this case, your original course is 235°, and you want to get around the ridge to your left, on the south side. Your first leg, then, will be 90° south of 235, or 145°. Shoot that azimuth with your compass, note down your exact departure time, and start walking leg A. As soon as you've traveled far enough south on the 145° leg to clear the ridge, again note the time, then use your compass to realign yourself with your original course (235°), and hike leg B until you've cleared the far side of the obstacle. All that remains now is to shoot an azimuth for and walk the final leg of the three-sided box—the *back azimuth*—which will be 180° opposite leg A (or 90° north of your original course). In this case, adding 180 to your first-leg course of 145 gives you a third-leg heading of 325°.

For this final leg, check your notes to determine the time traveled along leg A, then turn to your new heading of 325°, and walk for the same amount of time, trying to approximate the speed you traveled on the first leg. (If, for instance, leg A was slightly uphill and leg C is slightly downhill, you'll need to compensate by holding yourself back a bit on C.) When you've walked along the final leg for the specified time (or the same number of paces), stop. If your compass calculations have been accurate, you'll now be very close to directly opposite your starting point;

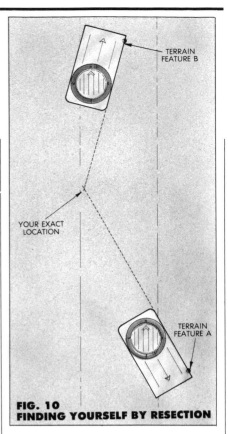

**FIG. 10
FINDING YOURSELF BY RESECTION**

simply reorient yourself to your original 235° course, and resume your march.

Intentional error: Another compass-following trick worth knowing is *intentional error*. This technique comes in handy when you're camped (or your vehicle is parked) along a road, stream, power-line trail, fence row or other longitudinal landmark, and you'll be exploring out from that point.

Begin your route planning, as always, by orienting your map to true north, then pinpointing and marking your starting position. In this case, let's say you're parked at a horseshoe bend in a Forest Service road. Let's further assume that you plot out a three-legged course: The first leg will take you several miles diagonally away from the road, the second leg will roughly parallel the road, and the final leg will shoot you directly back to your starting point. You hope.

But you've learned from hard experience that no matter how carefully you plot and follow a course, you rarely come out right on the money, especially when several legs are involved in the journey. In other words, though you'll have no problem getting back to the *road* at the end of the day, and though the point at which you cut the road will probably not be *too* far from where your vehicle is parked, you may have to guess which way to walk along the road to locate it. If you guess wrong, you could be trudging that dark byway half the night before you find your wheels. Let's hope it doesn't rain or snow.

In such a situation—when you're attempting to find a specific point along a longitudinal landmark—you can provide yourself with ironclad directional insurance by figuring an *intentional error* into the last leg of the walk. If you determine, for example, that a final-leg course of 150° will bring you out at your vehicle, simply add 5° or so to your heading and you'll know when you strike the road to turn left. No guesswork.

Finding Yourself

Plotting a route and following it through country you've never before traveled is the most common use of map and compass. But this pair of valuable backcountry tools can also help you locate your position when you know the general area you've been wandering through but have managed to become disoriented and unsure of your exact location. (Some call this "lost.")

Resection: Break out your map, spread it on the ground, and orient it to true north. That done, inspect the area of the map you suspect of including your present position, looking for terrain features that seem to match up with the country around you—mountains, lakes, canyons and suchlike. If you can spot just two visible landmarks and pinpoint them on your map, you're home free. It's a technique called *resection* (Fig. 10), and it involves using the back azimuth of two known points (the landmarks) to plot a third, unknown, point (your position).

Story time: Imagine two large vultures, one sitting atop each of the two distant landmarks you've chosen. Your goal in doing a resection is to plot on the map the heading from each landmark that the vulture in question would fly in order to join you for lunch. Where these two flight paths cross is your location.

Sources for Topographic Maps of North America

Topographic maps are available over the counter from sporting goods stores and bookshops in most popular hiking areas or can be ordered directly from their producers—the U.S. Geological Survey (USGS) in the United States and the Canada Map Office in Canada.

In the U.S., the first step in mail-ordering topos is to send for some free literature: an index map of the state you plan to visit and the pamphlet "Topographic Maps." The index will help you pinpoint the exact quadrangles you'll need to purchase and includes an order form with current prices; the pamphlet will provide you with additional map-ordering information plus lots of important topo trivia such as map editions, symbols, scale and the addresses of USGS offices around the country.

Since topo maps must be ordered by state and by quadrangle name, series and scale, you almost *have* to send for the index and pamphlet first.

For maps of the United States and U.S. possessions, write to

Distribution Branch
U.S. Geological Survey
Box 25286, Denver Federal Center
Denver, CO 80225.

Canada has three separate topo map indexes; all are free. When ordering, ask for a "Maps of Canada Index," and give the number of the index you want, as explained in the list below.

Index 1 covers New Brunswick, Newfoundland, Nova Scotia, Ontario, Prince Edward Island and Quebec.

Index 2 covers Alberta, British Columbia, Manitoba, Saskatchewan and the Yukon Territory.

Index 3 covers the Northwest Territories. Write to

Canada Map Office
615 Booth St.
Ottawa, Ontario, Canada K1A 0E9.

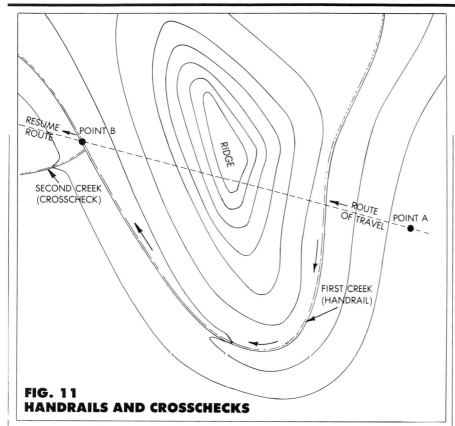

FIG. 11
HANDRAILS AND CROSSCHECKS

Sight along the DOT arrow of your compass to the first of the two landmarks you've chosen, then rotate the compass housing until the orienting arrow is aligned perfectly with the compass needle. The azimuth to the landmark can now be read at the base of the DOT arrow—let's call it 165°. Make a note of the heading, and then shoot an azimuth to the second landmark—let's say this one lies at 30°.

The next step is to compensate for magnetic declination. Sticking with our running example of 15° east declination, the 165° bearing becomes 150, while 30 less 15 is 15.

Now for the plotting: Turn the compass housing until the 150° mark is aligned with the base of the DOT arrow. Position a front corner of the compass base plate over the first landmark on your map (the one whose declination-adjusted heading is 150°). Now carefully pivot the compass around the corner that's sitting on the landmark until the orienting arrow is parallel with a true-north reference (such as a north-south map border) on the map. (Note: Take a moment to verify that the 0° mark on your compass dial is toward the top of the map.) Finally, draw a line along the edge of the compass base extending in the direction the DOT arrow is pointing.

Now repeat the above procedures for the second landmark: Align the 15° mark on the compass card with the base of the DOT arrow, position a back corner of the compass

base on the second landmark, pivot the compass around until the orienting arrow aligns with true north on the map, and then draw a line that extends along the edge of the compass base in the direction of the DOT arrow. Where the two back-bearing lines cross (you may have to extend them) is your location.

Orienteering Tricks

Orienteering is a competitive sport that combines map-and-compass skills with cross-country running. Orienteering has been popular in Europe since before World War II, but has only recently gained a significant following in North America. Since the object of this sport is to team brains and legs in order to make it around an assigned course faster than the next competitor, special tools (like the orienteering compass) and techniques to enhance speed and accuracy—both in calculating a heading and in reaching a goal—have evolved. A couple of these tricks can be put to good use by hikers, hunters and other backwoods types, no matter what speed they choose to travel.

Handrails and crosschecks: A straight line is the shortest distance between two points over a *level* surface, but not necessarily so on ground that may rise and fall several hundred feet within a few miles. And even when a particular route is relatively flat, if it's littered with obstacles, your progress will

be slowed and your energy drained. Enter the concept of *handrails*.

In the jargon of orienteering, a handrail is any longitudinal terrain feature—gully, road, stream, fence, ridgeline—that more or less follows your intended line of travel. In most cases, following a handrail will increase your travel distance, but it will also make for much easier going and free you from the necessity of keeping your eyes glued to map and compass.

Working in conjunction with handrails are *crosschecks*—obvious terrain features that can be pressed into service as stop signs or progress markers because of their location in relationship to your route of travel. Figure 11 illustrates how handrails and crosschecks can be used to save time and energy.

In this example, we've decided to skirt a steep hill that lies between Points A and B by following the dry bed (a feature known in navigators' jargon as an *intermittent stream*) of First Creek. The distance appears to be greater this way, and it may well be—but not by all that much when you consider the amount of ground covered were you to attempt going *over* the hill. In any event, following First Creek will be much easier than climbing up and down the hill, thereby making any extra mileage well worth it. First Creek, then, is a handrail.

Once around the hill, we'll want to leave the creek bed and rejoin our original course. As you can see, it just so happens (aren't hypothetical examples wonderful?) that another dry creek—Second Creek—cuts into our handrail just a few hundred yards before we intersect our original route. Second Creek is a perfect crosscheck—a prominent terrain feature that tells us when to stop following a handrail, sit down, take out map and compass and get reoriented. By measuring the map distance from the point where our route crosses First Creek to the point where Second Creek cuts in, then using the map's mileage conversion chart to translate map distance to ground distance, we know how far past the intersection of First and Second creeks we'll need to stop and reorient ourselves to our original course.

We've walked a bit farther by following First Creek, but we've saved time and energy by not having to tackle that hill.

Orienteering compass, handrails and crosschecks: Thank you, orienteers.

Outdoor Weather Forecasting

Predicting the weather during a wilderness outing is mostly a matter of noticing change.

When you walk in the woods or open country, where do your eyes play? If you're like a lot of hikers, you easily get wrapped up in plodding—figuring out where the next footfall will be—instead of observing. No wonder the weather catches so many people by surprise; they're just not paying attention. The sky, the greenery and the ground, as well as all the creatures that inhabit these environs, provide a constant flow of clues about what the atmosphere holds in store. All one needs to tap this 24-hour weather report is a sharp set of senses. Just look, listen, feel, and—yes—even sniff.

For example, have you ever noticed that the odor of rotting wood (maybe mixed with the scent of mint) seems more pungent some days than others? There's a perfectly good explanation: When atmospheric pressure is high, odors are subdued—held in; when it drops, they waft into the air. On its own, knowledge of the barometric pressure won't tell you much about approaching weather. But if you notice that smells are on the wane (barometer rising) and that the wind seems to be shifting from the south toward the west, you can be pretty sure you're going to stay dry for the next few days.

Predicting weather without the meteorologist's arsenal of instrumentation is mostly a matter of charting changes. A one-time viewing of clouds, for instance, isn't nearly as sure as a comparison of the current situation with the type of clouds present a few hours, even a few days, ago. In fact, any *single* predictor mentioned here is of little value. Weather has defied such simplification for eons. So look for evidence from every source available, and hazard a guess only when the majority of the symptoms point to the same prognosis.

Whether you record your observations on paper or you map systems in your memory, paying attention to the weather will help keep you in touch with nature's progress around you. And you're likely to stay much more comfortable, too.

Regional Weather

Lay weather forecasters who've lived in an area for many years often become quite proficient, because they've learned from experience what a particular condition tells about the future weather. Even if you've lived in one place for only a year or two, you probably know from what direction the wind usually blows.

When you pack into a wilderness many hours (or days) from home, you start without the benefit of experience: You don't know what the prevailing wind is, what direction storms usually approach from or how the topography affects the weather. Any information you can arm yourself with before hitting the trail will improve your weather-forecasting accuracy.

If you're heading into federally controlled backcountry, the regional ranger station may be able to offer a detailed weather history of the area. Perhaps locals—outfitters, the itinerant fisherman or even your friendly bartender—are willing to part with some of their accumulated weather wisdom. Barring the closer sources, the National Climatic Data Center is *the* repository for weather information.

Weather Basics

Before we can get down to specific prognostication, we'll need to review some basic weather principles. On a large scale, weather systems in North America—in fact, in all the middle latitudes of the Northern Hemisphere—are carried from west to east by the jet stream. Prevailing high-altitude winds are from the west. (Please note: It's all reversed in the Southern Hemisphere.) Regional lower-level winds, however, swing around the points of the compass as the air in higher-pressure areas moves toward lower-pressure areas in attempts to equalize pressure differences (see Fig. 1).

The process goes something like this: Air descends in a high-pressure system (literally a tall stack of atmosphere) and spirals outward in a *clockwise* rotation. Because the air has come from high altitude, it carries little moisture, giving high-pressure systems a reputation for fair weather. The air moves outward, continuing its descent, and the pressure becomes progressively lower. As the air mass passes close to the ground, it picks up moisture. At a certain point, the winds begin spiraling inward to the low in a *counterclockwise* direction. Accumulated moisture may form clouds and eventually drop out as precipitation. Hence the low-pressure system's reputation for inclement weather.

There are three important things to remember about general circulation and the movement of air from highs to lows: First, high-level winds carry weather systems west-to-east (usually from the southwest in summer and from the northwest in winter); second, lower-level winds (the ones you're most aware of) may be entirely different from the general circulation; and third, lower-level winds move counterclockwise around lows.

Clouds, wind, humidity and pressure are the symptoms of approaching weather. The mix foretells one of three conditions: stable weather, the arrival of a cold front or the arrival of a warm front. A front is simply the disturbance at the boundary between masses of colder and warmer air—a sometimes violently unstable region that produces most of our bad weather.

If it's a cold front, the heavier cold air will push under the warm, and there may be severe weather (thunderstorms in summer) of short duration. If it's a warm front, the lighter warm air pushes over the cold, and there's likely to be protracted (but usually not very heavy) precipitation. Most often, cold fronts come and go quickly, while warm fronts give more warning and last longer. Hence there's some validity to the old saw that bad weather lasts about as long as the time it warns of its arrival. But fronts sometimes become stationary (particularly in summer), which confounds such a simple rule.

On average, a cold front will pass through every five to seven days, so you're not being paranoid if it seems to rain only on weekends. An intervening warm front—arriving a couple of days after the cold—may not be strong enough to bring any precipitation. Nonetheless, two to three days (the usual interval between warm and cold) is the farthest in advance you can make a halfway reliable seat-of-the-pants weather prediction. And just like that questionable sage on the evening news,

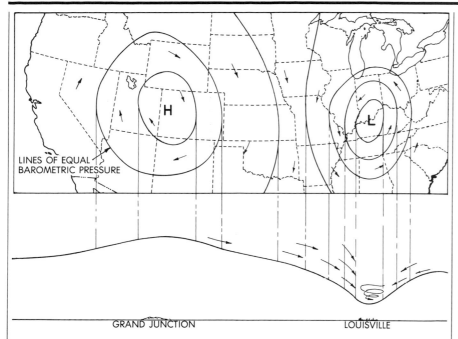

LINES OF EQUAL
BAROMETRIC PRESSURE

H

L

GRAND JUNCTION   LOUISVILLE

Figure 1: High- and Low-Pressure Systems

your accuracy will decline dramatically the further you look into the future. Still, since you're outdoors, at least you'll never get caught forecasting a chance of rain in the middle of a downpour.

Clouds

There are two basic types of clouds: heap (cumulus) and layered (stratus). These are further segregated by their altitude (cirrus for high, alto for medium) and their tendency to deliver precipitation (nimbus). Clouds often violate this neat categorization by being both basic types at once—the stratocumulus, for example—by changing from one to another or by adopting unique characteristics. As a result, descriptive words are often tagged onto a cloud's name, such as cumulus congestus (a cumulus trying to become a cumulonimbus) or stratocumulus mammatus (an unstable cloud with bags hanging down).

Fortunately, to predict the weather, we need to know only 11 of the hundreds of cloud permutations. The important 11 and what they portend are shown on page 150, and the sequences in which they occur in different types of weather are given on page 151. Interpretation of cloud types and sequences is the backcountry weather forecaster's single most valuable tool.

An important trend in any type of deteriorating weather is the lowering of cloud bottoms. As the system approaches, the clouds will form at lower and lower altitudes. Low clouds with irregular undersides most likely will produce heavy precipitation.

Clouds also affect the way the sky and celestial objects look, leading to some of the best-known folk weather predictors. Most people are familiar with the adage: "Red sky at night, sailor's delight; red sky at morning, sailor take warning." It's been with us at least since the time of Theophrastus in the 300s B.C. There's a lot to this one, as long as you're looking in the right direction; not into the setting or rising sun but at the opposite horizon. Red implies lower-level, water-bearing clouds. Thus, if the red is in the west, rain may be on the way; but if it's in the east, the system is beating a retreat. Likewise, a rainbow to the east or west tells you there's rain in that direction.

Another well-known and accurate portent of falling weather is a large halo around the moon, indicating a thin layer of cirrostratus clouds. If the winds are from any point between northeast and south, precipitation is likely within 24 hours. If the halo (around either moon or sun) changes to a frosted appearance, altostrati have moved in, suggesting precipitation within 12 to 20 hours. (This sequence of clouds also augurs an approaching warm front.) Some people assign importance to the appearance of the points on the crescent moon—sharp horns indicate fair weather, fuzzy horns signal rain—but there are too many causes for such a visual change for it to be considered reliable.

Winds

As a general rule, fair weather comes from the southwest in summer and the northwest in winter, but it's very helpful to know what the prevailing wind is in your locale. Nature

offers some clues: Trees show the undersides of their leaves when the wind shifts from its usual direction. Silver maples and cottonwoods are particularly helpful because the bottoms of their leaves are silvery white. To know what the wind direction is at the moment, look for a perched bird. It will almost always face into the wind.

Once you know where the fair-weather wind comes from, watch for change. If the wind shifts counterclockwise to between the south and northeast, there's likely to be bad weather in the next 24 hours. Likewise, if you notice that the wind is shifting in a clockwise manner from between south and northeast to the west, the weather is probably going to improve.

Armed with the knowledge that winds rotate counterclockwise around a low and that the storm system as a whole is headed east, you can be a lot more specific about the approach of bad weather. If you face into the wind and raise your right arm straight to the side, it points into the low. If you know which direction is which—and you should, if you're out in the sticks—you can figure out whether the storm is coming towards you, passing to the north or passing to the south, based on the assumption that the system as a whole is headed east.

Now we're going to embellish the "face the wind" axiom a bit, to make it more accurate and to learn even more about what's coming. Because of friction, the surface wind direction is different from the lower-level wind circulating around a low. If they're available, use low-floating clouds to determine the lower-level wind direction. Otherwise, adjust by using the following corrections. Over rough terrain, the surface wind is turned inward (toward the low's center) about 30°; over open water, the deflection is only 15°. Thus you should turn somewhere between 15° and 30° to your right to correct for surface friction.

Should the skies cooperate and allow you to see lower-level and upper-level clouds at the same time, it's simple to predict with the "crosswind rule." Face into the oncoming lower clouds (this saves having to worry about surface friction), and note the direction that the upper clouds are coming from. If they're coming from your right, the storm is approaching; if they're coming from the left, it has passed; if they're coming toward you, you're on the south side of the system, and the weather will not change much; and if they're moving away, you're to the north, and—again—the weather will be steady.

Humidity and Pressure

Cold and warm fronts have characteristic patterns of humidity and barometric pres-

Eleven Important Cloud Formations and What They Bring

A. Cirrus

Description: High, lacy, white ice cloud; often hairy appearance. *Weather:* Fair if lower-level wind is from west.

B. Cirrocumulus

Description: High, white layer of puffy or rippled clouds. *Weather:* Precipitation in 15 to 20 hours if wind is from between northeast and south.

C. Cirrostratus

Description: High, transparent, white clouds that put a halo around the moon. *Weather:* Precipitation in 15 to 20 hours if wind is steady from northeast.

D. Altocumulus

Description: Medium-height, white to light-gray layers. *Weather:* Precipitation in 10 to 15 hours if wind is steady from between northeast and south.

E. Altostratus

Description: Medium-height layer of gray, translucent clouds. *Weather:* Precipitation in 10 to 15 hours if wind is steady from between northeast and south; overcast for other winds.

F. Nimbostratus

Description: Light- to dark-gray monotonic, low-level cloud layers that obscure the sun. *Weather:* Precipitation of long duration if wind is from between northeast and south.

G. Stratocumulus

Description: Light- to dark-gray, variable-tone, low-level layers. *Weather:* Precipitation soon.

H. Stratus

Description: Usually lighter gray, low-level, flat layers. *Weather:* Heavy precipitation if wind is from between northeast and south.

I. Cumulus

Description: Separated, fluffy, white clouds. *Weather:* Fair weather unless developing into other cumulus.

J. Cumulus congestus

Description: Cumulus starting at low altitude, turning gray, billowing and beginning to develop vertically. *Weather:* May produce precipitation immediately.

K. Cumulonimbus

Description: Towering, billowing cloud varying from white to dark gray. *Weather:* The severe weather cloud. May bring high winds and thunderstorms.

sure. Before a cold front arrives, humidity will usually remain steady or rise only slightly, and the barometric pressure will drop fairly rapidly (depending on the storm's intensity). After the front's passage, the humidity will drop precipitously, and the pressure will shoot up. A warm front will be preceded by increasing humidity and steadily (but slowly) dropping pressure. Once the front has passed, the humidity will be steady or even increase slightly, and the pressure will rise a little.

Signs of change in humidity and pressure come from our own senses and from clues offered by plants and animals. In many cases, it's not easy to figure out which factor is causing the effect, so lumping humidity and pressure together at least lacks presumption.

People who are prone to the aches and pains of sore joints have more trouble when it's humid, and there's a statistical correlation between antisocial behavior and low barometric pressure. So, in general, we're likely to feel worse physically and mentally when the humidity is increasing and the pressure is dropping.

Sound travels farther when the air pressure is low; many people claim that distant noises seem almost to be coming down a tunnel. Another sign of low pressure is smoke that curls over toward the ground. Likewise, visibility often drops off in the haze of low pressure and high humidity. (Over water, though, high visibility may be a sign of unstable air that portends a storm.)

When pressure increases, smoke will rise straight up, odors will be subdued, the water level in dug wells will drop noticeably, ice on ponds may crack, and if you've toted any canned goods along on an outing, the tops might pop in. Though it may seem counter-indicative at first, dew, frost or ground fog in the morning is a sign of low humidity and good weather. Only when the air is dry and clear will the earth's surface give up enough heat to the night sky to cause condensation. (For the same reason, there's more difference between day and night temperatures in fair weather.)

Animal and plant indications of humidity/pressure abound. If you see significant numbers of deer moving down from the mountains to the valleys, expect snow within a day or two. Look for birds flying at high altitude in times of high barometric pressure. On the other hand, when hawks and vultures play on rising columns of air called thermals, conditions are ripe for forming cumulus congestus and maybe cumulonimbus clouds. It's also been variously reported that before bad weather insects swarm near the ground; swallows and other insect eaters fly low; frogs croak a lot; rodents such as mice and squirrels are frisky and noisy; birds chirp and may feed at unusual times; trout shun artificial enticements and leap for swarming insects; spiders will build up their webs eight hours prior to a storm but disassemble them if it's to be a bad blow; bees will stay close to home; ants will travel in columns rather than scattering; plants, including chickweed, clover, dandelions, hawkweed, indigo, African marigolds, tulips and scarlet pimpernel, close up; and the pitcher plant opens.

Weather or Not

Weather prediction skills can be vital in the backcountry, but they're also a heck of a lot of fun day to day. Even in town, a pause to study the atmosphere helps to restore, at least temporarily, an intimacy with the environment that bricks, beams and video screens too quickly steal.

Sequences of Clouds Before Fronts

1. Cirrus: If well developed, and lower-level winds are indicative, cirrocumulus will develop quickly.
2. Cirrocumulus: Indicator, if following cirrus by a few hours.
3. Altocumulus or altostratus: Look for frosted appearance and lowering.
4. Stratocumulus: Immediately before storm clouds. Sometimes this will be the first cloud seen and will stream in rows parallel to the wind; common in winter.
5. Cumulonimbus in summer, **nimbostratus** in winter; herald the arrival of the front.
6. After front passes, some **cumulus** may remain.

1. Cirrus: May be very thin at first and may persist with other cirrus forms for several days.
2. Cirrostratus: Will move across and cover the entire sky.
3. Cirrocumulus: May develop the classic "mackerel sky" of ripples.
4. Altocumulus.
5. Altostratus: May see red skies in western sunset or in west at sunrise.
6. Nimbostratus, occasionally **cumulonimbus;** the heaviest precipitation of the warm front.
7. Stratus: May develop as the front passes and continue light precipitation for several days.

Wilderness First Aid

Some times you have to heal yourself.

What starts out as a nice day of early-spring lake fishing ends up with "a catch" of three frostbitten toes. A slip on a mountainside hunt causes a shin fracture that almost leads to death from shock. A high-country snowshoe hiker suddenly becomes blind—*and* irretrievably lost.

Anytime you get away from the trappings of civilization, you also leave behind its medical services. Hence, a knowledge of basic first aid is just as important a survival aid as those matches in your pocket or that knife on your hip. Probably more important—you don't have to be far from home for a serious injury to mean serious trouble.

The information given here covers how to cope with the most common backcountry accidents and injuries. Remember, though, by far the best way to learn these skills is to take some of the widely available classes in first aid.

Be Prepared

First, a quick reminder: Most wilderness calamities are preventable, and it's a million times easier to prevent a disaster than to remedy it. The rules are simple. Wear proper clothing for the season. Know what weather you may experience, and be fully prepared for it. Take along at least a simple first-aid kit. Know your own physical limits, and abide by them. Know and act at the first signs of any potential health problem.

Follow such commonsense precautions and you'll rarely need the information that follows.

Three First-Aid Basics

1. Keep calm. Fear or panic will make any first-aid situation worse. They can lead to or increase shock. They can keep you from properly treating injury.
2. Do no harm. This is the golden rule of first aid. Don't risk a cure that may be worse than the trauma. (For example, don't move someone with a broken back unless absolutely necessary—or you may paralyze the per-

son.) This rule is a standard for doctors in hospitals; it certainly applies to amateurs in the backwoods.
3. Get help. In other words, first aid must not delay first treatment. Get the victim to professional medical help, or vice versa, as soon as possible.

Exposure Problems

Shock: A side effect of almost any injury—from heat exhaustion to snakebite—may be shock. Symptoms are paleness, weakness and rapid but weak pulse. Breathing may be shallow. The skin may feel sweaty or clammy. Unconsciousness may result, even death.

First identify and treat the cause of shock—such as severe bleeding or burns. Then have the victim lie down, kept warm in a sleeping bag (try to improvise, and add hot-water bottles). Unless the person has a head injury or difficulty breathing, elevate the feet and legs to improve blood flow. Give warm water. Comfort to reduce panic.
Trench foot: Due to exposure to wet, cool (but often not freezing) conditions, the foot becomes cold, swollen and waxy. It may become numb. The foot is *not* frozen, but if untreated, the flesh may die and amputation will be necessary.

Treat by drying and warming the foot. Avoid trench foot by bringing extra dry socks and using them.
Frostbite: Parts of the body will freeze if exposed to excessive cold and wind. The hands, feet, ears, nose and cheeks are most likely to be affected. Flesh first becomes discolored, turning gray or chalky white, and then becomes numb. Eventually, the flesh can freeze and die. Gangrene can set in.

Treat by warming the affected area. Blankets, clothes and warm hands will help, but the best remedy is to immerse the area in warm, not hot, water (approximately 110°F). Keep the frostbitten area clean against infection. And don't let it refreeze—that could result in substantial tissue loss. Once a limb is thawed, it can't be used until it has healed, so if you have a frostbitten leg

but must hike out, go *before* thawing it.

Several "home remedies" for frostbite will make things worse. Do not rub the part with snow, kerosene or oil. Don't force off frozen shoes or mittens. Don't give the victim alcohol or tobacco.
Hypothermia: This is one of the leading killers of outdoorsmen and -women. It occurs when the body loses heat faster than it can replace it—whether the temperature is below freezing or above. Wind, moisture and cold all contribute to cause hypothermia.

The warning sign is shivering. If untreated, the shivering will become intense and uncontrollable. The victim will then have trouble speaking. Thinking will become sluggish. When the shivering begins to stop (from muscle fatigue), the victim will become apathetic and helpless to save him- or herself. Muscles will become rigid, heartbeat and breathing will slow, and stupor will set in. Unless the person is quickly helped, death will result.

The best treatment is always to be on the lookout for hypothermia, avoiding serious symptoms by quickly warming anyone who has a bad case of shivering. Failing that, strip the victim and one or two helpers, and have all of them lie together in a sleeping bag. (The victim will not get warm if left alone in a sleeping bag.) Provide dry clothes, warm, nonalcoholic drinks (alcohol opens surface blood vessels, causing the body to lose more heat) and candy or other high-energy nourishment.
Snow blindness: Sunlight reflected off snow can cause serious eye damage. (Since the ultraviolet rays that cause the problem penetrate thin cloud layers, snow blindness can occur on an overcast day.) The eyes first burn or feel scratchy. They may tear readily and wince at light. Severe pain and headaches then lead to total blindness.

To treat, keep the eyes completely covered with cool compresses, take aspirin for the pain, and rest. Most people recover within a day. It's best, of course, to avoid the problem by wearing sunglasses with side covers in bright snow. You can improvise by rubbing soot on regular eyeglasses or by cutting thin eye slits out of bark, a bandanna or cloth and wrapping the material around your head.
Exhaustion: Muscles become like rubber, breathing becomes difficult, senses may become dulled, and the victim becomes weak and drowsy. If ignored, such fatigue can lead to serious complications.

Treatment is simple but important. Rest. Replace used-up salt and water. If necessary, treat for shock.
Heat exhaustion and stroke: Heat exhaustion is a form of shock caused by overexertion in hot weather. So much blood is

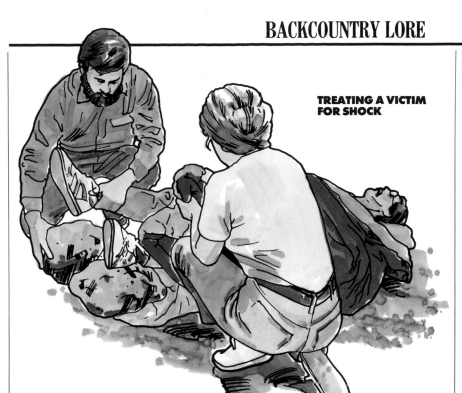

TREATING A VICTIM FOR SHOCK

diverted to the skin to help cool the victim that the blood pressure of the whole system weakens. The person feels tired or faint and may sweat heavily. The face pales, breath becomes short, and vision blurs.

Treat for shock—have the person lie down, and elevate the feet. Give the victim lots of unchilled drinking water (only if conscious—never give fluids to an unconscious person) and salt.

Heat stroke is more serious. Initial signs may be sweating, weakness, headache, cramps, confusion and irrational behavior. In the full stroke—a complete breakdown of the body's heat-control process—the victim may lose *all* ability to sweat. He or she looks pallid and clammy and falls into a coma. Body temperature rises rapidly and leads to death if not promptly treated.

The best remedy for heat stroke is to totally immerse the victim in cold water. Do whatever you can to cool the victim—pouring on cold water, fanning, wiping with wet cloths. Massage the limbs to promote blood circulation. Then keep a close watch on the victim's temperature (it may fall or rise again suddenly), and get the person to a physician immediately.

Altitude sickness: If you're not acclimated to exercising at high altitudes (8,000 feet and higher), you can be struck with an array of serious symptoms: headache, nausea, vomiting, shortness of breath, weakness, coughing, rapid heart rate, chest congestion, mental confusion, vision and coordination loss, coma and even death.

The cure is obvious but essential: Get the victim back to a lower altitude. Other helpful steps are to replace fluid loss, restrict salt intake and administer oxygen.

Animals and Plants

Snakes: There are four poisonous snakes in America: the rattlesnake, copperhead, water moccasin and coral snake. The first three inject their venom through two fangs; the last chews its victim.

First, keep the victim calm. Identify the snake to make sure it's poisonous. Even if it is, it may not have injected any venom: A fifth of the bites from poisonous snakes are not venomous. If venom was injected, the victim may feel a peculiar tingling and rubbery taste in the mouth, and then burning pain in the area of the bite.

All treatment procedures are based on slowing the body flow of toxin-carrying lymph. Keeping the victim calm and still helps slow lymph circulation. Do not give coffee, tea or alcohol—which would increase lymph flow.

There is disagreement about what treatment procedure is best. Most experts say that if you're within two hours of a hospital, to splint the snakebite area with an elastic wrap like an Ace bandage and get the victim to a hospital.

Another method—favored by some, renounced by others—involves placing a constricting band close to the wound, between it and the heart. (Don't apply a tourniquet,

which cuts off all circulation.) The risk here is that you can cut off blood flow and cause the person to lose a limb. So the band must allow blood flow—you should be able to see or feel pulse on both sides of it. It should also be released briefly every 15 minutes and refastened a bit closer to the heart.

Be alert for signs of shock, and treat the victim if necessary.

Rabies and other animal bites: Treat any animal bite for possible infection. Wash the wound thoroughly, and treat with disinfectant. If infection does occur, apply frequent hot compresses to draw the infection to the surface and promote drainage, then evacuate the victim to a hospital.

Rabies is transmitted by small mammals such as skunks, foxes, coyotes, wildcats, squirrels and bats. If you are bitten by a previously wounded animal or one that attacks with no provocation (*not* one merely trying to defend itself or its family), you'd better get to a physician for rabies immunization within two weeks. The immunization treatment is painful, but once symptoms appear, the disease is fatal. If you can capture the attacking animal and have it analyzed, you can find out for sure if rabies treatment is necessary.

Poisonous plants: This covers plants like poison ivy, which give you skin dermatitis on contact, and plants like foxglove or elderberry leaves, which are toxic when ingested. Treat the former by washing the afflicted area thoroughly with strong soap to remove the poisonous oil and by cleaning any clothes that may have absorbed any oil. Calamine lotion helps soothe.

The accepted treatment for ingested poisonous plants is to give a conscious (*not* unconscious) victim liquids and then induce vomiting (gagging the throat with fingers or a spoon is effective). Lower the face below the hips to keep any vomitus from entering the lungs.

Injuries

The standard first-aid sequence for treating injury is to 1) check airway, 2) reestablish breathing, 3) check circulation, 4) check cervical vertebrae for fracture, 5) stop bleeding and 6) treat shock. The first three steps—airway, breathing, circulation—are easy to remember by their initials: ABC.

Breathing: The best way to give artificial respiration is with the mouth-to-mouth technique (Fig. 1). First clear any obstructing material out of the throat by scooping it out with your fingers. Tilt the victim's head backward by putting one hand under the neck and pressing down on the forehead with the other. (If you suspect a broken neck, don't tilt the head; instead, use one hand to open the jaw.) This should open the air passage.

Pinch the nostrils shut with the same hand that is holding the forehead back (maintain the head tilt, keeping your other hand under the neck). Place your mouth completely over the victim's, and give four quick, full breaths. (If the victim's chest does not rise, check the airway again for obstructions.) Remove your mouth, inhale, wait for air to come out of the victim, then give another full, strong breath. The victim's chest should visibly rise and fall from your efforts.

Apply breaths every five seconds to adults. With children, cover both the nose and mouth with your mouth, and breathe (not as forcefully) every three seconds. If necessary, hit the victim sharply on the back to free a lodged obstruction. If the victim's stomach starts to bulge, turn the head sideways, and press the stomach briefly. This will force air out of the stomach, but it may also cause vomiting that you will need to clear.

Choking: If someone is conscious but choking, apply the Heimlich maneuver (Fig. 2). Grab the victim from behind by locking both arms around the person's waist. Then squeeze sharply, thrusting both fists into the upper abdomen and chest beneath the sternum. This should force air in the lungs to push the obstruction out like a cork from a bottle.

Bleeding: Serious bleeding can lead to death. Have the victim rest, and—if no injuries prohibit it—elevate the bleeding section above the level of the heart. To stop intense bleeding, apply firm pressure to the wound, preferably with a sterile pad but if necessary with the bare hand (Fig. 3). Add another dressing and more pressure if necessary.

This should stop the bleeding in almost all cases. Do *not* use a tourniquet unless all else has failed and you're willing to sacrifice a limb to save a life. Once bleeding is controlled, do what you can to prevent infection, or else serious complications may ensue. Puncture wounds should be washed out as deeply as possible with sterile (boiled, then cooled) water. The wound should be covered with a sterile dressing. If there has been a large loss of blood, the victim will need to be immediately transported to a hospital to receive blood transfusions.

Fractures: The basic first-aid treatment for fractures, i.e., broken bones, is *immobilizing* the injured part. First, though, you need to identify that a fracture has occurred. Obvious signs are a severely bent limb or when the victim hears or feels a bone snap. A less obvious indication is severe localized pain or tenderness: When you press gently on the injured spot, it hurts, but pressing a few inches away does not. A person with a broken neck will have trouble using his or her fingers; a broken-back victim will have trouble controlling toes. Early swelling may or may not be a sign of fracture. If you have any doubt, treat the injury as a fracture.

Stop the bleeding, and clean and dress any wounds before splinting a fracture. Be sure to—as first aiders say—"splint them where they lie," that is, immobilize the injured limb before moving the victim. Rig splints with bandages, clothes, wooden slats, ax handles, poles, etc., so that the joints above and below the fracture are fixed in place (Fig. 4). Pad the splints where needed. In some circumstances, as with a broken collarbone, the injured part should be splinted to the rest of the body.

Pelvis, neck and back fractures are very

serious. The best course of action is to keep the victim completely still (cover with blankets, and treat for shock or breathing difficulties if need be). Don't move the victim. If it is absolutely necessary to evacuate the victim, be extremely careful—movement of the neck or back could cause permanent paralysis or death. Move the injured person onto a rigid stretcher while keeping the hips, neck and back stiff and straight. Pad the person well, and carry the stretcher very carefully.

Sprains: A sprain occurs when ligaments, tendons or other tissue surrounding a joint are stretched or damaged. Sometimes it's hard to tell a sprain from a fracture—in both cases, the area may swell and be tender to the touch. When in doubt, treat as a fracture. If you're sure it's a sprain, elevate the injured area, and apply ice in cloth for 20 minutes at a time or cold rags for at least a half hour to reduce swelling. Keep the sprain immobilized if at all possible.

Burns: Treat the pain of a superficial burn by immersing the afflicted area in cold water. Then clean the burn with nonmedicated soap and water, and rinse thoroughly. Cover with a dry sterile dressing, and change that every 48 hours.

Serious burn victims are in danger of losing their lives. *Immediately* treat victims of deep or extensive burns for shock—even before you treat the burn itself. It's vitally important to replace lost fluids, giving the victim as much fluid (preferably tepid water) as he or she will tolerate—five quarts or more in the first eight hours. It's even more important to evacuate the victim promptly to a hospital.

To treat the wound, remove all clothing and jewelry from the burned area (but don't

FIG. 1
ARTIFICIAL RESPIRATION

FIG. 2
HEIMLICH MANEUVER

FIG. 3
APPLYING PRESSURE TO STOP THE BLEEDING

pull out any that is stuck in the burn). Cover the burned area with clean dressing—do not apply greasy ointments. Leave the dressing in place, and get the victim to medical help as soon as possible.

Heart attack: Symptoms of heart attack include chest heaviness or pain, shortness of breath, pale appearance, weakness, and pain radiating into the neck or arms. The main treatment is rest. Place the victim lying down or with the head and shoulders elevated. Keep the person calm (don't talk about "heart attacks"). Treat the person as a total invalid, and get medical help—don't transport unless absolutely necessary.

Check the pulse at the wrist or near the voice box, or listen to the chest for a heartbeat. If the heart has stopped, place your hands palms down at the base of the breastbone, one on top of the other (Fig. 5). With your arms straight and directly over the chest, press down one to two inches on the sternum. (Do not press too hard or onto the ribs or you may fracture them.) Relax the pressure so the chest can rise, then press again.

After each 15 chest compressions, stop and give two quick mouth-to-mouth lung inflations. Work quickly, about 80 chest presses a minute. If you have a helper, one of you give one lung inflation for every five chest compressions by the other, at a rate of about 60 chest presses a minute.

This last technique, cardiopulmonary resuscitation, is an advanced first-aid skill. You cannot really learn it from a book, but excellent first-aid classes in CPR are offered all over the country. Taking such classes is easy to do when you're in civilized country. Having such skills when you're not could save a life.

Distress Signals

A knowledge of the main backwoods distress signals can come in handy if you're injured, have someone in your party who cannot be moved or even if you're lost. (Most outdoor experts recommend staying in one place if you're seriously lost, and waiting for help.)

The two guidelines for signaling are to always make your signal stand out from its background and to signal in groups of three.

Any ground message must be big and contrast strongly with its environment if it's to be spotted by a passing aircraft. For instance, if you carve an SOS in snow, fill the letters with sticks or rocks, or at least make them so deep they'll form contrasting shadows. Likewise, if you use a signal fire on an overcast day, try to make it smoke as much as possible by throwing green branches on the flames—or make black smoke by tossing in oil-soaked rags. By the same token, don't expect gunshots to draw help in hunting season, but blowing on a whistle may.

Signals in threes are international distress calls. A sole campfire may not impress a passing pilot, but three fires placed in a triangle indicate distress. (Set the fires 100 feet apart if possible. And don't try to keep them burning all the time, but have them ready to light whenever you hear an airplane.) Three shots from a gun, three blows on a whistle (you can blow across an empty cartridge shell for a makeshift whistle) and three bangings of a stick on metal are all emergency calls. The Morse code signal for help—SOS—is three groups of three: dot-dot-dot, dash-dash-dash, dot-dot-dot.

Another good signaling aid is the helio-graph mirror, a two-sided hand mirror with a cross cut out of the center. These can be purchased or can be improvised out of scrap polished tin. Hold the mirror as illustrated, and face it approximately halfway between the sun and a rescue plane. Adjust the mirror so you see the plane through the cross and so the image of the cross on your face or hand is reflected back onto the center of the mirror. The mirror will then bounce sunlight directly at the aircraft.

If a plane comes overhead, do not wave with one arm—the pilot may think you're just saying hello. Instead, hold both arms straight overhead. This means you need to be taken aboard. An additional signal you may want to use is to lie flat on your back with your arms stretched together overhead —that means you urgently need medical assistance.

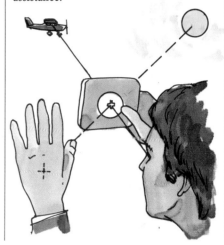

**FIG. 4
SPLINTING A FRACTURED LEG**

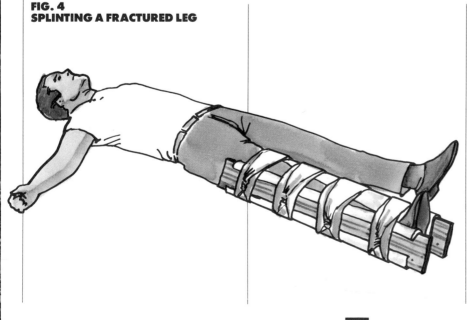

**FIG. 5
CARDIOPULMONARY
RESUSCITATION**

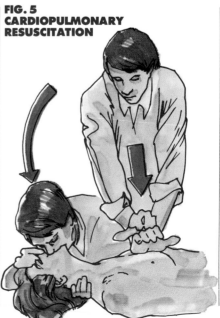

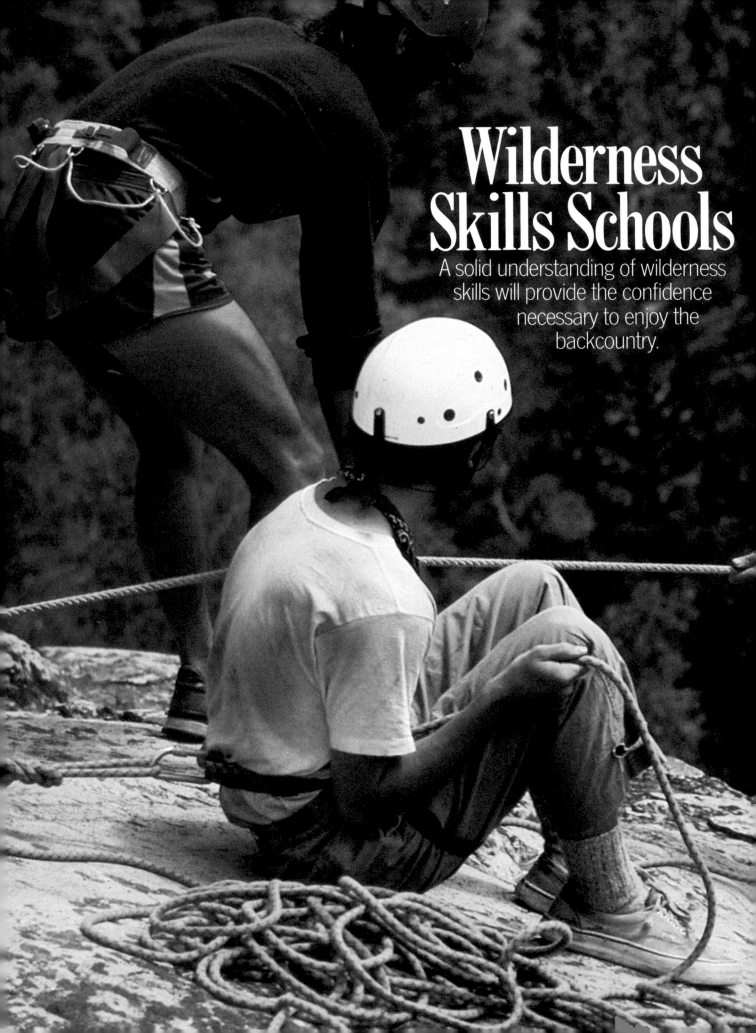

Wilderness Skills Schools

A solid understanding of wilderness skills will provide the confidence necessary to enjoy the backcountry.

Of the five outdoor schools examined here, three are distinctly *survival* oriented. They are Boulder Outdoor Survival School (BOSS), the Tom Brown School of Tracking, Nature and Wilderness Survival (better known simply as The Tracker School) and the Reevis Mountain School of Self-Reliance (RMS). Of that trio, BOSS and The Tracker School are pure in their wilderness skills and survival orientation, while RMS teaches a wide variety of outdoor-related topics, of which wilderness survival instruction accounts for about half.

The remaining two schools—the National Outdoor Leadership School (NOLS) and Outward Bound—place heavy emphasis on character-building and wilderness travel skills rather than survival.

("Survival Kits," on page 134 gives recommendations from four of these five schools on essential survival equipment.)

Boulder Outdoor Survival School

"BOSS" is an appropriate acronym for this most challenging of the hard-core civilian wilderness survival schools. Based at Rexburg, Idaho, BOSS has outdoor campuses in Idaho's Snake River valley and in south-central Utah near Boulder.

BOSS offers a variety of courses, but the class that has earned them their hard-as-rocks reputation is the 26-day Wilderness Expedition. According to David Wescott, director of BOSS, "This program is designed for the individual seeking to test him- or herself physically, mentally and emotionally. You'll hike hundreds of miles [the average is 200 to 250] and may lose 10 to 20 pounds in weight. The mental and emotional challenges come in facing and defeating obstacles and tasks set before you by nature and your instructors, and in adjusting and learning to live with nature in a harsh environment."

Sounds tough, and it is—nearly a month of intense foot travel across Utah's rugged and beautiful canyonlands, carrying a minimum of food, water and equipment. (Standard gear and rations per student include one army blanket and a nylon poncho, a couple of water bottles, a pocketknife and a few pounds of basic foodstuffs—flour, grains, fruit and vegetables.) Calories provided by the Spartan rations are supplemented with wild foods foraged along the way; even so, hunger and thirst are constants. Flashlights, matches, tents, sleeping bags, backpacks and other modern outdoor appurtenances are not allowed.

These outdoor institutions teach confidence and competence.

For prospective students who can't afford the time or cost of a month in the backcountry, or who simply don't feel the need for such a heavy dose of physical hardship, BOSS offers a 14-day condensed version of the longer course.

And then there's the tortuous seven-day Advanced Primitive Living and Nature Observation trek—advertised in the BOSS literature as being designed to satisfy the masochistic appetites of "hard-core rock-biters." The premise here is primitive simplicity itself: no gear, no food, not even a penknife. You walk into the wilderness with, quite literally, only the clothes on your back and, for seven days, survive by wits and gumption. Enrollment in this course is sensibly restricted to those having had previous survival training, and class size is limited to 12 students (accompanied by two or more instructors).

However, prospective BOSS students who would like to learn primitive wilderness skills, but can do without the hardships of a survival trek, might consider a seven-day Skills Clinic. Rather than hiking across great expanses of wilderness, participants attend the skills clinics at permanent base camps in Idaho (winter) and Utah (spring through fall). Here the physical challenge is lessened, with emphasis being placed instead on learning primitive crafts and survival skills in a relaxed and reasonably comfortable outdoor setting.

Although modernism is gently discouraged even in the skills clinics, students are at least allowed to bring along knives, backpacks, sleeping bags, water filters and other contemporary gear (within reason), and the rations are nutritious and filling, if not fancy.

In addition to the courses outlined above, BOSS also offers 12-day Adult Women's outings, a 14-day Mexico Desert and Marine Adventure, a seven-day Winter Skills course and others.

While BOSS doesn't give its services away, the primitive, low-impact nature of most of the courses helps to keep down overhead—and, thus, tuition—making BOSS a bargain relative to most other wilderness schools.

College credit can be earned for most BOSS courses, and a limited amount of tuition assistance is available to prospective students who can show financial need.

While BOSS isn't the only competent sur-

vival school around, it's the oldest, it may well be the most challenging, and it teaches wilderness skills as they should be taught—in the wilderness.

For a course schedule and complete enrollment information, write BOSS at P.O. Box 905, Rexburg, ID 83440, or call 208/356-7446.

Reevis Mountain School

Riddle: What do you get when you take a small group of people with a shared strong interest in communal living, organic gardening, appropriate technology, primitive crafts, New Age philosophies and wilderness survival skills and plop them down in an isolated valley in Arizona's rugged Superstition Mountains?

Answer: The Reevis Mountain School of Self-Reliance.

It all began with the incredible desert odyssey of Peter "Bigfoot" Busnack. Today, Bigfoot (he comes by the nickname honestly) is the honcho of RMS. But back in 1976 he was a construction worker with a healthy interest in edible and medicinal plants native to the Sonoran Desert. He also had a driving desire to test himself physically and spiritually. Bigfoot decided to undertake a solo survival hike across the hottest part of Arizona's lower Sonoran Desert during the hottest two weeks of the hot hot summer of '76.

For this grueling 85-mile trek, he carried a camera and basic survival equipment such as knife, compass and water containers, but no food or water. Midday temperatures pulsed up to well above 100°F. Bigfoot fell sick with hepatitis but cured himself with wild herbs. He got water from his food, from the occasional seep, trickle, spring or stream and, at the worst of times, from barrel cactus. He ate wild greens, bugs, frogs, a rattlesnake. He survived.

As word of this near-miracle of desert survival got around, Bigfoot quickly became a regional legend; the notoriety eventually prompting him, in 1979, to found RMS. Today, near the headwaters of Campaign Creek, at the foot of Reevis Mountain, Peter Bigfoot and the dozen or so other resident members of the RMS community (singles,

Food gathering can include spearing a fish with a homemade gig.

couples, families with children) raise their own food, produce their own electricity (with the generous help of the Arizona sun) and teach a wide variety of self-reliance topics.

A sampling of course titles: Primitive Skills, Land Navigation, Stone Masonry, Herb Study, Natural Remedies, Tanning Skins, Desert Survival Skills Trek, Vision Quest, Tai Chi Chuan, Meditation.

Reevis is a small and little-known school relative to the other four we're looking at here, but nonetheless has drawn students from as far away as New York. Most, though, come from Arizona's largest city, Phoenix. RMS courses are short in comparison to those offered by the other schools, averaging three to seven days.

If you enroll in a Reevis desert survival class, expect to study such subjects as dressing for desert comfort, selecting a practical survival knife and keeping it sharp, finding water in arid climates, starting matchless fires, making emergency shelters, mastering land navigation, identifying edible and medicinal wild plants and more. Some of these subjects are covered in-depth and hands-on, while others are merely discussed and demonstrated.

Tuition at Reevis is the lowest of any outdoor skills school and includes instruction, materials, a keeper copy of the funky but functional *Bigfoot's Survival Skills Manual*—and, for classes held at the Reevis campus, a place to unroll your sleeping bag, use of solar-heated shower facilities and an all-you-can-eat organic vegetarian dinner each evening.

For a brochure listing current class offerings and tuition rates, write RMS at HCO2, Box 1534, Roosevelt, AZ 85545. (There is no phone at RMS.)

The Tracker School

The story of this school is the story of one man, Tom Brown, Jr. Now in his late 30s, Brown is a teacher, author and survival celebrity. Over six feet tall, Brown stands ramrod straight, emphasizing his broad chest and powerful biceps.

Tom Brown became a national figure in 1976 with the publication of his first book, *The Tracker*, which tells the extraordinary story of his childhood, spent in the New Jersey Pine Barrens under the tutelage of an elderly displaced Apache. From the age of seven, Brown was trained by his adopted Indian grandfather in the traditional skills and philosophies of Native Americans.

In 1977, Brown founded what is today the largest wilderness survival and tracking school in the country. He has also written a set of field guides, two more autobiographical books, *The Search* and *The Vision*, and numerous magazine articles.

But even before he began writing and teaching, Brown was known to law enforcement and government agencies as The Tracker. His success in finding fugitives and lost children, sometimes staying on the trail without provisions for days, has been little short of amazing. Tom Brown, Jr., is widely acknowledged as *the* best tracker in the country.

During his welcoming talk to a group of some 40 students just arrived for a Standard (introductory-level) class, Brown says, "I pack this course with information. Time is critical here. I use every minute. When you're done on Sunday and you look at how much we've gone over, your head will reel."

He doesn't exaggerate: During a week of almost nonstop lectures and workshops—beginning at 8:00 each morning and continuing into the night, sometimes past midnight—Brown's Standard class covers an astonishing variety of survival skills, each in depth: matchless fires, emergency shelters, survival water, subsistence trapping, skinning and tanning, natural cordage, cooking, arrow and bow making, flint knapping, Eolithic rockwork, stalking, foraging, hunting and, of course, tracking.

When asked why he started The Tracker School, Brown replies, "I believe that teaching survival gets to people's hearts, that when a person learns how to enter the world purely, unencumbered by society, where you share a hand-to-mouth existence with the earth, a connection develops. That's why I run this school—to bring as many people as possible back to the earth and to send them out to teach other people."

Although advanced classes are held outdoors in New Jersey's Pine Barrens, the Standard class is conducted in the area surrounding Brown's home, a retired dairy farm near Asbury. A big red barn serves as the schoolhouse, with the hayloft doing for student sleeping quarters.

The Tracker's six-day Standard class is held once or twice a month throughout the year. For further information and a schedule of classes, write The Tracker, P.O. Box 173, Asbury, NJ 08802.

National Outdoor Leadership School

Unlike BOSS, RMS and The Tracker School, the National Outdoor Leadership School (NOLS) does *not* teach wilderness survival but rather how to avoid putting yourself in a survival situation. Neither is NOLS as heavily challenge-oriented as its chief competition, Outward Bound (discussed next). Rather, NOLS concentrates on teaching minimum-impact camping and outdoor leadership skills—those talents necessary to take yourself and others into and back out of true wilderness in safety and comfort.

Specific skills covered in NOLS wilderness courses include the selection and care of outdoor equipment, backpacking, horsepacking, campsite location, selection and use of portable shelters, fire building, camp cooking, sanitation and waste disposal, land navigation, river crossings, first aid, rescue techniques, fly-fishing, flora and fauna identification, geology, weather and wildlands ethics.

NOLS is headquartered at tiny Lander, Wyoming, hard beneath the spectacular Wind River Range. Although it wasn't officially chartered as a private, nonprofit school until 1965, NOLS's beginnings date back to the 1930s. It was then that a colorful western character named Paul Petzoldt noted that a single obstacle had caused problems on each of the many strenuous Himalayan treks he had made—a lack of competent leadership.

"He could find good climbers, good anglers and good biologists, but he couldn't find really good all-around outdoor leaders," explains Paul Calver, director of marketing and admissions for NOLS. Consequently, Petzoldt took it upon himself to train such leaders, eventually founding the National Outdoor Leadership School.

As the years wore on, Petzoldt took note that more and more people were visiting the mountains in search of physical recreation and spiritual re-creation. The time had come, he figured, to broaden the NOLS curriculum to include wilderness ethics and

From catching your dinner to cooking it with style, there's a course for each outdoor skill.

conservation.

On the subject of wilderness preservation versus public use, Paul Calver says, "There's a school of thought that feels the answer to saving the wilderness is to chain up the gates and not let anybody in. Of course, that can't be done. Wilderness will and should be used by the public, who, after all, own it. We at NOLS believe that educating users is the key to wilderness preservation."

In the more than 20 years since its beginning, over 25,000 people have been educated by NOLS in courses held in Wyoming, Alaska, Washington, Africa, Argentina and Mexico.

With the exception of special women-only courses, all NOLS programs are coeducational, with a minimum age requirement of 14—though some courses are designated as youth- or adults-only. In addition to its general wilderness skills classes, NOLS also offers single-topic courses in mountaineering, sea kayaking, cross-country ski touring, horsepacking, natural history and other subjects.

Course lengths vary from 14 to 95 days, with tuition including instruction, food and local transportation. College credit can be arranged.

Although having fun is an integral part of every course, NOLS takes itself seriously as a school. When you're not hiking or climbing or making or breaking camp or cooking dinner or fishing for it, you'll be attending classes.

For a current course schedule and enrollment information, write NOLS at P.O. Box AA, Lander, WY 82520, or call 307/332-6973.

Colorado Outward Bound

Founded in 1961, the Colorado Outward Bound School (COBS) was the first Outward Bound school in the Americas. Its philosophies are based on those of the original school, located in Aberdovey, Wales, which was founded during World War II to instill in young British sailors a tenacious spirit of challenge and an ethic of serving others. Today there are 35 Outward Bound schools operating on five continents.

COBS is a nonprofit educational organization and an affiliate of Outward Bound, Inc., the chartering authority of the five U.S. schools. About 6,000 students go through the Colorado programs each year, with the total alumni numbering some 70,000. The four U.S. affiliate schools—located in Oregon, Minnesota, Maine and North Carolina—offer courses designed to suit their geographic locations. For example, the Maine school specializes in sailing, while the Minnesota school highlights canoeing.

Colorado Outward Bound offers a wide variety of programs in Southwest-oriented outdoor activities, including summer mountaineering (23 days), winter mountaineering (18 days), desert trekking (10 and 23 days), multi-environment (mountain, desert and river) travel (21 days), whitewater rafting (four and seven days) and others.

COBS is not a survival school and is dedicated more to personal growth and development than to teaching specific wilderness skills—though plenty of the latter also are covered.

Outward Bound doesn't try to make seasoned mountaineers, river-runners or desert rats of its students. These high-adventure activities simply provide good settings in which to learn and grow. Consequently, if acquiring specialized wilderness survival expertise is your goal, Outward Bound is probably not for you. They're not going to teach you how to catch dinner with your bare hands or build a fire by rubbing together a couple of sticks. (In fact, you might not build a fire during your entire course, other than in a camp stove.) Moreover, if you want to learn enough about mountaineering to tackle technical rock or peak climbs on your own, you may also be disappointed with a COBS course—though you *will* get a good hands-on introduction to what mountaineering is all about.

If, however, you want thorough training in backpacking and camping skills—including first aid, cooking, land navigation and wilderness travel—along with the thrill of experiencing exciting outdoor activities such as rock climbing, rafting or cross-country skiing, then an Outward Bound course may be perfect for you.

The least expensive Colorado Outward Bound offering is a four-day whitewater rafting experience; the most expensive, a 90-day "semester" course. COBS offers a generous scholarship fund, awarded on the basis of financial need.

To qualify for enrollment in any COBS course, you must be at least 14 years of age (over 40% of students are 30 and older) and in good physical and mental health.

For more information, write Colorado Outward Bound at 945 Pennsylvania St., Denver, CO 80203, or call 303/837-0880. For information on any of the other four U.S. Outward Bound schools, contact the national office at 384 Field Point Rd., Greenwich, CT 06830 (800/243-8520).

Survival:
Shelter

A warm, dry place in a cold, wet, wild world.

When exploring the great outdoors, you can never be sure you won't suddenly be faced with a situation in which survival will depend upon your ability to make a shelter, find food and water and build a fire. In fact, even if you're "safely" ensconced in the security of a cabin, farmhouse or city apartment, any number of natural or manmade disasters can force you to keep yourself alive by using only what is available in nature.

However, any person who knows how to provide his or her necessities, without having to depend on manufactured commodities, can endure even if a calamity severs all ties with the rest of society. And wilderness living abilities are particularly important assets for the camper, sportsperson or other nature enthusiast who enjoys spending time away from the trappings of civilization.

But good survival skills include much more than the capability merely to live through a disaster. They can also approach a pure art form, and help individuals enter into a deeper kinship with all of creation. Consider how rewarding it would be to be able to build a shelter from natural materials; to make your own matchless fire; to gather, prepare and preserve wild edible plants for their nutritive and medicinal value; to find water where there seems to be none; to stalk, hunt and kill game with a bow and arrow made by your own hands from the materials around you, then to use every part of that animal, from the hoofs and hide to the bones and meat—in short, to be able to eliminate your dependence upon purchased goods and do without even such basic items as matches, candles and rope!

A person trying to live in the out-of-doors should experience no need to fight, feel no pain and endure no hard work. Indeed, whenever humans try to conquer the pure and natural, they are always defeated, and sometimes killed.

The most important rule for any person suddenly faced with a survival situation is to *keep from panicking.* The fear that overtakes someone who has just lived through a major disaster, or has abruptly realized that he or she is lost, can be beyond description. Remember, though, that panic is probably the biggest killer of all in such emergencies. Therefore, having confidence in one's skills during those first traumatic moments sometimes means the difference between life and death.

So, when you find yourself faced with a challenging situation, don't act like the fully equipped hunters—in those grisly stories that make headlines every deer season—who panic and then die of shock and exposure a few yards from a highway. Instead, follow the example of a nine-year-old boy who confidently weathered a two-day blizzard under a fir tree because he knew rabbits use firs for shelter and figured that their technique would work for him as well.

When calamity strikes, sit down and think things through *before* taking action. Relax, and realize that you can stay in the wilderness as long as you wish. Instead of giving in to panic, look upon the event as an opportunity to enjoy an unplanned vacation!

If you approach a survival situation with a negative attitude—thinking, "I can't stand sleeping in a smelly, bug-infested shelter in the middle of these damp, scary woods"— you will certainly have nothing but problems. But if you think, "Here I am all by myself in this magnificent forest, surrounded by the richest scents of nature, lying in the embrace of the earth and sleeping in a shelter I made myself," your experience can actually be grand and harmonious.

You'll also go a long way toward increasing your mental comfort by accepting the fact that you cannot immediately have everything you want, but *can* have everything you need. Most people, when lost, instantly become concerned about what they're going to eat. Yet of the four necessities for survival—shelter, water, fire and food—food is often the least important requirement. Most people can survive well over 30 days without eating.

Fire ranks next to last on the list because, if you have good shelter, you don't really need a fire. Water, of course, is essential (one can survive only a few days without it), but, if you know the ropes, you can easily collect water in almost any situation.

A person stranded in a harsh environment, though, may not live through a single night without an adequate shelter. Therefore, anyone interested in wilderness survival should begin by learning how to construct a protective emergency "dwelling."

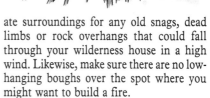

The simple leaf hut is among the best of emergency shelters. It's easy to construct in most locales and surprisingly comfortable.

Requirements for a Good Shelter

1. A shelter must give complete protection from the elements. It should be able to ward off violent storms, hot sun, high winds, frost and dampness.

2. A shelter must be able to keep you warm and dry even if you don't have blankets, coats, sleeping bags or heavy clothing (people in survival situations often find themselves equipped with only the clothes on their backs).

3. A shelter should provide a warm, dry work area and some storage space as well as a sleeping compartment.

4. A shelter should give a sense of security. It ought to be a sanctuary, a place where your cares drop off and you find rest.

Where to Put It

The location of your structure is just as important as the type of shelter you build. The best-constructed survival hut won't keep you comfortable, even in mild weather, if it's set up on a poor site. So, in choosing a suitable location, keep in mind that the natural surroundings themselves can supply a lot of protection.

When deciding where to erect your hut, first make sure the spot has adequate drainage and is a good distance from any large body of water. That way, you'll avoid the dampness that settles around water and the danger of having your temporary home washed away in a violent rain.

The area you choose should also be well protected, especially on the windward side of the locality's prevailing weather systems, by such natural barriers as vine tangles, trees or rock outcroppings. Inspect the immedi-

ate surroundings for any old snags, dead limbs or rock overhangs that could fall through your wilderness house in a high wind. Likewise, make sure there are no low-hanging boughs over the spot where you might want to build a fire.

Finally, it's a good idea to find a location that can be easily seen, so that searchers will have a good chance of spotting your position. Since natural shelters are hard to detect even if they're placed in the open, you should do whatever you can to make the structure more visible.

Positioning the Door and Fireplace

Whenever possible, the entrance to your shelter should face east. Aligning one's home in this direction has deep spiritual meaning to many Native Americans, and is also very effective as a survival practice. For one thing, an east-facing entrance will admit the first warming rays of the rising sun after a chilly night. In addition, since most weather systems travel from west to east, the wind will normally strike the *back* of such a shelter.

Your fire should be set in front of the hut's entrance, allowing you to sit in your home's doorway protected from the wind in back and warmed by the flames out front. This setup will also enable you to toss additional fuel on the fire without climbing out of your nest.

Be careful not to build your fire too close to the shelter, though: Since most survival huts are made of highly flammable materials, your wilderness heat source should be located a good six to 10 feet away from your door. You can increase the amount of warmth directed toward your home by backing the fireplace with a horseshoe-shaped reflector made of stones.

Natural Shelters

Natural shelters include any wilderness spots, such as caves or hollow trees, in which a survivalist can find temporary refuge. Such places usually make meager dwellings at best, though, and should be used only in dire emergencies.

When you must seek a natural shelter, simply do as the animals teach us to do: Find protection in shallow caves, beneath fallen logs, overhangs, brush tangles or next to the trunks of fir or spruce trees.

The Leaf Hut

There are many types of manmade emergency shelters, but the leaf (or debris) hut offers the longest-lasting and best-insulated protection of any, and is certainly one of the easiest survival homes to construct.

Basically, the debris structure is nothing more than a huge domed pile of leaves, with the foliage supported by a frame that completely surrounds the work and sleeping areas. In a way, the leaf hut functions like a sleeping bag, but the shelter is stuffed with leaves instead of down or synthetic fibers. What's more, unlike a bedroll, the hut is waterproof and will keep a survivalist dry in almost any downpour: The dome shape forces the rain to run off the structure's sides, and the leaf walls actually wick ground moisture up and away from the interior of the nest.

How To Do It

To build a leaf hut, first select a proper site and find some object—such as a stump, rising ground, the fork of a tree, a log or a large rock—that can support a sturdy ridgepole. (If necessary, you can build a wooden tripod as a prop.) Then place one end of the ridgepole on the support, and rest the other end on the ground. Next, gather sticks, and lay them against the sides of this triangle so that the branches lean at a 45° angle against the ridgepole. Leave a gap in the eastern side of the framework, toward the hut's high end, for your doorway.

Now, collect brush, and add that to the structure's skeleton until the entire frame is covered by a huge wooden web thick enough to prevent leaves and other debris from falling through. At this point, your domicile should look like a half-erect pup tent.

Next, gather up leaves, grasses, ferns, pine needles, green boughs or whatever is available. Pile the material to a thickness of at least two and a half feet on the sides and top of the structure's frame. (A leaf hut with two-foot-thick walls will keep you warm and dry in temperatures just below 0°F. In severely cold weather, make the structure's sides at least four feet thick.) Finally, complete the outside of the hut by laying more brush, sticks and poles over your wilderness home to hold its covering in place and keep the walls secure even in a high wind.

The sleeping area of the hut is completed by stuffing the lower end of the nest with leaves or other soft debris. Place only a light carpet of foliage on the floor of the remainder of the hut, though, so that you'll have a usable work area and a place to store dry kindling, food and so forth.

From start to finish, it shouldn't take an adult much more than an hour to construct a good leaf hut. And while gathering the materials for the nest, you can collect a supply of firewood as well. To lie down in the shelter's sleeping area, work your way feet-first into the packed bedding so that your head protrudes slightly into the work area.

Because the walls of a leaf hut contain plenty of insulating air space, the shelter will remain warm even when it's wet. So if you find yourself caught in a rainstorm, don't be afraid to use drenched materials to build a

hut. Your nest may be damp, but you'll still be warm and alive.

If you have to spend the night without a fire, stack a pile of leaves near the hut's doorway. When you turn in for the night, you can pull this foliage inward to block the entrance. Remember, though, that you'll need an opening to let in some fresh air. Otherwise, you might build up an unhealthful oxygen deficit during the night.

All things considered, the leaf hut is probably the best form of survival shelter. If you build one, try to make it a miniature Taj Mahal, a work of art as well as a good warm home. Careful crafting will improve your survival potential.

By the way, many of the natural shelters mentioned earlier can also be used in conjunction with leaf hut construction methods. Cave entrances, rock outcroppings and root networks can be blockaded with the basic dome-of-debris structure. Indeed, the resourceful survivalist will adapt the leaf hut to satisfy his or her particular needs.

Snow Shelter

A modified leaf hut can even serve you well in deep snow.

An effective wintertime shelter can be constructed by simply building a leaf dome over a depression in the snow. Evergreen boughs will substitute ably for the normal debris insulation, but if you can't find such limbs, just pack snow over the shelter's wooden frame. A snow-sided home may not be as comfortable as would a leaf- or evergreen-lined shelter, but at least it won't collapse on you.

Try It

Finally, keep in mind that the best time to learn how to build a leaf hut is *not* during a survival situation, when mistakes can be costly. Instead, simply leave your tent at home the next time you go camping, and make your own shelter. When you do so, please show respect for the earth, and don't break off any limbs or gather any woodland materials you don't absolutely need.

The job can be both easy and fun if you let your whole family join in on the shelter-building project. That way, you'll all have a chance to discover how comfortable wilderness survival can be.

Survival:
Water

When you're lost, food is a luxury; water is not.

Many early Native American people believed that water was the earth's blood. And the purpose of the sacred substance—in the minds of such individuals—was to give life to all the world's beings. Therefore, men and women were expected to be careful to avoid contaminating water in any way. Unfortunately, in these "modern" times, our feet have become far removed from the earth, and much of humankind has lost its respect for nature. Hence, more and more pollutants are being dumped into our water, and it's hard nowadays to find a stream, lake or river anywhere in this country that hasn't been contaminated.

In today's world, then, a survivalist who needs water faces a twofold task: finding the liquid, and rendering it potable. In spite of having to take purification precautions, obtaining good water is, with practice, perhaps the easiest survival skill to master. Yet the simplicity of learning the needed techniques does not take away from their importance, and, though people have survived for days without drinking, it's both uncomfortable and unhealthy to go more than 24 hours without water.

Always remember not to take chances with questionable drinking sources. Even streams in remote areas may be polluted. The possibilities of physical harm, dehydration and the draining of vital energy resulting from diarrhea just aren't worth the risk.

This chapter covers four techniques for obtaining safe water in the wild. If you practice and follow the courses of action described here—always working toward becoming part of the natural world—you'll never find yourself without this most precious resource.

Whenever possible, it's wise to filter or purify even the cleanest looking wilderness water.

Natural Catches

Any landscape feature that holds or channels water is termed a natural catch. Finding such a source is usually the easiest way to obtain water. However, it can be difficult to locate natural catches that haven't been tainted by pollutants.

Still, provided you take proper precautionary and purification measures, some natural catches can be viable drinking sources. Here's a list of the most common of these, with information on how you can best use them safely.

Water channels and holders: This category includes rivers, lakes, ponds and streams. The safest of the four are streams. Any drinking water drawn from such a source should, of course, be clear and running. Generally speaking, the higher up a stream you go, and the faster it's running, the safer the water will be for drinking. Examine the water channel before you sip. You should see no signs of man's presence, but, instead, plenty of aquatic vegetation, fish, small insect life and—along the banks—animal tracks. Remember

that such prints don't necessarily mean the water is safe for humans. Wild creatures frequently drink from polluted water sources and even eat deadly poisonous plants, with no apparent ill effects.

It's better not to drink directly from a stream, because by doing so you may stir up the bottom and ingest some debris. You can easily improvise a container—a rock basin or a hollowed log—to collect the fluid. To make a rock cup, simply chip a depression out of a very soft stone with a smaller, harder rock. You'll lessen your chance of cracking the cup if you use soft glancing blows.

You can turn a log or limb into a container by using hot coals to burn a hole in the wood, blowing on the embers to expedite the process. After the coals have burned down, it should be easy to scrape the charred wood out with a knife or sharp rock. A large cup can be made from softwood (such as pine) in less than an hour with this method, and a one-gallon container can be burned out just as quickly if you use a lot of coals.

If the stream's water is muddy or has large amounts of suspended particles, you can filter it. A piece of cloth will do the trick, or you can make a cup-shaped strainer from bunches of matted bark strips or grass. Or you can simply put clean sand in a hollow

The inner stem of the bull thistle can be chewed for moisture.

log with a grass mesh bottom, rinse the sand as often as necessary to make the water coarsing through come out clear, then pour your liquid through.

As the last step, you should boil the collected stream water for 20 minutes to purify it. (Many wilderness experts recommend cooking the liquid for only five minutes, but that shorter processing will not kill some spore-stage bacteria.) You can accomplish this task either by heating the water over a fire or—if you don't have a suitable pan or a concave stone—by dropping red-hot rocks, one by one, into your wooden water container until the liquid has been fully purified. (Caution: Use only rocks found on high ground. Stones from lowlands or waterways may contain trapped moisture and explode when heated.)

It's important to remember that while long boiling neutralizes any biological contaminants, it won't destroy *chemical* pollutants.

Stone and wood catches: A depression in a rock—sometimes called a kettle—or a shallow hole in the nook of a tree or stump may contain water. Such pockets are numerous both in forests and deserts, but these are generally undesirable catches because the water doesn't last long before it either evaporates or is contaminated by bacteria.

If you must drink from a pocket of water in a stump or a limb cavity, first make sure that no animals are living in the water, that a profusion of algae doesn't grow there and that it hasn't picked up a bad taste from wood

tannins and resins. Rock kettles, too, can contain toxins if the collected water has run down over higher, poison-containing stones. This is especially common around old mining areas.

Soak up the water from the catch with a piece of cloth or a bundle of dried grasses, wring it out into a container, then filter and boil the fluid as described above.

Lowland catches: These are areas where the soil is soft and damp. To collect moisture, simply dig a hole until water begins to seep into it, and gather the liquid with cloth or dried grasses. Again, wring the absorbing material out over a container—repeating the process until you've accumulated the amount of water needed—then filter and purify it. The work will often go more smoothly and efficiently if you dig and draw from more than one hole at a time.

In some areas, particularly sandy bottomlands, ravines and dry riverbeds, the water is usually pure and—in an emergency where purification is impossible—can be drunk as it's gathered. At the opposite extreme, though, avoid catches containing ocean, cave, timberland or farm water, any of which may well contain pollutants.

Water From Plants

Plants can also provide water, and usually don't contain the pollutants that natural catches can harbor. However, since most vegetation doesn't have enough available water to serve as a complete survival source, plants are best used to stay the pains of thirst or to obtain temporary, "quick relief" emergency water. It takes a long time to collect

In bright sunlight, a solar still can generate good supplies of water from moist soil or crushed herbaceous plants.

liquid from all but a few species of plants, many such sources are good only during certain seasons of the year, and you have to be careful never to utilize vegetation from a sprayed area or roadside.

Hardwoods: In early spring, walnut, maple, birch and hickory trees can all serve as sources of water. To get the fluid, you simply tap the tree, just as Vermont maple-syrup makers do, by boring a half- or quarter-inch hole into the trunk with a knife or sharp rock, inserting a hollow reed and collecting the thin sap in a bark or log cup. Or you can cut through the bark with diagonal slashes. Make sure that you cut into the sap wood, or cambium, which lies just under the bark, and that you don't kill the tree by cutting all the way around it.

Since water gathered by this method contains a high concentration of sugar, drinking large amounts of it can cause an upset stomach or cramps. For the same reason, the liquid tends to spoil when not drunk soon after collecting.

Sycamores: These trees can be tapped in the same manner as the hardwoods. The water from a sycamore, however, can be harvested any time of year except in the dead of winter and, since it doesn't contain much sugar, can be consumed in quantity or stored for a few days.

Thistles: All common species of North American thistle can provide water, though the bull thistle yields the most and best-

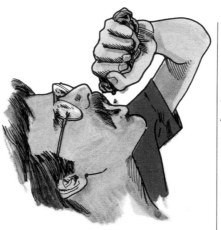

In most parts of the country, dew can be a reliable source of water.

Melt snow before using it, so as not to waste your body heat.

tasting. To get the juice, simply peel the thorns off young stems and leaves, and chew the watery food like celery.

Since thistles supply only a meager portion of liquid, they're best used to quench a thirst or to keep you going until other water sources can be found.

Cacti: A widespread variety of this edible water source is the common prickly pear. It has a high water content and is also a good vitamin-laced food source. Those who find the flavor or texture of the pulp objectionable can simply crush, squeeze and strain the plant for its water.

Solar Still

A build-it-yourself solar still is one of the best ways to obtain drinking water in areas where the liquid is scarce. Developed by two doctors in the U.S. Department of Agriculture, it's an excellent water collection device. Unfortunately, you must carry the necessary equipment with you, since it's all but impossible to find natural substitutes. The only components required, though, are a 5' X 5' sheet of clear or slightly milky plastic, six feet of plastic tubing and a container to catch the water. These pieces of gear can be folded into a neat little pack and clipped onto your belt or carried in a pocket.

To construct a working still, use a sharp stick or rock to dig a hole four feet across and three feet deep in a damp area, such as a gully or river basin. Place your container in the deepest part of the hole. Then lay the tube in place so that one end rests all the way in the container and the rest of the line runs up the side of the pit and out over the top.

Next, cover the hole with the plastic sheet, securing the edges of the material with dirt and weighting the center down with a rock. The plastic should now form a cone with 45°-angled sides. The low point of the sheet must be centered directly over, and no more than three inches above, the container.

The solar still works by creating a greenhouse under the plastic. Ground water evaporates and collects on the sheet until droplets form, run down the material and fall off into the container. When the container is full, you can suck the refreshment out through the tubing without having to break down the still.

A good solar still, located in a damp area, should keep collecting water for quite a few days. In drier regions, such as deserts, make the hole deeper and place crushed herbaceous plants (cactus and thistle are good choices) in the pit to increase the still's output.

Dew and Snow

Collecting dew is probably the simplest and safest way to obtain potable water in a survival situation.

The only equipment needed to gather dew is a rag, a piece of clothing or a handful of dried, nontoxic grasses. Collect the condensed droplets from grass, rocks, leaves and even sand, and wring the liquid into a container or directly into your mouth.

You'll have to get up early and work hard, since dew doesn't stay around very long, but

don't let the simplicity of this method lead you to believe that it's ineffective.

It's best to melt snow or ice and warm the water slightly before ingesting it. You can do so by building a fire and digging depressions in the snow nearby to collect the fluid, dropping a heated rock into a container of snow or simply placing a snow-filled cup in a snow pit and covering it over with pine or fir boughs; sunlight on the dark needles eventually will melt the snow in the cup.

Be Careful, Be Safe

As you might be beginning to realize, water can be simply and safely obtained in any survival situation, provided you follow the necessary precautions. Whenever you examine a newfound supply, ask yourself, "Would I stake my life on this water?" That's exactly what you'll be doing if you drink it!

If you find yourself in a situation where you have a limited reserve of water, conserve your supply to the utmost by following these few simple rules: Don't eat anything if you don't have water to drink with it; by consuming food you'll burn up your body's supply of vital fluids that much faster. Travel only during the coolest hours, and walk at an easy pace so that precious moisture doesn't get used up through perspiration. Finally, try to store as much water as you can in your stomach. People have died with full canteens as a result of trying too hard to conserve their water supplies!

Survival:
Fire

It may not be the most critical of survival needs, but a warming blaze can provide comfort and—that most important tool—confidence.

Shelter and water are the two most important requirements for anyone facing a survival situation; one seldom needs a fire in order to stay alive. But because a good blaze can be used to cook food, sterilize water, create tools and keep a survivalist warm and comfortable, it's important to know how to ignite that fire without the aid of a cigarette lighter or matches. After all, you might unexpectedly find yourself thrust into a situation where your lighter and matches are lost or too wet to work. What's more, no self-respecting outdoors purist would want to be dependent on a fallible lighter or a finite supply of matches.

The best all-around primitive flame starter is the bow drill. Learning how to work with this tool will give you a lot of satisfaction and will add to your feeling of security when traveling through the woods.

Whenever you practice this or any other outdoor skill, it's important to do the best job on the task that you can. Consistently careful craftsmanship, even in rehearsals, will not only insure good results but also improve your ability to get the job done under adverse conditions. Most Native Americans aimed at this same perfection of skill on an everyday basis. They felt that anything—including, but not limited to, living plants and animals—that they took from the earth was a gift from the Great Spirit. Doing a shoddy job of employing the gifts would, in effect, be showing disrespect for the Great Spirit's generosity, so they tried to make works of art of all things. Such actions were an integral part of these people's religious beliefs and served the purpose of greatly increasing their survival abilities.

Preparing the Site

Before starting to make a fire, choose an appropriate spot for it. Your site should be free of any combustible brush, dried grasses or leaves, away from low overhead branches, and should not be in an open, breezy area or on an exposed ridge. Set your fire some six to 10 feet—depending upon wind and weather conditions—away from your shelter entrance.

Once you've picked a site, dig out your fire pit. This dish-shaped hole should be about a foot deep and have gently sloping sides. The depression will cradle the fire with its coals grouped toward the center, and thereby help your embers burn much longer than they would in a flat fire bed. Be sure, though, not to make the hole so deep that the pit will prevent your fire's heat from reaching you. And if you're digging in rich, loamy earth or in soil that's full of root stems, line the bed with rocks to avoid the possibility of starting an underground fire. Use only stones gathered from a high, dry area for this, or any, fireplace job,

since water-logged rocks may explode when heated.

To increase the amount of useful warmth provided by the blaze, build a simple horseshoe-shaped reflector of rocks, damp wood or even earth around the side opposite your position. An experienced survivalist always builds fires with reflectors and tries to sit with his or her back against a tree, rock or shelter. That way, the reflector can help warm your front and (by bouncing heat off the rear barrier) your back as well. With such a setup, a small fire—which won't use up a lot of wood—can provide sufficient comfort.

An amateur, on the other hand, will often build a roaring blaze but leave it totally unbordered, and will therefore have to spend the night spinning at various speeds to keep one side of his or her body from freezing and the other from burning.

Finding Wood

Most people who attempt to start an outdoor fire are stopped in their tracks by one difficulty: locating *dry* wood. The cardinal rule to remember in this situation is that any wood found on the ground will have soaked up moisture and be difficult to light, so never collect ground wood for fire-*starting* fuel. Instead, gather dead limbs from standing trees. This wood will always ignite easily. (In fact, even in the Olympic rain forest—which receives 88 inches of rain a year—it's possible to pull a dead branch off a Douglas fir, whittle away only its outer surface and find dry fuel.)

Also, try to collect your wood from trees in open sunny areas rather than those near stream bottoms or lowlands where fog and moist air collect. You can easily determine whether the wood you're gathering is dead and dry by breaking off a piece: If the stick snaps cleanly and audibly, you've got good firewood. In most weather conditions, you can also find reasonably dry wood by touch. When your hands are too cold to be sensitive, you can press the fuel against your lower lip or cheek to feel for dampness.

You'll need four types, or grades, of fuel. The first is tinder, the light, airy, fast-burning material that's used to catch a spark. The dried inner bark of elm, cottonwood, willow, sage, cedar, aspen, walnut or cherry makes excellent tinder. Dry vegetation such as reeds and grasses, dogbane, velvet leaf, yucca, primrose, fire-

A WELL-PLANNED FIRE SITE

THE "TIPI" METHOD OF FIRE BUILDING

THE BOW-DRILL APPARATUS

MAKING TINDER

Gather dry inner bark.

Rub fibers vigorously.

Finished tinder fibers should be as fine as hair.

BOW-DRILL FORM
The right posture is essential.

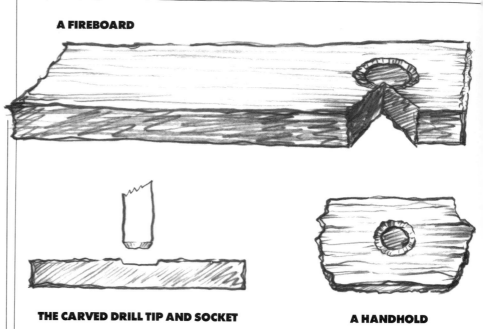

A FIREBOARD

THE CARVED DRILL TIP AND SOCKET

A HANDHOLD

weed, bulrush, milkweed, cattail and thistle also works well. In fact, with a little bit of effort, you can use just about any dried fibrous plant.

To prepare your tinder, remove all hard, crumbly bark or inner pith from the fuel, and rub the remaining fibers back and forth between your hands until you've created a fluffy bundle made up of filaments as small as thread. You can soften any particularly stubborn fibers by pounding them between two rocks.

The next type of fuel you'll need is kindling, tiny twigs or slivers that range from the thickness of a pencil lead to that of a pencil itself. You can either break kindling material off sheltered, dry branches or carve the fuel from larger pieces of wood. Always be sure to keep both this and your tinder absolutely dry.

Squaw wood, the next in size, gets its name from the fact that Native American women collected this pencil- to wrist-width wood as part of their daily routine. Rather than waste time and energy cutting huge trees for firewood, Indians burned the small and easy-to-gather sticks as often as possible.

The largest fuel is firewood, which is added to a fire only after the blaze is going strong. Don't waste your energy trying to cut up logs. Instead, shove the butt end of a log into your fire, then gradually feed the rest in as it burns down.

Don't try to take short cuts when gathering any of these four types of fuel. Take the time to obtain the best materials, and your fire will be easy to start and will keep burning no matter what the weather conditions. In addition, be sure to gather enough firewood to last through the night; there are few more uncomfortable wilderness tasks than having to leave a snug shelter and stumble around in the dark to replenish your supply.

Additional Fuel Tips

If you want to generate a tremendous amount of heat and adequate light from a slow-burning fire that results in fine cooking coals, use hardwood for fuel. On the other hand, should you need quick heat and a lot of light, it's best to find a softer wood such as cedar, tamarack or juniper. Wet wood, green leaves or pine boughs can be added to a fire to make a thick plume of smoke and steam that will help searchers pinpoint your location.

Damp fuel can also be used to help keep a

bed of coals burning overnight. (Green wood also works well for this purpose, but never cut living trees for fuel unless faced with a true survival situation.) Add a liberal supply to a strong blaze just before going to sleep. The slow-burning wood will keep the fire going for several hours, and produce coals that will possibly last through the night.

The Tipi Fire

Once you've prepared a fire site and gathered the necessary materials, it's time to lay the fire. Tipi-shaped stacking is best for this job, since the design allows the fuel to stand high and lean toward the center of the structure where the flames naturally rise. A tipi of small, dry fuel starts easily, burns efficiently and throws out quantities of heat and light. Furthermore, the slanting walls and resulting high flames help the blaze hold up even in rain or snowstorms.

Start with a bed of tinder. Then, working from your smallest materials up, build a cone-shaped structure. (You may want to lay down a tripod of firm sticks first, to give the design its form.) Also, be sure to leave an opening through which you can reach the interior of the pile to light the fire. This entrance should face the wind so that the prevailing breeze can help drive the flames up through the fuel.

One efficient technique is to place about six inches of tinder and kindling in the center and add a good supply of squaw wood—working carefully from the skinniest sticks to thicker—until the tipi is eight to 10 inches across and a foot or more in height. When it's raining, you can place small slabs of bark around the cone.

If you're carrying matches, you can simply thrust one into the "doorway" of the tipi and watch your blaze take off. However, if you have no matches, you'll need an effective alternate method—such as the bow drill.

Building a Bow Drill

There are five parts to a bow-drill apparatus: the bow, the handhold, the fireboard, the drill and a tinder bundle. The *bow* can be made by cutting a $2^{1}/_{2}$- to three-foot length of $^{3}/_{4}$-inch green sapling, preferably one having a slight bend. Fasten some cordage made from a shoelace, a strip cut from your belt or a tightly braided piece of clothing to the stick's ends ($^{1}/_{8}$-inch nylon cord is a good choice when you're practicing, since it will last through many trial runs).

The *handhold*—the object that fits in your palm and holds the drill in place—can be made from a small section of branch, a rock with a depression in it or a piece of bone. Almost any type of wood will do, but it's best to use a variety that's harder than the drill and fireboard material.

The next two pieces, the *fireboard* and *drill* (or *spindle*), should both be made from the same type of wood. Select a branch of dead wood that's dry, yet not rotted. It should be a wood of *medium* hardness. Avoid extremely hard species such as oak, hickory or walnut, and soft, resinous types such as pine, fir and spruce. Cottonwood, willow, aspen, tamarack, cedar, sassafras, sycamore and poplar are best.

After you've chosen your wood, cut off a branch for the spindle about $^{3}/_{4}$ inch in diameter and eight inches long. Now use a sharp

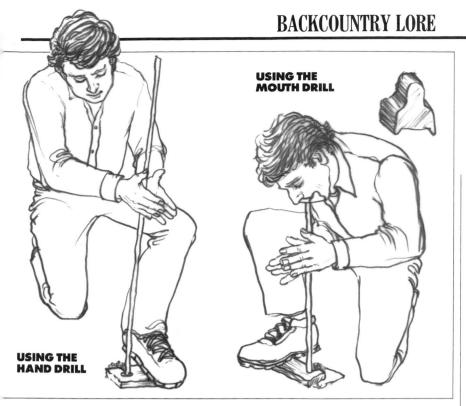

USING THE MOUTH DRILL

USING THE HAND DRILL

rock or a knife to smooth out the drill until it's as straight and round as you can make it, then carve points on both ends of the spindle.

To construct the fireboard, find a branch that's about one inch thick and 10 inches long, and whittle it flat on both sides; you want to end up with a board that's twice as wide as your drill and about ¹/₂ inch in thickness.

The last item needed to make fire with a bow drill is a small wad of very dry, finely textured tinder.

Burn and Notch

With the necessary equipment assembled, it's time to finish preparing it by burning holes in the handhold and fireboard and then cutting a notch in the board. To mark the holes' positions, place a small nick—which will serve as a starting point—in the center of the handhold and one in the fireboard. The latter cut should be far enough in toward the middle of the board to leave room for a side notch and for the depression that will be burned in by the drill.

Now, wrap the string once around the drill to secure the stick. Adjust the tension of the cord so that you can't slide the spindle back and forth along it. Next, set up the components as shown in the accompanying illustration of a bow-wielder.

Take careful note of the form shown in the illustration: If you duplicate it *exactly*, you should be able to start a fire under almost any weather conditions. The right-handed survivalist (a left-handed person would reverse these instructions) has placed his left foot across the fireboard, while resting his right knee on

the ground. His chest is set firmly on his left knee, and his left hand, braced tightly against his shin, grasps the handhold and keeps the spindle perpendicular to the fireboard. The bow is held in his right hand and moved in line with his body. From this position the firemaker can easily spin the drill while pressing down. In addition, his body overshadows the apparatus and thus creates a meager, though valuable, weather break.

When you've positioned yourself and your equipment properly, begin vigorously moving the bow back and forth while gradually increasing downward pressure on the handhold. This action will probably feel quite awkward at first, but after you've gotten the hang of it, you'll soon have drill, fireboard and handhold smoking and be able to burn good-sized depressions in both the board and hold.

Now it's time to add the most essential part of the entire bow-drill setup: the notch. This pie-shaped opening should be carved completely through the fireboard, with its point just short of center in the plank's burned-out pit. Make your notch a clean, well-manufactured cut.

Finally, grease the top of the drill and the handhold's socket to prevent friction-caused heat from making that depression any larger, and to help the drill rotate smoothly. You can use natural body oils by simply rubbing the end of the drill stem along the sides of your nose or through your hair. Pine pitch, animal fat and slime molds will also do the job, but don't use water or the drill will swell and bind up. And be sure *not* to mix up the ends of the drill. Otherwise, you'll get grease in the fireboard and ruin the friction.

Making a Fire

At last, you're ready to start a fire. Before you start though, check to see if the ground you're working on is damp. If it's moist, use a large flat rock or a piece of dry bark to provide a dry work surface. Now lay down your tinder, and position the fireboard directly over it, so that the notch opens to the exact center of the fiber bundle.

Next, set up the rest of the apparatus, and check to be sure your form is good, your handhold is firmly braced and your drill is straight up and down. Now move the bow back and forth quickly while pressing the drill downward. Press firmly until the lower part of the spindle and the fireboard are smoking. But don't apply *too* much pressure, or the drill will slow, the string will start to slip and the smoke will quickly diminish.

Once the board has begun to smolder, keep stroking the bow for 10 more complete repetitions. Now carefully dismantle the upper apparatus *without* jarring the fireboard. Next, carefully slip your knife blade down through the top of the notch to dislodge the burning dust formed by the abrasive action of the drill upon the board. Now remove the board, and wrap the tinder up around the glowing ember, taking care not to crush the coal. Gently blow the bundle into flames while turning the tinder as necessary to keep the ember in contact with fresh fuel—and thrust the burning mass through the doorway into the center of your firewood tipi. If you've built the tipi well, you'll be in business.

Practice Makes Perfect

All the cutting, burning, greasing and stroking involved in using a bow drill may seem troublesome, but with practice a survivalist can proceed from start to finish—including manufacturing the entire apparatus—in just under 15 minutes. Neither does the task require a lot of strength; form and coordination are much more important than are sweat and brute force.

Learning to use a bow drill may not come easily at first, but keep at it, and you'll soon master an important survival skill. Then you'll always have the security of knowing that you *can* make a fire, if necessary, at almost any time and in almost any place.

PART SIX

Campfire Cuisine

As Mark Twain
once said, "Nothing
improves scenery
like ham and eggs."

Low-Cost Backpacking Foods

Shop the supermarket for trail cooking.

There are many factors that have to be taken into consideration when deciding which foods to pack along on a hike. In addition to palatability, you must think about heft and bulk, ease of preparation and cost. In an effort to weigh all those variables and come up with the best backpacking meals for the least expense, let's begin by surveying the different products offered by the purveyors of specialty camp foods.

Foods

Freeze-dried foods—let's admit it—aren't all bad. Orange and grapefruit juice crystals, for example, are usually tastier than Tang. And some of these packaged dinners even taste sort of like food. Furthermore, there are times when freeze-dried meals offer some real advantages: For winter treks, preparation speed alone is reason enough to opt for this sort of grub; and on hikes lasting more than, say, 10 nights, every ounce of weight you can eliminate will most likely be considered cheap at *any* price.

Of course, the average backpacker's outings don't last as long as 10 nights. And it's extravagant to eat expedition-style when the trip could be provisioned better, and less expensively, from your pantry and the supermarket.

"Retort" meals are a newer wrinkle. Initially developed for the long-distance outings of NASA astronauts, these meals are precooked main courses, sealed in foil pouches, which keep without refrigeration. To prepare a retort meal, you simply dunk the pouch(es) in boiling water for about five minutes. Retort foods are easier to prepare than other freeze-dried foods. They also require no utensils other than a spoon or fork (if you don't mind eating out of a pouch). On the other hand, they're heavier, and one portion isn't much of a feast for most outdoor appetites.

Now let's review the kinds of food a typical hiker consumes throughout the day.

Think of this as the outline you'll be filling in as you plan and shop for trail meals.

Breakfast

When a long hike is pending and you're eager to break camp and hit the trail, preparation and cleanup time usually limit breakfast options. For an appetizer there's dried fruit, dried fruit rehydrated overnight or juice from crystals. For a main course you can choose either quick-cooking (or presoaked) hot cereal, cold cereal or something from the granola family. For a hot beverage you have about the same choices as at home.

On days to be spent in camp (or when short hikes permit late starts), there's time for slow-cooking cereals, pancakes or biscuits. Since most hikers prefer death to powdered eggs, many take enough fresh eggs and bacon for the first few days.

Lunch

There are two schools of thought concerning on-the-trail lunching: One school advocates nibbling off and on all day rather than eating a "real" lunch, while the other prefers taking a lunch break *as well as* nibbling off and on all day.

Most lunchers have yet to find anything better (or lighter) than no-cook meats such as salami or sardines complemented by cheese and crackers or bread—unless it's peanut butter and crackers. Popular luncheon desserts include nuts, candy, cookies, dried fruit or gorp (trail mix). Beverages include water. For reasons that baffle culinary psychologists, most hikers tire less of these simple menus than of all camp dinners combined.

While some backpacking books advocate a soup lunch, hikers rarely prepare cooked midday meals in summer. Doing so involves too much fuss. Winter hiking is another story altogether. Even folks who limit cross-

country ski treks to one day find that midday soup (or at least a hot drink) is worth the trouble.

Dinner

Most respectable camp dinners start with soup and end with a simple dessert and a beverage. The soup brightens spirits and holds starvation at bay while the main course is cooking. Soup also helps hikers replenish their body fluids—which is especially important in parts of the American West, where the typically dry air evaporates body moisture rapidly.

Viewed broadly, main courses follow a single pattern: An expandable, fast-cooking starch is blended with (or served under) a mixture of meat and such enhancements as vegetables, sauces, spices and toppings to produce a hearty dish.

In fact, you can map out a main-course planner on one page. Split the sheet into three or four columns. Head one column "Starches" and another "Meats." Either lump the rest together as "Flavorings" or give "Vegetables" a separate column. If you can list 10 items in each of three columns, you'll have 1,000 combinations, not counting those that use two foods from the same

legumes simply won't rehydrate. The higher you climb, the more slowly *all* starches and cereals will cook. And because of the lower temperatures at high altitudes, cereals left to soak overnight may turn into whole-grain Popsicles—even in summer.

Will water be in short supply? If so, choose your dinner starches from among those that require little more liquid for cooking than the small amount they'll absorb. Forget water-hungry pasta.

How about wild foods? If you're in an area that lends itself to foraging, a copy of a good plant-identification book and a break-down spinning or fly rod can be worth three times their weight in processed and packaged meat and vegetables. Of course, don't ever eat a plant if you have the least doubt about its identity. (After a few seasons' worth of foraging experience, you'll probably have enough sure identifications locked in your head to make the book optional.)

Hint 2: Loot Your Larder

A backpacking trip is the perfect time to make use of home-dried garden produce. Dehydrated vegetables will glorify any trail dinner (most hikers come home craving green stuff). Hiking also presents a good opportunity to use such homemade treats as jerky, your pet granola mix, candies and sturdy cookies. (A tip on packing homemade granola bars: Overbake them a little. Crispier bars are lighter and hold up better in jouncing packs.)

Be sure to prepare your own gorp; store blends always leave out at least one thing you love.

Hint 3: Shun Boutique Foods

There are two differences between the Mountain Macho Backpacker Blend–type soup mixes sold at camping-specialty outlets and Knorr-type supermarket soup mixes: 1) Knorr tastes better, and 2) Knorr is cheaper. Likewise, no Packer Cracker from the camping boutique is better than Triscuits. (IBM is said to be doing research to determine why Triscuits break so little when slept on.) And no designer-priced Camper Cookies are as tasty as plain-Jane Oreos, let alone Pepperidge Farm, let alone homemade.

And if circumstances demand that any meat you carry be freeze-dried, you can still save money by buying *only* the meat and adding your own starches and flavorings.

Hint 4: Treat Yourself Kindly

When Colin Fletcher ambled the length of the Grand Canyon, each of his air-dropped food packets included one gourmet goody. Take a lesson from *The Man Who Walked*

Between specialty trail food and practical off-the-shelf choices, camp meals are better than ever.

column. Of course, many of these wheel-of-fortune combos will be real gaggers (imagine fried-rice-style Rice-A-Roni with tuna and chili powder), but you'll also have hundreds of *real* possibilities.

Dinner desserts include the lunch varieties, plus instant puddings and other easily prepared sweets (such as no-bake cheesecake).

Notice that we've presented no detailed menus, but only broad guidelines for getting better—and better-*tasting*—backpacking meals for your money. Along the same lines, the following nine hints will help in planning better, cheaper trail meals.

Hint 1: Analyze Your Trip

Every outing presents its own culinary opportunities and limitations. Smart cooks plan precisely—day by day, meal by meal—for the trip at hand. So before you go out to shop, make a detailed list, asking yourself questions like these:

How many days? If several strong backs will be dividing the load for a weekend trip,

you needn't worry about how much your food supply weighs.

Nutritional balance is important on long trips (you may even want to include vitamin pills). But for short outings, diet is a matter of choice; after all, you *could* survive three days on nothing but Fritos and water without seriously threatening your health—though it's difficult to imagine that anyone would want to do so.

Unless every ounce counts, carry enough fresh foods for the first day or two on the trail. Frozen steaks in zip-topped plastic bags will thaw as you hike. Carrots and other sturdy vegetables will keep fine for the second day's lunch. So will hard-boiled eggs. In your pack's cool center, leftover home-cooked meat should keep well for the second night's dinner. Tightly wrapped smoked ham should keep until the third night or longer.

Will you have lazy days in camp? Will you build fires? Foods that need lengthy soaking before or during cooking (beans, lentils, regular brown rice, etc.) are fine for in-camp days and campfires—but they won't do for fast meals after hikes or for trips when you must carry and ration stove fuel.

Will you be cooking at high altitudes? If the answer is yes, then forget about dining on anything requiring dried beans, because the

Through Time, and pamper your own wilderness stomach. Remember—almost anything short of caviar is a bargain when compared with freeze-dried grub.

To stave off culinary boredom, carry the best meat you can afford. If you know you'll have to lunch all week on salami, it should be the tastiest Italian variety you can find. And why carry processed American when it can be provolone or New York Cheddar?

You can splurge on beverages and still not spend a lot. Instant tea doesn't belong in camp, because it tastes nasty; carrying your favorite bagged tea won't sprain your shoulders. Since brewed coffee is usually too much trouble, treat yourself to *good* instant coffee—your favorite brand, a gourmet type you've been hankering to sample or even one of the Continental-style flavored coffee mixes.

And while you're blending your gorp, why not make it a gorp fit for royalty? (You never know *whom* you'll meet out there.)

Hint 5: Two Cautions

Before you hasten off to turn the neighborhood grocery store into your safari supplier, two warnings are in order:

Read labels carefully. Be sure the cooking time won't require more stove fuel than you can spare. And check those "just add" ingredients: Anything that says "just add two eggs" is a bad bet if you're going to be five days from the nearest hen (unless you know for a fact that the eggs aren't essential). Brand differences matter, too: Some brands of "quick" rice are quicker than others; some gingerbread mixes *don't* need an egg.

Perform your big experiments at home, not on the trail. Don't attempt your very first cake in a fireside reflector oven. Likewise, if you're a Mexican-food innocent, don't plan to have your first brush with "jalapeño destiny" halfway up Mt. Whitney.

Hint 6: Stay Alert When Shopping

Backpacking demands lightweight foods that taste good, keep without refrigeration, are quick and easy to prepare, and dirty a minimum of utensils. Consider only those realities, and forget any notions about "what backpackers eat."

It's all a matter of attitude. For instance, the person seeking trail food finds little good bread. So much of it is bulky, crushes easily and goes stale fast. But the alert shopper heads for the deli section and finds lots of cocktail ryes and firm, European-style pumpernickels. Such breads are ideal pack fare. But even to consider them, your mind's eye must be focused to see that "party food" can also be camp food.

Search the supermarket for light, quick-fix foods that keep well. Ask yourself how long each dairy product will hold up. Hard cheese keeps better than soft, but a wax coating or foil wrap matters more than the type of cheese. If you bake, try using powdered buttermilk.

What about condensed mincemeat for desserts? If you've got the space, how about popcorn balls? And remember that "chocolate" chips come in other flavors, too.

Notice *all* the canned meats, gourmet varieties included. Summer sausage (often sold as "beef stick") keeps well. So does pepperoni, and a few ounces of it will ignite lots of spaghetti. Salami that's left over from lunch can also be used to add zest to pasta dishes.

After you've scoured the grocery, take your well-sharpened eyes to health food and gourmet stores, and even ethnic food shops.

Finally, keep your eyes peeled. Wise old camp cooks are ever alert. Even when browsing through cheese catalogues for possible Christmas gifts, they pounce on anything that might jazz up next summer's camp cooking.

Hint 7: Welcome to Starch Trek

For the frequent packer, the discovery of one new *starch* is more blessed than three other finds. The pasta and rice, Hamburger Helper and dried-potato sections are only the first places in the supermarket to look. Did you remember Japanese ramen and Chinese chow mein noodles? Quick-cooking barley?

For a real starch treat, consider *couscous*—semolina wheat in granular pasta form. The Near East brand is ready to eat in five minutes. Look for it in the gourmet section. (And while you're there, look for *spätzle*—little German noodles.)

Health food stores are laden with pastas and grains, including bulgur (parched cracked wheat), *kasha* (buckwheat groats) and millet.

Hint 8: Spice It!

Seasonings are the lightest trail foods and among the most versatile. A clever seasoner can overcome many of the pack kitchen's limitations. For instance, when preparing soups, adding a few dried mushrooms and a sprinkle of marjoram can make quite a difference.

Seasonings also include bacon bits and other salad toppings; poppy, sesame and other seeds; flavored crumbs and croutons; bouillon cubes and soup mixes; and all those foil packets of sauce mixes, taco spices, marinades and gravies.

Grated Parmesan (or Romano) cheese is a superb trail food. It travels perfectly for weeks and will drive the drab out of countless main courses and soups.

Another must-have seasoning is Squeeze Parkay or a similar liquid margarine. Many main courses require some form of oil, and most can use a bit of a flavor boost, too.

Dessert? No one ever called instant chocolate pudding the high point of a gourmet meal, but it's better when you add malted milk powder or, perhaps, a little instant coffee.

Drinks? Try cinnamon or another sweet spice in tea, coffee or cider mix. Take miniature marshmallows for cocoa.

Breakfast? If you've brought along instant oatmeal that you've "customized" and prepackaged with chopped dates, banana chips, raisins, brown sugar and powdered milk, you'll have a cereal worth crawling out of the sleeping bag for.

Hint 9: Be Adaptable

When you select foods that will allow you to eat a whole dinner from a Sierra cup, you're making a sensible adjustment to camp dining. Keep looking around for other smart adaptations.

Try presoaking grains and hot cereals. For dinner, you needn't cook bulgur at all. Instead, make tabbouleh salad by mixing bulgar with dried vegetables and spices, pouring boiling water on top and letting it sit for an hour.

Never reject a food idea simply because you won't be able to add some suggested frill, such as browning the dish on top after it's cooked. And unless the idea of pressing graham cracker crumbs into the bottom of your Sierra cup excites you, spread the crust mix *over* your no-bake cheesecake.

If you don't like messing with a reflector oven, keep in mind that many baked goods can be prepared pancake-style in a skillet. (So what if your gingerbread comes out looking weird? You want it to *taste* good, not to grace the cover of *Bon Appetit*.)

Just Like Home Cooking? Dream On!

The cold reality of trail eating is that a camp stove is *not* a range, a backpack is *not* a refrigerator and science has yet to find a way to dehydrate Caesar salad, leg of lamb or bourbon on the rocks.

Nevertheless, by planning carefully and shopping creatively, you can make your camp meals more enjoyable to prepare and eat, you'll have extra traveling money jingling in your hiking shorts, and the camping boutiques and designer trail-food manufacturers will be left holding the foil bags.

A Trio of Trout Treats

Trout carry the aura of legend, in the water as well as on the table.

It's likely that more paeans have been written to trout—be they rainbows, cutthroats, browns, brookies, Dolly Vardens, goldens or any of the other various true trouts, chars or salmon—than to any other group of fishes.

Perhaps part of the charm, at least in many sections of the U.S., is that trout season opens in the very early spring, making it the start of the angling year for great numbers of enthusiastic fisherfolk. In popular streams in some parts of New York State, for example, it's common to see men and women lined up elbow to elbow on opening day, despite the fact that the water around them rolls black and cold, snow often spots the spring fields and the still pools are rimmed with ice.

Trout carry the aura of legend, are sometimes almost heartbreakingly beautiful and have a well-deserved reputation as flashy and powerful fighters when hooked on tackle suiting their size. They are also, in the minds of many people, one of the finest foods that swim. The following recipes are offered to help *you* celebrate the anglers' rite of spring with a delectable and nutritious meal, whether your catch is the stuff of a streamside supper or the centerpiece of a full-scale sit-down banquet!

Charcoal-Baked Trout
4 fresh trout (11″–14″)
2 lemons (or 1 orange)
Chopped fresh parsley
Curry powder
Salt and pepper to taste
4 tablespoons butter

Clean the trout, and place 4 lemon wedges in the cavity of each fish. Sprinkle the inside of each with parsley, curry powder and salt and pepper. Season the outside with salt and pepper, and coat generously with butter.

Wrap the fish individually in heavy-duty aluminum foil, and once the charcoal fire has burned down to glowing embers, set the fish on the grill to cook for about 5 minutes on each side, or until the meat flakes easily. Serve garnished with a sprig of fresh parsley and more lemon wedges. Serves 4.

Beer-Fried Trout
2 pounds filleted or pan-dressed trout
1 can warm beer
1 cup all-purpose flour
¼ teaspoon garlic powder
1 teaspoon pepper (or to taste)
Salt to taste
Oil for frying

Mix the ingredients other than the fish, and let stand 30 minutes at room temperature or until the beer flattens. Whisk the mixture until it's frothy, and dip the fish in the batter. Heat the oil in the pan until it's hot, and fry the fish about 1 minute on each side, or until the batter is browned and the flesh flakes easily. Serves 4.

Broiled Trout
1 pound fillets
Salt and pepper to taste
3–4 tablespoons oil

Preheat the broiler. Cut the fillets into serving pieces, and sprinkle with salt and pepper. Grease the rack of a broiler pan, and place the fillets on the rack, skin side up. Brush with oil. Broil the fish 5–8 minutes, about 3″ from the heat, until they're brown. Baste with more oil. Turn, and baste the other side. Broil until brown and the flesh flakes easily. Serves 4.

Using Nature's Bounty

Give yourself a course in "culinary botany."

Identifying and foraging wild edibles is a versatile woodland skill. Many people find it an enjoyable, worthwhile family activity. Others appreciate the novel tastes and nutritional superiority of most edible wild plants. And wise campers, hunters and anglers know that a practical knowledge of wild foods can turn a survival crisis into a forager's feast.

While some woodland delicacies require exacting identification (best learned from an expert), here are several key wild plants that any outdoor explorer can spot. They will provide tasty backcountry eating almost anywhere in the U.S.

Treat all wild foods with respect and kindness. For instance, never clean out an entire stand of wild greens, but leave plenty of plants to spread and replace what you took.

Letting nature's bounty feed us has long been a dream of humankind. Wild foods provide us with an opportunity to partake for a moment in that rare—and spiritual—experience.

Lamb's-Quarters
(*Chenopodium album*)
True to its Latin name, "white goosefoot" leaves are shaped like goose feet and are whitish underneath. Lightly steam and gently season this spinach substitute.

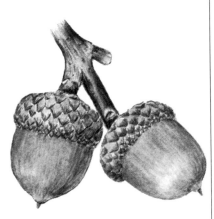

Acorn
(*Quercus* species)
All acorns are edible. Boil the peeled nuts (change the water when it turns dark brown) until any bitter taste is gone. Serve with batter and seasoning. Acorns can also be dried and ground into flour.

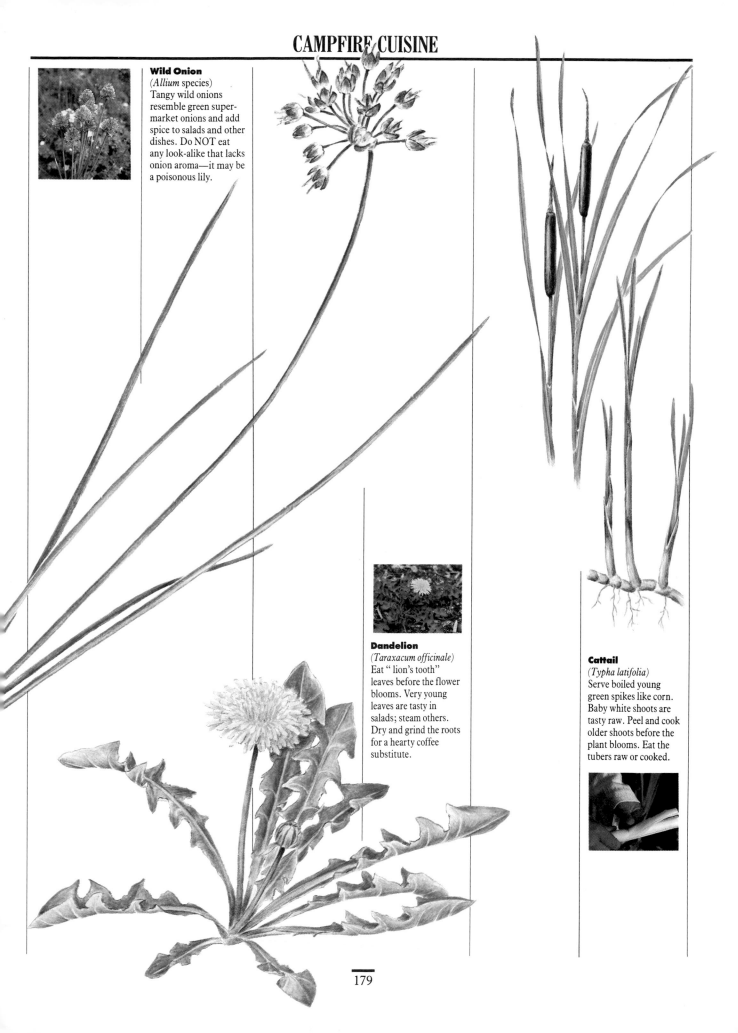

Wild Onion
(*Allium* species)
Tangy wild onions
resemble green super-
market onions and add
spice to salads and other
dishes. Do NOT eat
any look-alike that lacks
onion aroma—it may be
a poisonous lily.

Dandelion
(*Taraxacum officinale*)
Eat " lion's tooth"
leaves before the flower
blooms. Very young
leaves are tasty in
salads; steam others.
Dry and grind the roots
for a hearty coffee
substitute.

Cattail
(*Typha latifolia*)
Serve boiled young
green spikes like corn.
Baby white shoots are
tasty raw. Peel and cook
older shoots before the
plant blooms. Eat the
tubers raw or cooked.

Take a Wok!

When East meets West around a campfire, good food and convenience come together, as well!

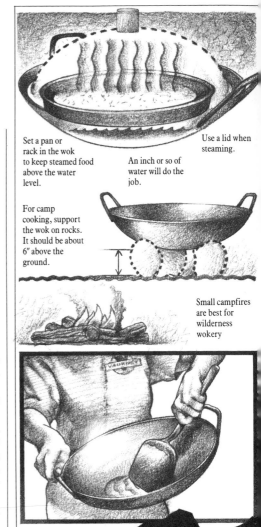

Set a pan or rack in the wok to keep steamed food above the water level.

Use a lid when steaming.

An inch or so of water will do the job.

For camp cooking, support the wok on rocks. It should be about 6" above the ground.

Small campfires are best for wilderness wokery

When you go camping, you don't have to take along a Dutch oven, reflector oven, griddle, iron skillet, nesting pans or any of the other cooking gear common to backcountry kitchens. But you can still bake brownies, make grilled cheese sandwiches, cook French toast, steam trout, fry tortillas and prepare just about any other dish you want. How? You can do it all in a wok—the traditional Oriental all-purpose utensil. It's the ideal campfire cook pot.

Unlike cast iron (which requires a lot of fuel just to get up to temperature) or aluminum (which can literally burn up on hot coals), the wok is designed specifically for high-heat cooking. So it performs beautifully over an open fire, on a park fireplace, with a backpacking or a propane stove or on a hibachi.

Traditionally the wok is used for stir-frying vegetables, and it serves that function just as admirably on the trail as in the kitchen. But it also makes a terrific oven: Just wad up a few pieces of foil, put them in the bottom of the wok, place a cake pan with batter on top of the wads, and put on the cover. Before you know it, *voilà!*—brownies, coffee cake, cobbler, biscuits.

A wok can also deep-fry foods to crispy golden perfection—with less than half the oil it takes to use a "real" deep fryer. With a little water in the bottom, and vegetables or fish in a pan (or on a small grate) set over the water, a wok becomes a steamer. It makes a fine stewpot, too.

There's another big advantage to using a wok for camp cookery: Cleanup takes just seconds (yes, seconds!). Simply scrape the surface with a metal spatula (the kind made especially for woks works best), and rinse the pan in hot water—or for more stubborn cas-es, fill the pan with hot water, and let it soak until the food particles can be wiped off. As any stir-fry cook can tell you, a wok should *never* be washed with soap or scrubbed with a scouring pad. A wok will blacken with use; it's supposed to. The blacker the wok, the better seasoned it is.

Taking a wok camping saves time, fuel and cooking oil. There's less gear (and weight) to carry and fewer dishes to clean. Thanks to the versatile wok, there's more time to really *enjoy* the outdoors—along with some really good eating!

Recipes

Here are a few favorite wok-prepared camping recipes. When preparing food over an open fire, keep your wok at least six inches off the ground; either use a grate or arrange a few rocks in a circle to cradle the pan over the fire. Remember, there are a lot of variables at work (the kind of wood used, the size of the fire, etc.) that will affect cooking times. A small fire is easiest to control to produce a steady, even temperature. Stay with the food while it's cooking, and watch it carefully. You may need to remove the pan from the heat for a minute or two to let the fire cool down or to build the fire up.

Most of the recipes use just a few basic ingredients. Feel free to add or substitute.

Acadian Breakfast Hash

$1/4$–$1/3$ cup cooked rice per person
$1/2$ tablespoon butter or margarine
1–2 eggs per person
$1/4$ cup grated or diced Cheddar cheese per person
Optional: Chopped green pepper or onion, mushrooms, raisins, diced cooked ham, sausage, bacon

Keep the cooked rice warm by pushing it to one side of wok. Melt butter or margarine. Sauté green pepper, onion or mushrooms, if using. Push to side. Break eggs into wok, and add half the cheese. Scramble eggs with a spoon or fork. When eggs have partially set on the bottom, gradually fold in rice and any optional ingredients, and cook till eggs are done. Top with remaining cheese, and cover until topping melts. Serve immediately.

Camping suggestion: This basic recipe can also serve as the foundation for a delicious evening meal. Just stir-fry some carrots, broccoli, pork or chicken (or any combination), and set them aside. Cook the egg-rice mixture completely, then fold in the additional ingredients.

Wok Popcorn

1 tablespoon salad oil
$1/4$ cup popcorn
Place wok on a campstove (use the pan's

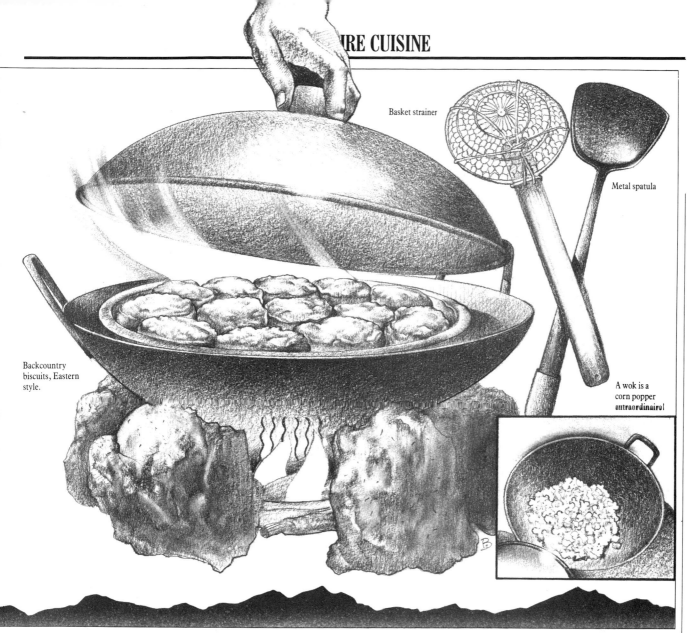

Basket strainer

Metal spatula

A wok is a corn popper entraordinaire!

Backcountry biscuits, Eastern style.

ring stand if you have one), on a backpack stove or on a circle of rocks over a campfire. Add salad oil and 2 or 3 kernels of popcorn. Cover. When kernels have popped, add remaining popcorn, cover, and cook. It isn't necessary to shake the wok. When popping stops, remove wok from heat, and season popcorn with salt, melted butter or grated cheese. Makes about 4 cups.

Indian Fry Bread

1 cup flour
1/4 teaspoon salt
1 teaspoon baking powder
2 tablespoons powdered milk
1 teaspoon sugar
1 tablespoon butter or margarine
1 beaten egg or equivalent powdered egg
3–4 tablespoons water
Vegetable oil for frying

Mix flour, salt, baking powder, powdered milk and sugar together. Cut in butter with the back of a fork. Add beaten egg, and mix well. Add water to make a firm dough.

Flour your hands, and pat dough into a flat cake about half an inch thick. Fry in hot oil until brown on both sides, 2–3 minutes. Serve hot with butter, honey or jelly.

Camping suggestion: Mix the dry ingredients at home, then add water, egg and butter at the campsite. The dough can be made using only flour, salt, baking powder and water, but the other ingredients improve the flavor and texture.

Greenbelt Breakfast Frizzles

1/2 pound bulk pork sausage
8 slices bread
4 ounces Cheddar or mozzarella cheese
6 eggs
1 tablespoon water
1/2 cup seasoned bread crumbs
Oil or shortening for frying

Using the rim of a cup or glass, cut each slice of bread to form a round. Divide sausage into fourths, and shape each portion into a ring large enough to enclose a bread circle. Start cooking sausage in the wok.

Slice cheese, put a fourth on each of 4 bread slices, and top with a second bread slice. Beat together 2 eggs and the water. Dip each sandwich into egg mixture, soaking both sides and pressing edges together. Then dip both sides into bread crumbs, and roll edges of the sandwich in crumbs to help seal them.

When sausage is thoroughly cooked, remove from heat, and pour off grease. Add oil or shortening to wok, and fry sandwiches, 1–2 minutes per side or until golden. Remove and drain.

Fry remaining eggs, and put one on top of each sandwich, which is served nestled in the center of a sausage ring. Makes 4 frizzles.

Camping suggestion: Don't throw away the bread crusts. The next morning, make "Leftover Frizzles French Toast": Soak the crusts in an egg-milk mixture, and fry them in melted butter or margarine.

More Backcountry Cooking

It's surprisingly easy
to bake breads and cakes
in the wilderness.

Wilderness fare doesn't have to be limited to instant oatmeal, freeze-dried dinners and scrambled powdered eggs. Instructors for the National Outdoor Leadership School (NOLS) teach expedition techniques for preparing such treats as fresh-baked cinnamon rolls, fruit fritters and egg drop soup. Dishes like these have a way of changing your whole attitude toward "roughing it" in the wilderness—especially when you consider that these delights are not only delicious but easy to make.

Essential Utensils

Start with a backpacking stove, a necessary piece of equipment. It offers reliable cooking even in uncertain weather. Also, campfires aren't allowed in some wilderness areas. You'll also want two three-quart stainless-steel pots and a 10-inch nonstick frying pan. All pans should be free of plastic parts and should have flat lids that fit tightly. For mixing and flipping, you'll need a spatula and a large stirring spoon, both plastic. Oven mitts and a pot grip (pliers make acceptable substitutes) are absolutely necessary for baking.

For dining, take an insulated 12-ounce mug with a lid (available at many convenience stores), a bowl, a spoon and a knife—preferably a pocketknife—for each person. The fewer utensils you have to mess up, the less cleanup is involved.

Backcountry Baking Methods

For many, camp baking consists of building a fire, letting it burn down to coals and

A sleeping-bag pad provides a clean surface for kneading the dough (right) which rises to the occasion as delicious rolls (above).

burying a cast-iron Dutch oven in the hot remains. Usually this procedure means scraping burnt crust off the bottom or top of camp bread before serving. Fortunately, NOLS instructors teach a more dependable baking method. They call this technique a "twiggy fire," and it's used in conjunction with a backpacking stove.

Regulate the stove's temperature until it produces a low flame. To allow room for ris-

ing, fill your skillet no more than half full with the dough or batter you want to bake. Cover the pan, and set it over the stove flame. Using twigs only, create a small fire on top of the skillet lid. (Now you see why no plastic parts.)

Let your bread or cake bake undisturbed for at least 10 minutes before checking on it. That will keep it from "falling."

When you do inspect the progress, carefully brush off the coals, and blow the ash dust from the lid before lifting it. Once satisfied the baked goods are cooking properly, replace the cover, and reestablish a twiggy fire on top, replenishing it as needed until the food is done.

Rocky Mountain Rolls

1½ teaspoons yeast
1½ cups lukewarm water
2 tablespoons oil
2 tablespoons brown sugar
2 cups whole-wheat flour
⅓ cup cocoa mix
1 teaspoon cinnamon
2–2½ cups white flour
1 teaspoon salt
½ cup raisins, optional

Add yeast to warm water, oil and brown sugar in a 12-ounce mug with a lid. Let sit 5 minutes until foamy. Combine remaining ingredients in a bowl. Stir in yeast mixture, adding more flour as needed to form a stiff dough. Knead in the bowl or on a floured flat surface 8–10 minutes. Return dough to oiled bowl, flipping once to coat both sides. Let rise 1 hour or until doubled in bulk. If it's really cold, put pan over hot water to rise. Form into balls. Bake in a greased frying pan,

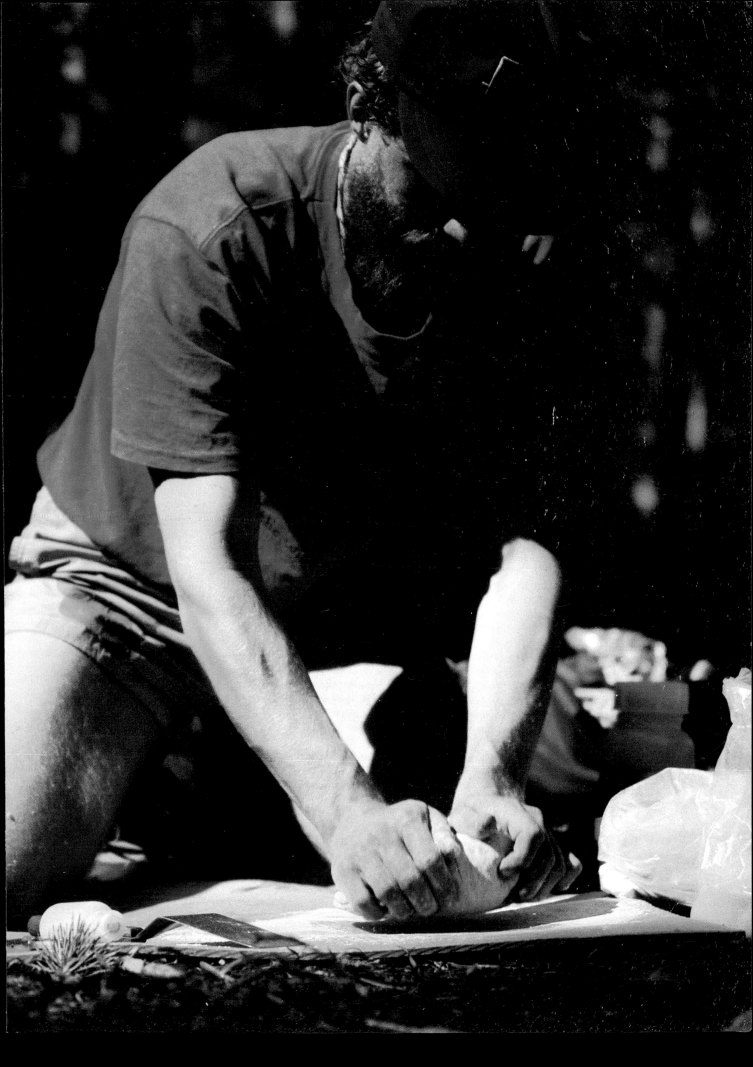

using twiggy fire, 40–60 minutes. Remove from heat. Let cool 10 minutes before serving. Makes 12.

Sunrise Cakes
1/3 cup cornmeal
1/2 teaspoon salt
2 tablespoons powdered milk
1/2 cup water
1/3 cup whole-wheat flour
1 teaspoon baking powder
1 tablespoon brown sugar
2 tablespoons margarine

Combine all ingredients except margarine in a bowl. Stir until blended. Melt margarine in skillet, and spoon batter onto the hot oil. Flip once to brown both sides. Serve with honey. Makes 8–10.

Eggzactly Milk
1 tablespoon powdered eggs

Honey or brown sugar to taste
1/2 teaspoon vanilla
1 1/2 cups milk made from powder

Add egg, sweetener and vanilla to milk. Shake vigorously in a 12-ounce mug with a lid for 1 minute.

Fritters
1/2 cup margarine
1/2 cup cornmeal
3/4 cup flour
2 teaspoons baking powder
1 1/2 tablespoons powdered eggs
1/2 teaspoon salt
2 tablespoons powdered milk
1/2 cup water
2 tablespoons honey

Melt margarine in frying pan. Mix all dry ingredients together. Add water, 2 tablespoons melted margarine and honey, and mix. Spoon batter into remaining melt-

Build a small fire atop your Dutch oven for even baking heat.

ed margarine in pan. Flatten slightly. Fry on both sides, being careful it does not burn. Serve with honey or syrup. If car camping, add a drained can of whole kernel corn to batter before frying. Makes 12.

Fruit Fritters
Chop 1/2 cup of fruit (raisins, apricots, dates, pineapple, etc.). Let stand in 1/2 cup water. Drain and use water in above recipe. Make up the batter as directed, then add chopped fruit and 1/4 teaspoon cinnamon. Fry as above.

Gnocchi (Potato Dumplings)
Boiling water
1 cup potato pearls
3 tablespoons powdered eggs

¹/₂–1 teaspoon salt
1 tablespoon oil
4 tablespoons powdered milk
¹/₄ teaspoon oregano, basil and/or garlic powder (optional)
¹/₄ teaspoon black pepper
1 cup whole-wheat flour

Add enough boiling water to the potato pearls to make a mashed potato consistency. Add about 3 tablespoons water to powdered eggs, mixing well to form a liquid, not a paste. Mix into potatoes. Add remaining ingredients, one at a time, mixing well after each addition. Let dough sit for a few minutes. Pinch off 1-inch pieces, and drop into boiling water. Simmer, covered, until they come to the surface, about 5 minutes. Because gnocchi are bland, they are best served with a well-seasoned sauce, such as a spicy spaghetti sauce. Serves 3–4.

Fideo ("FEE-they-oh")
3–5 onions, chopped, or 2–4 tablespoons dried onions
1 can green chilies, chopped, or 2 tablespoons dried green and red peppers
1 pound spaghetti or noodles
Oil or margarine for frying
Garlic, salt and black pepper to taste
1–2 cans tomato paste or 8–10 tablespoons tomato base
3–4 cans water (2 cans = 1¹/₂ cups)

If using dried onions and peppers, cover them with water to rehydrate. Break spaghetti into 1-inch lengths, and fry about ¹/₃ of the amount at a time in hot oil, stirring until brown. Do not burn. Remove each portion to a pot as browned. Add more oil as needed. Reduce heat, add onions to oil in frying pan, and fry until translucent. Add chilies or peppers, garlic, salt and black pepper, and cook for a few minutes. Dilute tomato paste with water. (Try 1 can paste to 2 cans water to start, or if using tomato base, put 4 tablespoons in a 12-ounce mug, add water to top while stirring—do this twice to begin with, stirring in more paste or base if you want thicker sauce and stronger flavor.) Add this to frying pan, and cook a few minutes. Pour into pot with fried spaghetti. Liquid should cover pasta. Cook, stirring often to keep from burning, adding more water if necessary, 20–30 minutes. Remove from heat when done, and allow to sit covered for

5 minutes before serving. Serves 3–4.

Oriental Egg Drop Soup
5 cups water
1–1¹/₂ cups broken spaghetti pieces
1 heaping tablespoon chicken base
¹/₂–1 teaspoon curry powder
¹/₄ teaspoon pepper
2 tablespoons powdered eggs
2 tablespoons powdered milk
Thin strips Swiss cheese for garnish

Bring water to boil; add spaghetti. Cook for a few minutes, then add chicken base, curry powder and pepper. Continue cooking until spaghetti is done. Mix powdered eggs and milk with enough water to form a fairly thick paste. Drop by small spoonfuls into hot soup; let cook for a few minutes. Serve with slivers of Swiss cheese for garnish. Serves 4.

Streusel Coffee Cake
Cake:
1–2 tablespoons margarine
2 cups baking mix
2 tablespoons brown sugar or honey
1 cup water
Topping:
5 tablespoons brown sugar
¹/₃ cup oatmeal
4 tablespoons margarine
1 teaspoon cinnamon

Cut margarine into baking mix. Add other cake ingredients, and mix well. Spread in a greased pan. Mix topping ingredients, and sprinkle on batter. Bake, using a twiggy fire, 20–25 minutes or until done. Fills a 10-inch frying pan.

Variation: Cook 1 cup fresh blueberries with 1 tablespoon sugar or honey, 1 tablespoon margarine, 2 tablespoons flour and 1 cup water until thick. Spread over cake batter, and bake as above.

Valencye (car-camping recipe)
2 tablespoons brown sugar
¹/₂ cup flour
³/₄ teaspoon baking powder
¹/₂ teaspoon cinnamon or apple pie spice mix
Pinch of salt
1 tablespoon plus ¹/₃ cup oil
1 tablespoon powdered milk
2 large oranges, peeled and sectioned
Mustard and brown sugar for dipping

Combine all ingredients except oranges,

¹/₃ cup oil and mustard and brown sugar for dipping. Let batter sit 15 minutes. Heat ¹/₃ cup oil in frying pan. Dip orange sections in batter. Fry on both sides in hot oil. Serve as is, or dip in small amount of mustard and brown sugar. Makes about 20 pieces.

Where to Learn More

Backcountry cooking can be much more than instant this and powdered that; roughing it can be a gourmet experience. If these recipes tempt you into wanting to learn more about open-air baking, NOLS has a new cookbook available, which is a practical guide to creating nutritious meals in the outdoors. *The NOLS Cookery*, with over 170 recipes and variations, is loaded with information on ration planning, cooking hints and ways to use up extra food. The book costs $6.95 postpaid from NOLS Publications, Box AA, Lander, WY 82520.

Essentials Checklist

1 backpacking stove and fuel
2 3-quart stainless-steel pots with lids
1 10″ nonstick frying pan with lid
1 pair oven mitts
1 pot grip
1 plastic spatula
1 plastic mixing spoon
1 spice kit (see below)
1 12-ounce insulated mug with lid*
1 bowl*
1 spoon*
1 knife*

*per person

The NOLS Spice Kit
To enhance your backcountry cooking:

2 ounces each	Cayenne
Salt	
Black pepper	**1 ounce each**
Garlic powder	Curry powder
Cinnamon	Chili powder
Spike	
Cumin powder	**¹/₂ ounce each**
Powdered mustard	Oregano
Apple pie spice	Basil
	Dillweed

Camp Coffee Traditions

"Hot, black as a bat cave and strong enough to walk off on its own."

"If you are a connoisseur," advised Horace Kephart in his classic 1917 guide, *Camping and Woodcraft*, "you will never be tempted more than once by any condensed coffee or substitute." Kephart's book is one of those great old manuals on traditional woodlore, illustrated with etchings and replete with advice on such subjects as building lashed-together lean-tos and making cups and kettles from peeled tree bark. These days, most of Kephart's ax-intensive methods would have you handcuffed to a park ranger before sunset, but his counsel on coffee holds true. If there's any old-time outdoor tradition worth hanging onto, making proper camp coffee is it.

"Proper camp coffee" is not perked, dripped or instant, not freeze-dried, not syruped, not filtered, not anything but real grounds-and-water-in-the-pot coffee. You make it by combining coffee and water in a ratio of roughly one generous tablespoon of coffee per cup of water (plus one, two, three, four or more tablespoons of coffee "for the pot").

Naturally, the fresher the ingredients you use, the better the brew. If you really want to follow in the footsteps of the old-timers, start with unroasted, green coffee beans. Toss them into a skillet over a fire, and give 'em a stir now and again with a stick till they're brown and smelling good (be careful not to let the beans burn). Then wrap the beans up in a piece of cloth or your shirt, pound on them with a rock until they're pretty well pulverized, and brew them right away. If you don't have access to green beans, buy roasted whole beans. And if you're not fond of rock-pounding, grind the beans fine just before you leave home (or—if you must—use preground coffee), and keep the coffee in an airtight container. As for water, take no chances on untreated stream water—boil it, or put it through a portable purifier, before adding it to your coffeepot.

It's not so much the ingredients, but the means by which they're added to the pot and brewed, that sparks debate around campfires. There are two basic approaches: 1) Start with a measured amount of cold water in the pot, then bring the water to a hard boil, take it off the heat, stir in the coffee, and let it steep, tightly covered, in a warm place for 10 minutes. Or 2) put the cold water and grounds together in the pot, then bring the water to a boil, immediately take the pot off the heat, and let the coffee steep for five minutes. In either case, wrap the pot in a coat or shirt while the coffee's steeping, to keep the flavor and aroma in.

Note that in neither method is the finished coffee allowed to boil, a practice bordering on sacrilege, something akin to overcooking filet mignon. Old-timers used to say that boiling coffee made it taste like rotten boot leather. Food scientists put it another way, explaining that coffee beans contain both flavorful oils and bitter tannic acids, and that the water temperature at which the oils are fully released is 205°F, just below boiling, while the bitter acids are released at or just above boiling.

Still another area of controversy, if not consequence, among camp-coffee followers is the matter of how best to settle the grounds out of steeped coffee. If you've made your coffee in a pot that has a wire handle, and if you have faith in centrifugal force, swing the pot up and around in a full circle a couple of times to pull the grounds to the bottom of the container. This technique is especially good when you've made a lot of coffee in a large pot.

Adding an eggshell or two to the finished brew also will help clear the coffee; in fact, some folks mix an egg—yolk, shell and all—into the grounds before brewing them. Others merely tap on the pot a few times to make the grounds settle. Or, just put a cold spoon or other utensil—or a pebble or two, for that matter—into your cup of coffee. The grounds will be drawn to the object in just a few seconds. Adding a teaspoon or so of cold water to your cup will also do the trick.

Any way you brew it, camp coffee should be consumed fresh and steaming hot. Never drink it lukewarm, and never drink it reheated. If there's any left over, add it to the evening's stew, or mix it into gravy to go with a batch of biscuits.

Camp coffee, like flannel shirts and old jeans, just naturally belongs in the outdoors. Next time you strike a trail, leave your jar of instant coffee behind—with the rest of civilization's bland trappings—and treat yourself to the real thing, the same sort of eye-opening brew a Rocky Mountain trapper affectionately described over a century ago: "hot, black as a bat cave and strong enough to walk off on its own." Now *that's* coffee.

Credits

Cover: Michael Soluri
Table of Contents: Clyde H. Smith/ F-Stop Pictures, Inc.
p. 6: Spencer Swanger/Tom Stack & Assoc.
p. 8: Dean Abramson/F-Stop Pictures, Inc.

Part I
pp. 11-15: George Olson **pp. 16-17:** Jim Corwin/Aperture Photobank **pp. 18-19:** Don Osby **p. 21:** Alan Carey **p. 22:** Brownie Harris **pp. 23-25:** Michael Soluri **pp. 26-27:** Bart Henderson/Sobek Photo File **p. 28:** left photo, Paul Ratcliffe/Sierra Shutterbug; illustrations: Jonas Kyle/ American National Red Cross **pp. 28-29:** S.C. Reuman/Conundrum Designs **pp. 30-31:** S.C. Reuman/ Conundrum Designs **p. 31:** Barry Rosen; illustrations, Jonas Kyle/ American National Red Cross **p. 33:** Photographs, Ken Forsgren; illustrations, Don Osby **pp. 34-35:** Brownie Harris **pp. 36-37:** Ken Forsgren **pp. 38-39:** The Bettmann Archive

Part II
p. 41: Jacqui Morgan **p. 43:** Alan Carey **pp. 44-47:** Illustrations, Kay Holmes Stafford **pp. 48-49:** Photo, Bill McRae; illustrations, Don Osby **pp. 50-51:** Jacqui Morgan **pp. 52-53:** Michael Soluri **p. 54:** Kay Holmes Stafford **p. 55:** Michael Soluri **pp. 56-57:** Kay Holmes Stafford **pp. 58-59:** William Waldron **pp. 60-61:** Kay Holmes Stafford **p. 62:** Heather Smith **p. 63:** Tom McHugh, 1973/

Dallas Aquarium/Photo Researchers, Inc. **p. 64:** Steve Price **p. 65:** Kay Holmes Stafford **pp. 66-67:** Michael Soluri; illustration, Kay Holmes Stafford **pp. 68-69:** Bud Titlow/F-Stop Pictures, Inc. **p. 70:** Kay Holmes Stafford **p. 71:** Michael Soluri **p. 72:** Illustrations, Ernest Lussier **pp. 72-73:** Clyde H. Smith/F-Stop Pictures, Inc. **pp. 74-75:** Craig Blouin/F-Stop Pictures, Inc.; illustration, Ernest Lussier **pp. 76-77:** Illustrations, Kay Holmes Stafford; photos, Michael Soluri **pp. 78-79:** Illustrations, Ernest Lussier **pp. 80-82:** Illustrations, Kay Holmes Stafford; photos, Michael Soluri **p. 83:** Illustrations, Ernest Lussier

Part III
p. 85: Thomas Kitchin/Tom Stack & Assoc. **p. 86:** California condor, Tom McHugh/Photo Researchers, Inc.; Cisco, Tomas Todd/U.S. Fish & Wildlife Svc.; Palila, H. Douglas Pratt; Tecopa pupfish, U.S. Fish & Wildlife Svc.; Mad Tom, Reprinted with permission © 1981 by Ohio State Univ. Press.; Black-footed ferret, Dean Biggins/U.S. Fish & Wildlife Svc. **p. 87:** Mouse, U.S. Fish & Wildlife Svc.; Seaside Sparrow, P.W. Sykes, Jr./Vireo; Song Sparrow, John Ward; Whale, Richard Ellis/ Photo Researchers, Inc.; Blue Pike, From *Inland Fishes of New York State* by C.L. Smith, 1985/NYDEC **pp. 88-89:** Alan Carey **p. 90:** Map by Don Osby **p. 91:** Alan Carey **p. 93:** Map by Don Osby **pp. 94-97:** Thomas Kitchin/Tom Stack & Assoc. **p. 97:** Map by Don Osby **pp. 98-99:** Jim Brandenburg/Woodfin Camp and Associates; right photo, M.A. Chappell/ Animals Animals **p. 100:** Don & Esther Phillips/Tom Stack & Assoc. **p. 101:** left, 1988 E. P. I. Nancy Adams/Tom Stack & Assoc.; right, Joe McDonald/Tom Stack & Assoc. **p. 103:** Gray Milburn/Tom Stack & Assoc.; Map by Don Osby **pp. 104-105:** Alan Carey; bottom, Ted Levin/ Animals Animals **p. 106:** Map by Don Osby **p. 107:** top, Tom McHugh/ Photo Researchers, Inc.; bottom, Joe McDonald/Animals Animals **p. 108:** top, Leonard Lee Rue III/Animals Animals; bottom, Map by Don Osby **p. 109:** Joe McDonald/Tom Stack & Assoc. **pp. 110-111:** Illustrations by Kay Holmes Stafford; Map by Don Osby; top photo, Zig Leszczynski/ Animals Animals; bottom photo, Ted Levin/Animals Animals **p. 113:** Alan Carey; Map by Don Osby **pp. 114-115:** Herbert Lange/Westlight **p. 115:** Map by Don Osby

Part IV
pp. 118-121: Illustrations, Clarence Goosen **pp. 122-123:** Ken Forsgren **p. 124:** Illustrations, Don Osby **p. 125:** Illustrations, Kay Holmes Stafford **pp. 128-129:** Illustrations, Don Osby **p. 130:** Illustrations, Kay Holmes Stafford **p. 131:** Illustrations, Don Osby

Part V
p. 133: Spencer Swanger/Tom Stack & Assoc. **p. 137:** Spencer Swanger/ Tom Stack & Assoc. **pp. 138-139:** Spencer Swanger/Tom Stack & Assoc. **pp. 140-143:** Illustrations, Don Osby; photograph, Michael Soluri **pp. 144-147:** Don Osby **p. 149:** Don Osby **p. 150:** Grant Goodge **pp. 153-155:** Kay Holmes Stafford **pp. 156-157:** Susan Biddle **pp. 158-159:** William Waldron **p. 161:** Will Waterman **pp. 162-163:** William Waldron; illustrations, Kay Holmes Stafford **p. 165:** Spencer Swanger/Tom Stack & Assoc. **pp. 166-167:** Kay Holmes Stafford **pp. 169-171:** Kim Belger

Part VI
p. 173: The Bettmann Archive **pp. 174-175:** Steven Ledell **p. 177:** Marvin E. Newman **pp. 178-179:** Photographs: Cattail, Christopher Nyerges; Dandelion, Christopher Nyerges; Wild Onion, Jack Wilburn/ Earth Scenes; Acorn, L.L.T. Rhodes/Earth Scenes. Illustrations, Bobbie Angell **pp. 180-181:** Illustrations, John Breakey **p. 182:** Deborah Binder **pp. 183-184:** Will Waterman **pp. 186-187:** The Bettmann Archive **p. 192:** Dean Abramson/F-Stop Pictures, Inc.